W9-BGC-030

The U.S. Financial Crisis: Analysis and Interpretation

Cheng Siwei

Long River Press
San Francisco

Published in the United States of America by

Sinomedia International Group

Long River Press

360 Swift Avenue, Suite 48

South San Francisco, CA 94080

ISBN: 978-1-59265-147-4

Cover design: Tiffany Cha

Printed in China

10 9 8 7 6 5 4 3 2 1

Library of Congress Cataloging-in-Publication Data

Cheng, Siwei.
 The U.S. financial crisis : analysis and interpretation / Cheng Siwei.
  p. cm.
 ISBN 978-1-59265-147-4 (hardcover)
 1. Financial crises--United States. 2. Financial crises--China. 3. United States-
-Economic policy--2001-2009. 4. China--Economic policy--2000- 5. Global Financial
Crisis, 2008-2009. I. Title. II. Title: US financial crisis.
 HB3722.C447 2012
 330.973'0931--dc23

                              2012013568

Contents

Preface

The subprime housing mortgage crisis (abbreviated as subprime mortgage crisis hereinafter), which originated in the United States in the spring of 2007, has developed from a debt crisis to a liquidity crisis, and further into a credit crisis. This financial storm, caused by the bankruptcy of subprime mortgage institutions, a meltdown of investment banks and funds and great turmoil in the stock market, has spread from the United States to the whole world, arousing turbulence and panic in the international financial market; it has also spread from the fictitious economy to the real economy, triggering a rapid slowdown of the global economy and economic recession in many countries. The scale, scope and rapid spread of the crisis are all beyond people's expectation and it is considered as the most severe and extensive global financial crisis since the Second World War.

Karl Marx once pointed out in *Das Kapital* that financial products such as negotiable securities based on loan capital and the credit system of banks are fictitious capital. For the last ten years or more, fictitious capital, mainly in the form of MBS, CDO and CDS, has greatly expanded, the leverage ratio of investment banks in the United States has exceeded 25×, and necessary and effective regulation has been absent, thus eventually causing a serious financial crisis.

Due to the globalization of trade, investment, division of labor and asset allocation, financial risks have also become increasingly globalized. Risks, on the one hand, spread through a series of micro-mechanisms of financial transactions and linking of balance sheets in financial institutions; on the other, they pervade worldwide through real economies. It is right through these two channels that the U.S. subprime mortgage crisis spread to the whole world and evolved into a global economic crisis.

Over the past 30 years since reform and opening up, China's economy has enjoyed a steady and sound growth, making more and more contribution to the safeguarding and promotion of economic prosperity and sustainable development in the world. With China's considerable GDP, rapid development and the largest foreign exchange reserve worldwide, countries held high expectations of the role China would play in the financial crisis. However, China is still a developing country, our GDP accounts for only 8% of world total and per capita GDP ranks below 100th worldwide, so we can only assume our due responsibilities in accordance with China's national strength and development. President Hu Jintao has clearly pointed out that in order to handle the financial crisis effectively, countries should strengthen confidence, intensify coordination and step up cooperation. China is willing, with a responsible attitude, to continue to participate in international cooperation in safeguarding the stability of global finance and boosting world economy. China's steady and sound economic growth itself is an important contribution to the stability of global finance and the growth of the world economy.

The author started studies on the financial crisis in 1997 and published the book "Analysis and Inspiration from the East-Asia Financial Crisis" (Democracy & Construction Press, 1999) as the chief editor and first author in 1999. Since 2007, the author has been paying close attention to the development of the subprime mortgage crisis; in recent years, the author has put forward personal opinions on how the crisis emerged and developed as well as what measures to take in many speeches at home and abroad. On April 30, 2009, the author submitted the essay on "Global Financial Crisis and China's Measures" to leaders of the CPC Central Committee, analyzing the causes of the financial crisis with theories of fictitious economy and its implications for China, and conducting initial studies into the measures China should take and the direction of China's future financial reform. The essay was read and commented on by relevant leaders and two of its paragraphs were published in the 25th issue of special reports by State Council Group on International Financial Crisis on May 22, 2009.

In order to carry out in-depth analysis on the causes and impacts of the financial crisis, evaluate the measures taken by China, and accumulate experience and draw lessons, leaders of the China Academy of Sciences supported the CAS Research Center on Fictitious Economy & Data Science to set up the key project of "Analysis on Causes of U.S. Financial Crisis, its Impact on China's Economy and Measures" and the author worked as head of the project. On September 14, 2009, the project was approved by the Bureau of Planning and Strategy of the Chinese Academy of Sciences; on December 1, 2009, funding for the project was available. After one year's efforts, the research group of the project has completed their studies.

The study in the project was conducted according to the study framework designed by the author and the study method of "Four Integrations" (integration of opinions and arguments, qualitative analysis and quantitative analysis, statistical inference and case study, reductionism and holism) proposed by the author. Apart from the general report, five specific reports are also provided as follows: (1) analysis on the cause and evolution of the U.S. financial crisis and its impact on the world economy; (2) the balance between financial innovation and regulation in light of the financial crisis; (3) the impact of the U.S. financial and economic crisis on China's real economy; (4) evaluation of the effect of China's policies towards the financial crisis; (5) prices of financial assets, inflation and monetary policies. The general report is not just a simple summary of the specific reports, but includes an overall view developed by the author by integrating the specific reports and his past studies, which should help people have a deep understanding of the causes of the financial crisis and draw lessons from it. The study has also enriched the theories and practice of the fictitious economy, contributing to the development of that discipline.

In order to make the results of the study available to more readers at home and abroad, the author decided to write a book based on the general report and publish it in both Chinese and English. In so doing, the author has more than doubled the content of the general report and tried his best to update relevant data and facts by the end of September, 2011.

Speaking frankly, much of the book reflects personal opinions of the author, so your criticism or comments will be warmly welcomed.

On the publishing of the book, I'd like to thank those who have participated in the study, including Professor Yang Haizhen, Professor Shi Minjun, Professor Long Wen, Dr. Guo Kun, Dr. Yu Jing and relevant colleagues in CAS Research Center on Fictitious Economy & Data Science. My gratitude also goes to Ren Ruo'en and Wang Huiwen, the part-time researchers, for the contribution they have made. Furthermore, I'd like to extend my thanks to Ma Yue, editor in charge in Science Press, whose great efforts have made the book as elegant as it is. I would also thank Mu Qin and Zhao Feifei, the translators, and Mr. Norman A Pritchard, the senior proofreader, all from Beijing Foreign Studies University, for their hard work.

1.

The Evolution and Spread of the U.S. Financial Crisis

A debt crisis generated by the subprime crisis

The subprime crisis was a financial crisis triggered by the sharp increase of mortgage loan defaults leading to credit austerity in the United States. Subprime lending means that the banks make loans to lower income groups and/or people with lower credit for purposes of house purchase. With the encouragement of government and the Congress, American commercial banks loosened the standards of mortgage loans. As a result, the market in subprime lending prospered. The down payment was quite low, even zero (in 2005, the median down payment for purchasing the first house was 2% in the U.S., and 43% of lenders did not make any down payment[1]). Usually, they paid back the banks with a combination of fixed and floating interest rates. It meant that, in the first few years, the lenders would pay back the loan based on a favorable fixed interest rate (they didn't even need to pay the principal.). After these years, the payment would be based on a floating rate. The interest rate for subprime loans was often higher than normal loans. As time went by, it was possible for the floating rate to increase dramatically.

After making the loans, American commercial banks did not have the responsibility of collecting the interest and principal. They packaged and sold the loans to maintain fluidity. Relevant institutions would issue Mortgage-Based Securities (MBS). Mortgage loans were therefore changed into securities and a secondary market was formed.

Between 2002 and 2006, there was continuing prosperity in the American property market. Due to a lower interest rate and minimal risks in many procedures, American subprime loans developed rapidly. From 2001 to 2006, the average annual growth rate of subprime loans was 38%. Lending institutions were over-optimistic about the market, because when there were defaults, the institutions would withdraw the house and put it on bid. In other words, there was no loss for them. Therefore, they were more than willing to lend. The borrowers also hoped that their house would appreciate in value. They would either re-mortgage it to borrow money from banks or sell it when they were under financial constraints. While prices in the American property market experienced continuing increase, the ratio of default was quite low. MBS, CDO (Collateralized Debt Obligations), CDS (Credit Default Swap) and other financial derivatives enjoyed rich profits and low risks. Rating institutions rated them and their institutions as AA or above. Therefore, many investors jumped in without hesitation and investment banks, investment funds and insurance companies also bought into the market to gain huge profits.

However, the good times did not last long. From the second half of 2006, along with the cooling of the American property market, it became difficult for buyers to sell their houses or re-mortgage them. Moreover, the interest rate was increasing (from June 30, 2004, the Federal Reserve increased the interest rate 17 times, and the interest rate of the federal fund grew from 1% to 5.25%). The interest rate of subprime mortgages echoed the increase. Lower income borrowers began to feel the stress of paying the loans and defaults started. In addition, the economy was slowed down by soaring oil prices. Many borrowers were laid off and were unable to continue their repayments. The ratio of defaults increased sharply. All of the above reasons led to the defaults of subprime mortgages. Banks could not collect the loans. As a result, many banks faced loss or even bankruptcy. The "subprime crisis" had been triggered.

February 22nd 2007 is usually considered to be the beginning of the subprime crisis. On that day, HSBC released its report about its loss due to subprime loans and reduced its holding of $10.5 billion subprime mortgage related MBS[2]. When the crisis broke out, subprime mortgage institutions experienced severe losses and some of them applied for bankruptcy. On April 2, 2007, the second largest mortgage company in the U.S., New Century Financial Corp, announced its application for bankruptcy and cut 54% of its workforce. Later, the tenth largest, the American Home Mortgage Investment Corporation, went the same route on August 6. In 2007, at least 100 mortgage lenders had to stop their business or be closed or sold[3].

Along with further property price reduction and the downturn of the American economy, some regular mortgage loans started to default, too. The loan crisis was expanding. Rating institutions added fuel to the fire and quickly downgraded financial institutions and financial products. Hedge funds took the opportunity to sell short. Many lending institutions, investment banks, insurance companies, investment funds and other financial institutions experienced a sudden fall of their stock price and suffered dramatic losses. Some were even forced to go bankrupt. Many investment funds in the U.S. and Europe had bought large volumes of derivatives of subprime loans and they were damaged as well.

On July 16, 2007, the fifth largest American investment bank, Bear Stearns, had two bankrupt hedge funds, namely the High-Grade Structured Credit Fund and the High-Grade Structured Credit Enhanced Leveraged Fund. On October 30 and November 5, 2007, both Stan O'Neal, CEO of Merrill Lynch, and Charles Prince, Chairman and CEO of Citigroup resigned over the huge loss sustained by their CDO. Between December 2007 and January 2008, Morgan Stanley, Citigroup, JP Morgan, Merrill Lynch, UBS and other major financial institutions all announced huge losses due to subprime loans.

Investors were panicking and the American security market shrank. In the first quarter of 2008, the market had a loss of 28.27% over the same period the previous year. CDO were reduced by 93.73% and asset-backed security by 82.58%, while at the same time, the American stock market dropped by 45%. Some commercial banks not only faced a loss because of default on mortgage loans, but also because of non-payment of credit card loans.

After a protracted struggle, the fifth investment bank on Wall Street, Bear Stearns, could not overcome the crisis of fluidity and at 9 am March 14, 2008, received investment of $30 billion from JP Morgan [4]. Eventually, it got the support of government. On May 30, JP Morgan purchased Bear Stearns at $10 per share. At the same time, those financial institutions of CDO and CDS which had a close relation with MBS also experienced problems of fluidity, and sold their financial assets and looked for mergers.

After the outbreak of the subprime crisis, the United States adopted many measures focusing on generating liquidity. On August 10, 2007, the Federal Reserve provided $38 billion to save the market, in addition to a $24 billion plan. On February 13th 2008, President Bush signed a $168 billion worth economic incentive plan. On March 11, he announced a $200 billion program, aimed at allowing financial institutions, including major American investment banks, to exchange their highest risk bonds for safe national treasury which guaranteed returns. The American Financial Services Commission of the House of Representatives, on April 29, decided to provide $300 billion as a subsidy to finance people who were about to lose their homes. From September 18, 2007 to April 30, 2008, the Federal Reserve lowered interest rates seven times, from 5.25% to 2.0%. On July 16, the U.S. Security and Exchange Commission issued an emergency ban to preventing major financial companies, including Fannie Mae and Freddie Mac, from playing short in the stock market. Another 30 days ban was issued on July 18, 2008, forbidding 19 companies, including Fannie Mae, Freddie Mac and Lehman Brothers, from playing short. President Bush signed an aid act for the property market which had a value of $300 billion. Such acts aimed at helping the two major American mortgage institutions, Fannie Mae and Freddie Mac, to get out of difficulty and also gave support to home-buyers.

During the period of subprime crisis, risks were spread among financial institutions in terms of their balance sheet. An intertwined financial sector meant the globalization of financial assets ownership. Financial institutions possessed assets of other countries, and countries with advanced financial systems all had assets relevant to American subprime loans. Therefore, when defaults appeared, the foreign financial institutions which had such assets were negatively affected. As the crisis was deteriorating, financial institutions in other countries all announced a steep decline and losses in mortgage-related assets.

On February 22nd 2007, HSBC released its loss due to the subprime crisis and reduced its relevant MBS by $10.5 billion. The German Industrial Bank rang the alarm bell for profits on August 2, 2007, when its Rhineland Funding, which had a size of €12.7 billion and a small amount of its business in American subprime market, experienced a severe loss of €8.2 billion. The German Central Bank convened a conference of banks to discuss a plan to save the German Industrial Bank. On August 9, the largest bank in France, BNP Paribas, froze three of its funds for the same reason. On August 13, the Mizuho Group which has the second largest bank in Japan, the Mizuho Bank, announced a loss of 600 million yen related to the subprime crisis. The crisis expanded into the global financial system. On October 23, the largest Japanese security company Nomura Securities, announced a quarterly loss of $620 million. On October 30, UBS, which has the largest volume of assets in Europe also announced a loss due to the subprime crisis. The total loss reached 830 million Swiss francs in the third quarter of the year, the highest for the five previous years [5].

The American subprime crisis deteriorated further in 2008. Investors were still panicking and the American bond market had shrunk by a large margin. At the same time, bad news also came from important foreign financial institutions. On February 18th 2008, the UK decided to nationalize the Northern Rock Bank. On April 18, the Mitsubishi UFJ Financial Group in Tokyo estimated that its subprime crisis related loss up to March 31 in that financial year was 95 billion Japanese yen ($921 million). On April 29, the Deutsche Bank announced its first net loss in five years.

To summarize, in this period, economies with advanced financial systems such as the EU and Japan were directly impacted by the American subprime crisis because of financial globalization. In order to cope with the crisis, nations adopted various measures focusing on increasing liquidity. For example, on August 10, 2007, central banks around the world together injected more than $320 billion to the financial system. On December 18, 2007, the European Central Bank also provided €248 billion. In addition, in this period, panic spread amongst investors, stock markets experienced great turbulence and the forecast for the future became pessimistic.

Financial crisis on Wall Street

The economic growth rate of the U.S. in the second quarter of 2008 reached 2.9% which was 0.9% higher than that of the first quarter. U.S. Treasury Secretary Henry Paulson and other experts agreed that the major risks of the subprime crisis had been attenuated and the American economy was taking a turn for the better. Contrary to their optimism, the crisis worsened and ultimately produced the Wall Street Financial Tsunami in the first half of September, 2008.

The two largest mortgage enterprises to receive support from the U.S. government were Fannie Mae and Freddie Mac. The MBS issued by them took mortgage loans as their foundation and had clear and strict standards for granting loans. However, with the encouragement of the government, the influence of hedge funds favoring higher risks, and pension and other funds, such standards had actually been violated. In 2007, the two enterprises held a subprime MBS of $394.8 billion. Counting on government support, they borrowed money from banks and other institutions and accumulated a debt of $5.2 trillion which was 62.5 times their core capitals ($83.2 billion). There was a continuous decline in property prices, while the payment capacity of regular borrowers revealed weaknesses. The MBS rating of the two companies quickly dropped and so did their share price. Problems of liquidity appeared.

Their market price was reduced from $38.9 billion and $22 billion in 2007 to $7.6 billion and $3.3 billion in 2008, respectively. They were collapsing and could not survive to the November election[6]. The bond issued by the major two accounted for 92% of all institutional bonds. On one hand, fewer institutional bonds led to the shrinking of the American bond market; and on the other hand, central banks were likely to sell the bonds because institutional bonds were a main part of their foreign reserve. As a consequence, the American government took over Fannie Mae and Freddie Mac to help them overcome their difficulties. They each issued $1 billion preferred stock to the U.S. Treasury. By buying the stock, the Treasury injected $100 billion to them to maintain their net book value. The purpose was to release the information that these two would not go bankrupt and this ensured the safety of their bonds. In this way, it expected to restore market confidence, stimulate a market boom, and stabilize ratings and prices while trying to drag down the mortgage interest rate and re-invigorate the property market. The Federal Reserve, together with the top ten banks, established a $70 billion reserve on September 14, to provide a guarantee for financial institutions on the edge of bankruptcy and ensure the liquidity of the market.

Unfortunately, all these efforts could not stop the crisis from spreading. Within 24 hours between the nights of September 14 and 15, 2008, three pieces of shocking news were released from Wall Street, arousing the attention of the world. First, on the night of September 14, Bank of America acquired America's third largest investment bank, 94-year-old Merrill Lynch, for $44 billion[7]. Second, the fourth largest investment bank on Wall Street, Lehman Brothers Holdings Inc. (with $639 billion of assets), had a debt of $613 billion. Since the federal government and the private sector refused to provide financial guarantees, it had to apply for bankruptcy on the morning of the 15th [8]. Third, America's largest insurance company, AIG, was downgraded, because many of its due contracts had defaulted. When it was clear that there would be no loan provider to help it avoid bankruptcy, AIG urgently applied for a short-term loan from the Fed. In this way, it tried to prevent a further drop in rating, a rising cost of financing, the need for additional financing collateral or a claim on capital from competitors which would lead to bankruptcy within 48 to 72 hours. The Fed responded to AIG, and announced on the night of September 16, that its New York Federal Reserve Bank would unprecedentedly provide $85 billion of credit facility in exchange for 79.9% of AIG's equity capital. Moreover, the Fed had the power to suspend the bonuses and dividends of the issued common stock and preferred stock, in the hope that these measures would tide AIG over the crisis [9-10].

Significant events between September 7 and 16, 2008 damaged the confidence of investors. The subprime crisis deteriorated into a general credit crisis. The Wall Street Financial Crisis or Wall Street Financial Tsunami therefore came into being.

Accelerated spread across the world

The credit crisis was at core a crisis of faith or trust. Many people could not believe the economy would recover and so lost their trust in financial institutions, the financial system, and even the government itself. Even though this financial crisis started from the U.S., similar problems could be found in many other countries. Eventually, a global financial crisis broke out.

Influenced by the Wall Street Financial Crisis, the global stock market plummeted dramatically. On September 15, 2008, while the American Dow Jones Industrial Average and S & P Index fell by a large margin, indicators in other stock markets were impacted. London's FTSE index dropped by 3.29%, 212.5 points lower than the previous day. Frankfurt's DAX declined by 2.74%, or 170.3 points lower than the previous day and reached a two year low. The average index of the Paris CAC 40 showed a decrease of 3.78%, and the RTS index declined by 4.78%. Major Latin American countries all had a stock market decline on the 15th. The market drop in St. Paul, Brazil and Buenos Aires, Argentina was over 5%, while on the 16th, major stock markets in the Asia-Pacific region also had a gloomy day. The Chinese Shanghai Composite Index retreated down through the 2000-point mark and closed at 1986.64 with a 4.47% decline. The Shenzhen Composite Index dropped by 0.89%; the HK Hang Seng by 1052 points or 5.4%; the Nikkei Stock Index fell by 4.95%; and the Korean KOSPI by 6.1%. In other words, the Wall Street Financial Crisis had evolved into a global crisis.

After the global stock market had been severely hit, the financial crisis rapidly spread to other countries. Many of them immediately launched measures with huge sums of money to save the market. On September 15, the European Central Bank and the Bank of England injected €70 billion and €20 billion respectively into the market. On September 22, right after the U.S. had carried out its $700 billion bail-out, the British government made available £200 billion to tide over the banks which were at the edge of crisis. On September 28, Belgium, the Netherlands, and Luxembourg provided €11.2 billion to Ageas which was a joint venture between Belgium and the Netherlands. This plan would nationalize part of the group and help it avoid bankruptcy. On the same day, the British mortgage giant Bradford - Bentley was national-ized and split up for sale. At the end of September, the Hypo Real Estate Bank in Germany experienced a severe liquidity shortage. The German government and several financial institutions jointly provided it with debt a guarantee of €35 billion to rescue it from the fate of bankruptcy.

Entering October 2008, the liquidity of banking systems deterio-rated and governments adopted countermeasures. On October 2, the Japanese Central Bank put ¥22.7 trillion into the financial market. On the next day, Ireland passed an emergency act, providing the six larg-est domestic banks with a personal deposit guarantee of €400 billion for a two-year term to maintain the stability of its financial market. On the same day, the Greek Ministry of Finance announced that it would guarantee the personal deposit of all domestic banks to calm those who were eager to withdraw their money. The British government agreed to increase their personal deposit guarantee from £35,000 to £50,000. On October 5, BNP Paribas reached an agreement with Belgium and Lux-emburg to buy the branches of Ageas in the two countries. On the same day, the Danish government came to an agreement with commercial banks that a risk fund would be established and 35 billion DKK (1USD to 5.4 DKK) would be added to the fund. In this way, account holders would not lose money when banks went bankrupt. The Swedish government increased its guarantee for personal deposit and promised that its Central Bank would provide more loans to banks. On October 6, France said it would guarantee all personal deposits. On the next day, Ministers of Finance in EU countries agreed to raise the bottom line of deposit guarantee to stabilize the financial market and protect the interests of account holders. On October 8, the British Chancellor of Exchequer put forward a bail-out plan for British banks. £50 billion would be supplied to the banking sector. As part of the plan, the British Central Bank provided an additional credit loan quota of £200 billion to the banking and construction sector to increase their liquidity. On the same day, for the first time in history, six major Central Banks jointly lowered their interest rate by 50 basis points; the banks were the Fed, the European Central Bank, the British Central Bank, the Swiss Central Bank, the Canadian Central bank and the Swedish Central Bank. On October 9, Belgium's Prime Minister Lai Temu announced that Belgium, France and Luxemburg would together provide guarantees for Dexia Bank, a joint venture between Belgium and France. Such a plan would allow the bank to collect €4.5 billion from the market. Days later, Mexico, Chile, Australia, Portugal, Portland, and Korea all carried out countermeasures. Although many countries adopted plans to prevent the financial crisis from changing into an economic crisis, the real economy could not resist the trend of recession.

As the financial crisis spread, Iceland was the very first to collapse. The Icelandic krona depreciated greatly and the liquidity of its banking system worsened. On October 6, Prime Minister of Iceland Haarde warned his people: "…my fellow citizens, this is a real danger. In the worst case, the national economy would be sucked into the whirlpool by the banking sector. And the result would be the bankruptcy of the nation [11]." Three days after that, three of the largest banks were taken over by the government. On October 7, the second largest bank of Iceland, Landsbanki, was taken over by the government because of the crisis. Its on-line bank Icesave, which was running in the UK, closed all its business. On the same day, Iceland announced that the exchange rate of the krona would be changed into a whole set of trading partner currency exchange rates. According to the new system, the exchange rate of krona against the euro was pegged at 1:131 [12]. Such adjustment was not accepted by the market, however, and the exchange rate of the krona against the U.S. dollar continued to decline. On October 8, Iceland's government took over the third largest bank, Glitnir Bank, and started to restructure it. All its businesses in Finland and Sweden would be sold. On October 9, the Icelandic government took over the largest bank, Kaupthing, and suspended its trading in the stock market to prevent a larger financial panic. Because of the severe financial and economic situation in Iceland, many rating institutions downgraded all of its ratings. Moody's downgraded its sovereign credit rating by three grades to A1. Fitch Rating also downgraded its long-term foreign currency issuer default rating, and maintained its outlook as negative on the next day. On October 14, Russia and Iceland negotiated in Moscow about providing a 4 billion euro loan to Iceland. On October 24, Iceland applied to the IMF for an aiding loan of about $2 billion to cope with the financial crisis. Iceland became the first western country to receive aid from the IMF since 1976. On October 27, Iceland's Prime Minister Haarde pointed out in Helsinki that the $2.1 billion loan from the IMF was insufficient to help Iceland to overcome the crisis, and that an additional $4 billion was needed [13].

Facing a real global financial crisis, all countries joined hand in hand to deal with it together. On November 15, 2008, leaders of the G20 member states convened the Washington Summit on financial markets and the world economy. Participants reached consensus on the origins of the financial crisis, enhancing cooperation and fighting against trade protectionism and supporting economic growth. The topics included increasing the transparency of financial market and improving accountability, strengthening administration, facilitating the integrity of the market, emphasizing international cooperation and reforming international organization. The summit made a statement on fighting the financial crisis, emphasizing cooperation among countries when facing the challenge to the world economy and the international financial market. Similar crises should be prevented through re-stimulating world economic growth and reforming the world financial system [14]. On November 23, 2008, APEC closed its 16th Economic Leaders Informal Meeting in Lima, Peru, with a statement saying that it estimated that the global financial crisis would be over within 18 months [15].

After that, governments continued to carry out measures to save the market, including the economic incentive plan passed by the U.S. House of Representatives and the Senate on February 13th 2009. The value of the plan was as high as $787 billion. Unfortunately, this plan did not stop the development of the financial crisis and its spread to Eastern European and developing countries.

In this crisis, emerging countries, which have relatively more closed capital accounts, more independent financial systems and a better balance of payment could nevertheless not be shielded from the negative effects. Dramatic decreases of domestic demand in European countries, the U.S. and Japan led to the decrease of their imports from other countries. Korea, Singapore, Malaysia and other countries which focus on investment products and consumer durables were severely harmed. In addition, with the declining demands for energy, raw materials and other bulk commodities, their prices fell and the producer countries, such as Russia and Brazil, had their income, purchasing capacity and economic growth reduced.

Another important cause of further globalizing the financial crisis was the decline of capital input. In recent years, financial globalization had developed gradually. Many developing countries became increasingly dependent on foreign private capital, and as a consequence, any sudden withdrawal of foreign capital would damage those countries severely. After the breakout of Wall Street Financial Storm, investors of all countries lost their confidence and sold their risky capital and shifted to "safe assets". With this background, for fear of losing more in the harsh economic environment, institutional investors withdrew from emerging markets. The net private capital inflow in developing countries shrank sharply, and the demand for external financing could not be satisfied. Moreover, large scale capital flight led to the depreciation of currencies against the U.S. dollar in those countries. Some developing countries had their currency depreciate by as much as 50% [16]. Therefore, this crisis hurt many developing countries in Eastern Europe and Central Asia which heavily rely on capital input. On October 17, 2008, Ukraine and Hungary received loans from the IMF and the European Central Bank respectively to stabilize their financial markets. In 2008, Hungary and Lithuania had negative growth. In 2009, seven of the eight Central and Eastern European countries had negative growth. Three Baltic countries had two digit negative growth rates, namely Estonia -14.1%, Latvia -18.0%, and Lithuania -15.0%, while Hungary registered -6. 3%, the Czech Republic -4.1%, Slovakia -4.7%, and Slovenia -4.7%. The statistics showed a clear recession. Only Poland had a positive GDP growth rate of 1.8%.

On April 2, the G20 held the second Financial Summit. Participating leaders reached an agreement on strengthening the coordination of domestic macro-economic policies, stabilizing international financial market, enhancing financial supervision, reforming the international financial system and many other fruitful results [17]. After the summit, a G20 Declaration was made which approved the provision of $1.1 trillion to the IMF, the World Bank and other multilateral financial institutions. The fund flow to the IMF was increased from $250 billion to $750 billion. The summit recognized that it was necessary to carry out regulation and supervision of those financial institutions, products and markets which had systemic influence. For the first time, it put hedge funds under supervision. Against "tax havens" which refused to cooperate, actions and sanctions would be launched. The summit also decided to build a new Financial Stability Committee to replace the current Financial Stability Forum.

In order to cope with the crisis, governments adopted super loose monetary and fiscal policies, implementing a portfolio of quantitative easing, super low interest rate and high fiscal deficit. This macro control had unprecedented power. In the second quarter of 2009, policies started to produce a good momentum: the financial system was stabilized to some extent and the economy was turning positive. On September 1, 2009, Nordea Bank issued a forecast report, saying that the world economic recession had ceased and the world economy was recovering [18]. On September 3, OECD estimated that the speed of halting the current recession would be faster than expected and that the downturn might have already came to a halt [19].

From September 24 to 25, 2009, financial leaders of the G20 held a meeting in Pittsburgh, PA. During the meeting, leaders of major economies discussed how to facilitate world economic recovery, reform international financial institution and improve supervision over such institutions. Progress was made. Suggestions, such as reforming financial executives' compensation, administration of financial derivatives and establishing transnational supervision were put forward in the meeting. Meeting documents pointed out that even if there were signs of recovery, the momentum was not strong. The major problem was high unemployment rates and insufficient consumer demand. The world economy was returning to the normal path, but we could not be self-satisfied. The meeting emphasized that the current policy should stand and enough support should be provided to increase employment. Countries needed to avoid withdrawing suddenly from the mechanism, but should prepare a strategy based on their situation for any withdrawal. At the same time, coordination was required among countries. Participating leaders also highlighted the problem of economic imbalance and the need to achieve sustainable development in the long run [20].

Breakout of sovereign debt crisis

Just as countries and international organizations were beginning to be optimistic about economic recovery, the outbreak of the Dubai debt crisis followed by the European sovereign debt crisis cast a shadow over the world economy.

On November 25, 2009, Dubai, United Arab Emirates, in the

Middle East experienced a debt crisis. Dubai's Ministry of Finance announced that Dubai World and its property company Nakheel would postpone the repayment of more than $1 billion debt for at least six months to gain time for restructuring.

After the crisis broke out, the world stock markets were affected greatly. On the next day, the London market had a dramatic fall. The index of the FTSE 100 closed at 5194.13 points which was 170.3 points or 3.18% lower than the previous trading day. This was the lowest in three weeks and the largest single-day drop in eight months [21]. On November 27, the New York stock market dropped as well. Three major indexes all decreased by more than 1%, namely the Dow Jones 154.48 points or 1.48%, S & P 19.37 points or 1.78% and the Nasdaq 38.22 points or 1.75% [22]. Major stock markets in the Asia-Pacific region dropped too. Tokyo's Nikkei 225 stock average price had a decline of 3.22%, the Seoul composite index 4.69%, Indian Bombay SENSEX30 1.32%, the major stock price index of Manila Philippines 1.45% and Hong Kong's Hang Seng index 4.84% [23]. After the decline of the 26th, the Shanghai and Shenzhen stock markets continued to fall, the Shanghai Composite Index to below 3100 while the Shenzhen Component Index dropped by 3% [24].

On the 27th, Abu Dhabi, the largest of the seven emirates of the UAE provided $15 billion support to Dubai through the UAE Central Bank and two private banks. On December 1, Dubai World which had been trapped in debt said that restructuring its "problem debt" would need 26 billion, less than half of the total $59 billion while the rest would have "stable repayment". Negotiations were held with relevant banks for restructuring. On December 10, HSBC Holding, Standard Chartered, Lloyds Banking Group and the Royal Bank of Scotland agreed to restructure Dubai's debt. On December 14, the Dubai government released a "final rescue plan" through the Supreme Fiscal Committee, including $10 billion from Abu Dhabi and an act of bankruptcy. Dubai World would use this $10 billion to repay debt. If the restructuring was not successful, it would go into the procedures of bankruptcy according to the new act [25]. On March 30, 2010, one of the largest creditor of Dubai World, HSBC Holding, supported its restructuring plan and expressed hope for a positive result. The Dubai government prepared to restructure Dubai World with $9.5 billion. It was planned to repay the creditors within five to eight years. On May 20, Dubai World made a statement, saying that it had reached a $23.5 billion principle agreement with major bank creditors for restructuring debt. Such agreement cleared a big barrier on the path of escaping from difficulty [26].

The Dubai crisis had aroused people's vigilance about sovereign debt crisis and such a crisis broke out in Europe immediately afterwards. Up to the present, three waves have swept over Europe.

Wave One: Greece

While crisis broke out in Dubai in November 2009, the Greek Minister of Finance announced that the 2009 fiscal deficit was not 6% of GDP as expected, but 12.7%. The market went into panic and the CDS price relevant to the Greek national debt rocketed. In December, the three major rating companies all downgraded their Greek sovereign credit rating. The debt crisis could only deepen [27]. On January 28, 2010, for the first time the gap in the interest rate of ten-year national bonds between Germany and Greece surpassed 400 basis points, reaching a historical high.

The problem of sovereign debt did not exist solely in Greece, but was present in many other European countries as well. On April 22, 2010, Eurostat released their findings that fiscal deficit and public debt in all member states had exceeded the EU ceiling. In 2009, the fiscal deficit of 16 countries in the eurozone accounted for 6.3% of GDP, much higher than the 2% in 2008. It is more than twice the limit (3%) required by the EU's *Stability and Growth Pact*. The public debt ratio increased from 69.4% in 2008 to 78.7% [28]. Among all member states, Ireland had the highest fiscal deficit in 2009, being 14.3%. Besides Greece, the UK, Spain and Portugal also had high rates, 11.5%, 11.2% and 9.4% respectively. According to the statistics, in 2009 no member state had fiscal revenue. In addition, among the 27 member states, 12 exceeded the requirement of the *Stability and Growth Pact* for public debt ratio. Italy had the highest, 115.8%, and Greece took second place at 115.1% [29].

Entering 2010, the sovereign debt crisis in Europe became prominent. On January 11, 2010, Moody's warned Spain that without any effective measure, its national bond rating would be downgraded. On January 29, the Spanish government announced that its fiscal deficit, reaching 11.4% of GDP, had exceeded expectation. On February 4, the Spanish Ministry of Finance admitted that the general public budget deficit would be 9.8% of GDP. The following day saw a general panic and the Spanish stock market crashed by 6%, the largest fall in 15 months. On March 4, the Italian National Bureau of Statistics reported that in 2009 the Italian GDP had shrunk by 5% (its largest decrease since 1971). On March 6, the Portuguese government passed an economic stability and growth plan for the coming three years, which made it the second eurozone country with a fiscal austerity policy after Greece. On April 14, the EU Committee warned that Portugal had exceeded the fiscal deficit requirement and urged it to cut its deficit. In order to deal with its financial and economic crisis, the Portuguese government invested huge sums of money which led to the increasing ratio of fiscal deficit to GDP from 2.8% in 2008 to 9.3% in 2009.

On April 21, 2010, the premium on Greek ten-year bonds against German public debt increased by 5.01 percentage points, reaching its highest point since March 1998. At the same time, the ratio of Portuguese ten-year public debt against German national bond expanded to 172 basis points, reaching a 13-month high. Such figures fuelled doubts amongst investors about the uncertainties of solving the Greek debt crisis and the global market experienced a sell-off [30].

The European sovereign debt crisis continued to deteriorate. On April 23, 2010, Moody's adjusted the credit and deposit rating of the National Bank of Greece, which had the highest rating in Greece, from A2/P-1 to A3/P-2. On April 26, the Spanish Central Bank issued its report on public debt, revealing that the unpaid national bond in 2009 was €461.996 billion, 33.9% higher than previous year. The net debt was €116.881 billion, also much higher than the €51.751 billion of the previous year [31]. On April 27, S & P downgraded the Greek sovereign credit rating from BBB+ to BB+ and gave it a negative forecast. For the first time since the birth of the euro in 1999, Greek national bond was considered to be "junk bond" in eurozone countries. At the same time, S & P adjusted the rating of Portugal to A-, two grades lower. On the next day, S & P downgraded the Spanish sovereign credit rating from AA+ to AA which cast a shadow on the future.

In order to avoid degradation of the crisis into disaster, government leaders and Finance Ministers of EU member states had an emergency meeting and agreed on an aid scheme of €750 billion. This was the largest bail-out plan in European history. €440 billion of the total amount would be provided according to the agreement among eurozone countries and had a term of three years. Another €60 billion was based on items of the *Lisbon Treaty* and raised by the EU Committee from the financial market. The remaining €250 billion would be from the IMF [32].

After the plan was made, the European countries all carried out fiscal austerity plans, aiming at stabilizing the market by joint action. On May 13, the Portuguese government agreed to adopt tough measures to tighten fiscal policy. On May 25, Italian Prime Minister Berlusconi approved a plan of fiscal budget cuts worth €24 billion, aimed at reducing its budget deficit. On May 27, Spanish Prime Minister Jose Luis Rodriguez Zapatero put forward a €15 billion fiscal austerity plan and had it approved by Parliament. On June 8, the cabinet of the German coalition government supported the austerity plan proposed by Chancellor Merkel. According to the plan, Germany would cut its fiscal deficit by €80 billion by 2014, setting another historical record. The reduced deficit would account for 3% of GDP [33]. On June 10, the Madrid Savings Bank and Valencia Savings Bank decided to merge which was an important step in restructuring the banking sector. On June 22, British Chancellor of Exchequer George Osborne handed in an emergency fiscal budget by the new administration to reduce public expenditure and increase taxation in order to cut its deficit. According to this emergency budget, from 2010 to the fiscal year 2014~2015, the British government would reduce its annual expenditure by £32 billion[34]. On June 29, the Greek Parliament passed a five year fiscal austerity plan. These joint actions calmed the market to some extent.

In addition, to avoid the decline of national bond price, the European Central Bank had already purchased about 40 billion euro bonds by May 28, including government bonds of Greece, Spain, Portugal and Ireland of which €25 billion was for Greek sovereign debt [35].

Because of the uncertainties of the European sovereign debt crisis, investors had clearly lost confidence in the European economy. From November 2009 to June 2010, the (monthly average) exchange rate of the euro against the U.S. dollar dropped from 1.492 to 1.221. In other words, the euro continuously depreciated and hit its lowest point. It is shown in Chart 1-1.

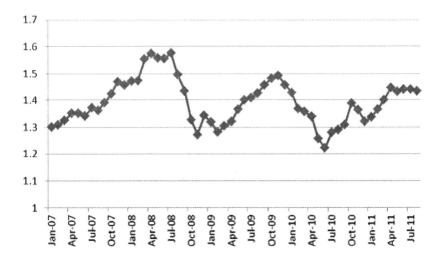

Chart 1-1 2007.1.~2011.8 Change of Monthly Exchange Rate of euro against USD. (Statistics from OECD)

With the aid of the EU and the IMF, the Greek sovereign debt crisis had been eased. According to the Greek Ministry of Finance, fiscal deficit in the first half of 2010 declined by 46% compared with the same period of the previous year. In 2009, it had been €17.8 billion euro and in 2010 it was reduced to €9.6 billion. Such information increased investors' confidence. Out of all expectation, on July 23, it was reported that the banking stress test in the eurozone only had 7 banks out of 91

sistance. On April 9, EU Finance Ministers held an informal meeting, agreed to provide aid and estimated that in the following three years the total amount of capital needed by Portugal would be €80 billion. The EU would provide €54 billion and the rest would come from the IMF. The EU also required the Portuguese government to present a plan to cut its expenditure and deficit.

As 2011 was ushered in, the European debt crisis was developing and there were many uncertainties.

First, the sovereign debt crisis in Greece was deteriorating. Three major rating institutions further downgraded its sovereign credit rating. On January 14, after Moody's, Fitch Rating rated Greece as "junk" level, from BBB- to BB+ with negative outlook. On March 7, Moody's reduced Greek national bond rating from "BB+" to "BB-". On May 23, the Greek government carried out a privatization package as part of a scheme to collect €50 billion to pay the debt by 2015. On June 29, the Greek Parliament passed a five year fiscal austerity plan, hoping that it would encourage more aid from the eurozone. The rating institutions did not buy it. Moody's lowered the long-term rating of Greece from "B" to "CCC" on July 4 and pointed out that incurring new debt to pay back the old might lead to selective default.

On July 11, the Greek Ministry of Finance announced that its deficit was €12.78 billion in the first half of 2011, which exceeded the limit of €10.37 billion. The major reason was that revenue had not been enough and the interest rate had increased. *Welt* of Germany reported on that day that Finance Ministers in the eurozone did not exclude the "extreme choice" which would restructure Greek sovereign debt to end the crisis. On July 21, the eurozone loaned Greece €109 billion after a summit meeting. The term of the loan was extended from seven and a half years to 15 to 30 years. The interest rate was lowered from 4.5% to 3.5%. In addition, private sectors such as banks agreed to aid Greece by purchasing €50 billion of bond from it. On July 27, S & P further cut Greek sovereign credit rating to "CC" with negative outlook. S & P thought that the EU's restructuring plan was a "cheap exchange" and that it was "unfavorable to investors". The restructuring was the equivalent of a "selective default". On September 23, Moody's downgraded eight Greek banks by two grades and defined the rating outlook of its long-term debt as negative.

Second, there were concerns about the sovereign debt in Spain. Spanish banks had more than $100 billion of risk exposure in Portugal, so Moody's downgraded 30 Spanish banks on March 24, 2011. Furthermore, the sovereign rating of Spain might be downgraded as well, since it held one third of all Portuguese national bonds (€105 billion). Even though the Spanish government had cut its expenditure and launched reforms, its economy could not achieve development. The public debt in Spain accounted for 55% of GDP and the 2011 budget deficit was 6.2% of GDP. In other words, the situation was not totally dangerous. However, individual and corporate debts were 178% of GDP and the unemployment rate was as high as 20%. Therefore, many people were concerned that Spain might be the victim of the next debt crisis. It would increase Spain's financing cost in the international capital market and cause a further downgrade of its credit rating. Spain is the fourth largest economy in the EU and its total volume is larger than that of Greece, Ireland and Portugal combined. The EU would do its best to stop it from collapsing. EU Commissioner Olli Rehn, German Minister of Finance Wolfgang Schaeuble, and the Spanish Minister of Finance all expressed the opinion that Spain had a small "chance of being infected by the debt crisis."

In addition, there was the possibility that the sovereign debt crisis would breakout in Italy. This country is the third largest economy in the eurozone, accounting for 17% in total. Therefore, economic stability in Italy is crucial to the survival of the eurozone. The size of Italian public debt reached 1.9 trillion euro in 2010, 120% of its GDP. If assistance were needed, the EU would bear a greater burden. There were other opinions, saying that the ratio of foreign debt in Italy (20%) was small; it had strong liquidity; its banking system was stable; and the share of its private debt was not large. Moreover, on May 25, 2010, the Italian government decided to cut government expenditure by 24 billion euro between 2011 and 2012 through fiscal austerity measures. By 2012, the ratio of fiscal deficit to GDP would drop to 2.7%, lower than EU's ceiling of 3%. By the end of September 2010, the total amount of credit loan in Italian banks relevant to Portugal was €3.4 billion, much lower than that of Spain (€86 billion), Germany (€40 billion), France (€37 billion) and the UK (€25 billion). In other words, the sovereign debt crisis in Portugal would have little influence on Italy.

However, the assets price of Italy crashed in July 2011. Optimistic views were mocked by reality. On July 8, 2011, the yield of Italian ten-year national bonds reached an unprecedented 245 basis points as premium against German national bonds. The yield of the Italian bond was 5.28%. On July 11, Italian President Giorgio Napolitano said, "the whole nation should unite together to overcome the current difficulty."

On September 13, Italian Prime Minister Silvio Berlusconi said at the joint press conference with President of the Council of Europe, Herman Van Rompuy, that the Italian Parliament would approve the second fiscal austerity plan of €54 billion ($73.86 billion) and would strike a balance in its budget by 2013. Such moves did not ease the tension of the market. On September 13, the Italian Ministry of Finance sold five-year national bonds of €6.5 billion ($8.89 billion) at an interest rate of 5.6%. On September 19, S & P downgraded Italian long-term sovereign debt rating from A+ to A and defined its outlook as negative. Two days later, it lowered the long-term credit rating of 7 Italian banks and defined their outlook as negative also, along with a further 8 banks.

Finally, other EU countries had all kinds of problems. For example, Belgium had a public debt as high as 100% of GDP, right behind Greece and Italy. Moreover, its June election in 2010 did not bring about a new administration. People suspected that it might be the next one facing a sovereign debt crisis. However, others considered that its deficit was only 5% of GDP. Consequently, in November 2010, the yield of its ten year national bond (3.7%) was much lower than that of Ireland (9.2%), Portugal (7%) and Spain (5.2%). As a result, there might not be sovereign debt crisis in Belgium. On the other hand, because of the in-fighting among parties, it had been without an official government for more than a year. According to its law, the caretaker cabinet has no power to decide national affairs. Hence, fiscal austerity policy and economic reform could not be launched. Fitch Rating announced on May 24, 2011, that the sovereign credit rating outlook of Belgium had been reduced from stable to negative. It also confirmed Belgium's "AA+" long-term foreign and local currency issuer default rating, defined as "F1+" its short-term rating and "AAA" its country ceiling rating.

In addition, eurozone countries paid a heavy price for saving Greece and other countries which were trapped in sovereign debt. For instance, in May 2010 the Czech Republic was dragged into heavy debt because of paying its quota for saving Greece.

Zig-zags on the road to economic recovery

On November 23, 2008, in the "2008 Xiaoguwei Financial Forum" held by the South China University of Technology, I said, "I am confident that the financial crisis will pass away in two to three years. By 2011, world economy will recover for sure [39]." This coincided with the statement of the 16th informal APEC leaders meeting which was issued that night saying that the global financial crisis would end in 18 months [40]. On November 15, 2009, I attended the 6th International Financial Forum and said in the opening speech that "as a cautious optimist, I think that with the joint efforts of all countries, the most difficult days have passed. The Chinese economy has touched bottom and become better and more stable. The world has embarked on the tortuous path of recovery. I believe that, in 2011, it is possible for the world economy to have positive growth[41]." The sovereign debt crisis in Dubai and some European countries delayed that recovery. However, if we define recovery as positive growth for three continuous quarters, the prediction was quite close.

In January 2010, the IMF stated in its World Economic Outlook that after experiencing a 3.2% economic recession in 2009, developed countries would only have a growth rate of 2.1% in 2010. In sharp contrast was the high speed of emerging economies. As a whole, developing

Table 1-1 2010~2011 Quarterly Economic Growth Rate of G20 Nations

Nations	2010Q1	2010Q2	2010Q3	2010Q4	2011Q1	2011Q2
Australia	2.37	3.05	2.66	2.65	1.04	1.38
Canada	2.07	3.62	3.82	3.35	2.85	2.17
France	1.05	1.48	1.63	1.37	2.10	1.60
Germany	2.39	4.05	4.03	3.77	4.63	2.76
Italy	0.67	1.43	1.39	1.51	1.04	0.82
Japan	5.52	3.32	4.80	2.48	-0.72	-1.09
Korea	8.44	7.29	4.37	4.71	3.92	3.39
Mexico	5.12	7.25	5.11	4.24	4.41	3.64
Turkey	11.26	9.99	6.85	9.68	10.14	..
UK	-0.27	1.62	2.54	1.54	1.65	0.74
US	2.17	3.30	3.51	3.14	2.24	1.55
Brazil	9.31	9.10	6.80	5.03	4.15	3.11
India*	9.30	8.92	8.35	7.77	..	..
Indonesia	5.62	6.11	5.80	6.87	6.49	6.48
Russia	2.88	5.12	3.59	4.32	3.81	..
South Africa	1.44	2.89	3.36	3.71	3.73	..
Eurozone	0.90	2.05	2.00	1.95	2.37	1.60
Spain	-1.38	-0.01	0.22	0.60	0.89	0.73
China	11.9	11.1	10.6	10.3	9.7	9.6
Argentina*	6.86	9.57	9.74	10.43	9.63	..
Singapore*	16.41	19.45	10.48	11.96	8.26	..

(Statistics are mainly quoted from the OECD. Nations with * had their statistics from the IMF database. Chinese figures are from the National Bureau of Statistics of China.)

countries would have a growth rate of 6% in 2010 among which India's would be 7.7% and China's 10%. The report also pointed out that countries and regions would differ because of specific initial situations, level of impact and their counter measures [42].

As shown in the above table, the IMF's prediction is close to reality. Most developing nations had smaller impact from the American financial crisis and their economy has basically revived. Nations such as China, India, Indonesia and Turkey, even though experiencing a slowing down of their economy in 2009, realized a relatively high growth rate in 2010. On the other hand, developed economies, such as the U.S., Britain, Japan and the EU, were seriously hurt by the financial crisis. Their economy had been reviving gradually, but there were still problems and uncertainties.

The Fed's Beige Book, issued in late July 2010, pointed out that even if the American economy had enjoyed positive growth in the first and second quarter of 2010 and its economy was coming back to good shape in general, the growing momentum remained weak because of the inactive property and automobile market. The American financial sector had been seriously harmed in the crisis and had taken a further hit from the European sovereign debt crisis. Now it was still weak in general with occasional problems. Unemployment rate was high at 9% and would not drop in the short term. Both consumers and corporations were cautious. Enterprises slowed down their recruitment of new staff. Consumer spending shrank. The tension of state and local government could not be eased, and budget shortfall in state governments would pose a threat to the American economy. There was a huge public debt which presented certain risks. All of the above mentioned reasons set barriers for American economic recovery. On October 1, 2010, the U.S. government issued a report expressing the opinion that the incentive scheme of Obama administration was running well, but that there were still uncertainties. After the mid-term election, the Obama Democrat administration faced more resistance from Congress now dominated by the Republican Party. In July 2011, the fierce bargaining between the two parties about raising the limit of national bonds shocked the world.

The biggest problem faced by the EU was the turbulence of the European financial market caused initially by the sovereign debt crisis in Greece and some other countries. Although in the first and second quarters of 2010 economic growth had been better than anticipated, European banks had achieved good results in the stress test (84 out of 91 passed the test), and the divergence between national bonds and corporate bonds in most EU countries had been narrowed, the confidence of investors had still not been restored to the level at the beginning of the year. They were still cautious. European banks were worried about the European economy and were not willing to loan money. The real economy of Europe had "insufficient blood supply" and could not move forward. In some EU member states, the unemployment rate remained high as they launched fiscal austerity plans. Because of fears for the future, consumers were not willing to buy. The conclusion is that in 2010 European economic growth was driven by exports. Economic recovery still faced the shadow of the sovereign debt crisis. In addition, it should also be noted that even if the European Central Bank was a convenient tool to coordinate monetary policies in EU countries, financial policies are quite different among those countries. Some of them had to consider the negative influence of tightened policy on politics. Monetary policy might hence be less effective.

On October 6, 2010, the IMF pointed out in its World Economic Outlook that Japan had enjoyed its economic recovery driven by growing exports which were based on the demands of western countries and China. However, the Japanese economy remained weak. Insufficient domestic demands and political stress over policies cast a shadow on its future, and economic growth might therefore slow down. Overseas capitals further purchased Japanese yen and sold U.S. dollars because of an estimated narrower gap between Japanese and American interest rates. Consequently, the price of the Japanese yen rose continuously until the exchange rate was close to one U.S. dollar to 80 yen. This was disastrous to Japanese exporters. Investors who had no faith in Japanese banks and the nation's highly reliant economy shifted their money to the bond market. On August 4, 2010, the yield of newly issued ten year national bonds, which can be taken as an indicator of long term interest rate, dropped to less than 1% for the first time in seven years. It even worsened the negative forecast for the future of the economy. Moreover, the Japanese premiership changed too frequently (from 1992 to today, there have been 15 Prime Ministers). Hence, the Japanese government could not maintain the stability of its economic policy under the stress of deflation. People predicted that the downturn of the Japanese economy would be sustained for two decades. This would be a "lost two decades" for Japan.

Even though China is still a developing country, it fought together with other countries to overcome the financial crisis. China declared that it would not reduce its holding of euro bonds but would support the stability of the euro. Measures adopted by the EU and the IMF were welcomed by Chinese government. It sent a trade and investment mission to Europe and signed many important contracts. China not only bought large amount of American and Japanese bonds, but was also increasing its imports from those developed countries.

Even though there are uncertainties for the world economy, many developing nations have recovered and the developed ones have taken a turn for the better, lessening the chances of another worldwide financial crisis. However, it is necessary to remain vigilant and not to be overoptimistic based on the scenario in the U.S., Europe and Japan. On September 22, 2010, the Fed declared its interest rate policy, stating that the goal was for the rate to remain at the current level of 0-0.25%. If necessary, it would provide additional accommodating support to the American economy. The European Central Bank announced on October 7, that the leading interest rate in the 16 eurozone countries would be kept at 1%. On the same day, the British Central Bank, the Bank of England, also decided to keep its leading interest rate at 0.5% which was a historical low, as well as not increasing the currency supply. On October 5, the Japanese Central Bank lowered its benchmark interest rate from 0.1% to between 0 to 0.1%. This was the first time for Japan to have a zero rate policy in the previous four years.

The Fed released a new round of quantitative easing plans on

March 3, 2010. National bonds worth $600 billion would be purchased before the second quarter of 2011 to revive the economy. Such a plan would cause pressure towards appreciation of some currencies and lead hot money to these countries in arbitrage.

After careful consideration, the Fed did not launch QE3 after QE2 as expected. Instead, it announced, on September 21, that it would maintain its federal funds rate at between 0~0.25% after the Federal Open Market Committee had finished its meeting. At the same time, the FOMC planned to have Operation Twist which meant that it would adjust the structure of the American national debt and try to lower medium- and long-term interest rates by buying and selling short-term and long-term bonds. Eventually, this would promote the recovery of the American economy. The schedule is that by June 2012, Fed will sell $400 billion medium- and short-term national bonds which have a maturity date of no more than three years while it will purchase the same amount of medium-and-long-term bonds whose remaining maturity is between 6 and 30 years. Is this going to be effective? Only time will tell.

On April 7, 2011, European Central Bank increased the key rate in the eurozone from 1% to 1.25%. This was the first time for it to raise the interest rate since July 2008. On July 7, 2011, it further increased the rate to 1.5%. Britain, at the same time, declared that it would maintain its benchmark interest rate at 0.50%. The Japanese central bank announced on September 7, 2011, that the inter-bank unsecured overnight call rate, which is also the benchmark interest rate, would remain at between 0.0-0.1%. It is estimated that developed countries will sustain these low rates for some time which means that economic recovery will not be stable.

Dominique Strauss-Kahn, President of the IMF at that time, gave an interview on October 7, 2010 with French journal *Le Monde*. He said that along with the trend of recovery, countries were developing different policies based on their individual situations, especially in terms of monetary policy. Since there was insufficient coordination among monetary policies, he was worried about a possible "monetary war". In order to achieve an overall global economic recovery, all countries should cooperate closely, be confident, overcome difficulties and stop fighting a trade war or currency war. At the same time, experience and lessons should be drawn from this financial crisis. We need to promote global financial system reform and build a stable, balanced and fair international monetary system.

Summary

1. The American financial crisis originated from subprime loan defaults, developing from a loan crisis to a crisis of liquidity and ultimately to a crisis of credibility. Starting from the U.S., the crisis spread to every corner of the world and led to sovereign debt crisis in some countries and a worldwide financial crisis.

2. The crisis extended from the virtual economy to the real economy and triggered severe economic crisis. World economic growth rate therefore decreased to 2.8% in 2008 and -0.6% in 2009. The global economy fell into recession.

3. According to the statistics of the first and second quarters of 2010, most developing nations had a smaller impact from the American financial crisis and their economy has basically recovered. Nations, such as China, India, Indonesia and Turkey, even though experiencing a slowing down of their economies in 2009, realized a relatively high growth rate in the first half of 2010. On the other hand, developed economies, such as the U.S., Britain, Japan and the EU, were seriously hurt by financial crisis. Their economy has been reviving gradually, but there are still problems and uncertainties in financial, economic and political areas. Since developing nations have recovered and the developed ones have set foot on the rugged road to recovery, there are smaller chances of another worldwide financial crisis. However, it is necessary to remain vigilant and not to be overoptimistic.

4. In order to achieve a global economic recovery, all countries should closely cooperate, be confident, overcome difficulties and abstain from

fighting a trade war or a currency war. At the same time, experience and lessons should be drawn from the current financial crisis. We need to promote a global financial system, reform and build a stable, balanced and fair international monetary system.

2.

An Analysis of the Origins of the American Financial Crisis

People hold many different views on the causes of the American financial crisis. Some argue that it was loose supervision and under-regulation by government or financial institutes that led to this crisis, while others consider over-innovative financing or operational confusion as its origins; yet others believe that it was overcapacity of production in the financial industry that did so or even, finally, that the crisis itself was a huge conspiracy deliberately plotted by America. The interpretation of these causes remains a matter of academic discussion. In my opinion, we should probe, objectively rather than subjectively, into the internal causes in order to clarify the sources of the crisis instead of limiting our focus to some exterior phenomena or external reasons for this situation.

Some Chinese scholars, basing their argument upon Marxist theory of the crisis of capitalism, attribute the origins of the American financial crisis to the capitalist mode of production, which, however, is too general an argument for this analysis since it cannot explain the reason why the crisis only occurred in America at that particular time nor can it provide any valuable lessons from experience, albeit theoretically correct. In respect of other scholars' belief that it is China's socialist system that has allowed her to maintain relatively high growth leading to unique prosperity despite the global crisis, I would myself argue that this cannot be the case, since capitalist countries such as

India and Indonesia have also maintained their high growth during this gloomy time.

In my view, one important cause of this financial crisis is the over-inflation of fictitious capital from excessive borrowing and speculation.

The concept of fictitious capital

'Fictitious capital' is mentioned in Chapter 25 of the third volume of Karl Marx's *Das Kapital*, in which he wrote that negotiable security and other financial products occurring from loan capital and the bank credit system could be considered as fictitious capital. Hence, if investors bought stocks or bonds, then these could be regarded as titles of ownership as they have given their capital's right of use to others while maintaining its ownership. Investors could, via this warrant, demand that the bond issuers repay capital with interest and share issuers give bonuses as well as protecting the rights and interests of their shareholders. Remember that the value of this title of ownership relies greatly upon credit such as the repayment of capital with interest and the distribution of dividends or shares holding as promised by those who enjoying the right of use. Yet the warrant of ownership is just worthless paper once the credit has been broken. Karl Marx believed that 'real' capital must have its own value and produce surplus value at the same time. However, negotiable security itself does not have any value yet produces surplus value in some form, so for this reason he referred to it as 'fictitious capital'.

It is my view that fictitious capital refers to trust-based resources that produce profits and have indefinite prices rather than being in real forms or sharing monetary features. The appearance of warrant of ownership embodies the dual characteristics of capital ownership as it separates right of use and ownership of capital. Hence the occurrence of fictitious capital, which includes three types of capital, namely, credit capital, knowledge capital and social capital. Holders of the above three fictitious capitals do not have real capital themselves, yet they can obtain right of use of real capital. Warrant of ownership simply means ownership of fictitious capital with no value in itself, and thus referred to as secondary fictitious capital.

Inflation is one trait of fictitious capital

Inflation based upon the bank credit system is one prodigious trait of fictitious capital. Karl Marx cites a simple example in *Das Kapital:* a London merchant A, by means of middleman B, books an array of commodities from a Manchester manufacturer C to sell it to client D in East India. In such a case, each one of A, B, C or D could discount bills issued by one another to banks for the purpose of obtaining spendable funds within a short time, thereby causing an inflation of their fictitious capital.

Let us extend and extrapolate from this case: assuming there was 1 million demanded with a 1 year time of delivery (TOD). After a series of contracts being signed between B and C, A and D as well as A and B, they could each discount to a bank by means of bills or might borrow money from a bank in the name of these contracts. Manufacturer C could discount to his bank with bills issued by B or might borrow money, in the name of contracts signed with B, from the bank for the purpose of purchasing materials, hiring employees and organizing manufacture. Middleman B could discount to his bank with bills issued by A or might borrow money, in the name of contracts signed with A, from the bank. Similarly, A could borrow money in the name of contracts signed with D and vice versa. Under such circumstances, the 1 million of A has turned into 4 million spendable funds within half a year. Undoubtedly, this is a simplified case because, in practice, banks will definitely give a discount when they are providing loans and also manufacturer C is not fool enough to organize manufacturing before he or she has received some earnest money.

Let us suppose A, B and D, within half a year, are trying to do some business with the money borrowed from the bank for the purpose of earning more money. If each merchant earns a profit, then B may give the 1 million to C, deliver commodities obtained from C to A and return the 1 million taken from A to the bank. A delivers the commodities to D via marine transit and returns D's 1 million payment to the bank. Also D may return the 1 million loan to the bank as soon as the commodities are sold in India. Yet the whole capital chain would be broken if there were any problem occurring in one link, i.e., one merchant could break the contract or promise, and in that case, the bank would face bad debts while the contract breaker would be punished by law.

Currently, inflation of fictitious capital is much greater than the above mentioned description in Karl Marx's time (the 19th century). There are endless dazzling financial derivative products in today's world accompanying the development of science and technology in combination with advances in financial innovation. The original intention of introducing financial derivative products was to satisfy different investor preferences regarding security, profitability and liquidity as well as to decrease risk by making good use of hedging. However, construction of financial derivative products could also result in swift inflation of fictitious capital as these derivatives might offer various opportunities for speculation in financial markets.

The inflation of fictitious capital has several characteristics, as follows.[1]

Overvaluation: Inflation of fictitious capital occurs when investors overvalue a particular warrant of ownership. Take stock markets as an example: if investors are overoptimistic as to the profitability of a listed company, they will purchase shares in that company at a relatively high price. In particular many investors, in a bull market, will pursue one stock out of following suit or fooling mentality, namely, they believe someone else will take over the same stock at a much higher price, thus forming a stock market bubble, from which investors will inevitably suffer heavy losses.

Excessive Liabilities: If those who seeking financing believes its return on asset (ROA) are higher than the rate of borrowing, they will borrow a great deal of money for much greater profits via the purchase of more assets. This will make the ratio of their liabilities versus self-owned capital as great as several tenfold or even hundredfold. Yet if investors become pessimistic in this regard, they may demand recovery of the loans or refuse to grant new loans, in which case, the party seeking financing will, more often than not, face a risk of bankruptcy.

Small Investment for Large Deal: Investing a small amount of capital for guaranteeing large deals. Taking commodities futures markets as an example, initially one might buy a futures contract with only 5% earnest money in advance.

Multiplier Effect: A well-known result of the influence of the multiplier effect is that an initial currency offering of a Central Bank can be expanded several times into a socially circulating quantity of money. Similarly, fictitious capital can also be expanded gradually via the multiplier effect. For instance, bond holders may obtain cash, by means of pledging their bonds to banks, for the purpose of using this amount of cash as earnest money to purchase futures and financial derivative products. Hence the fund initially used for the purchase of bonds may be calculated into outstanding bonds, open interest futures (the amount of money being possibly as much as 20 times that of the earnest money) and open interest derivatives, thus being magnified dozens of times in book value. Yet the bond holders' risk will increase from former bonds to current futures and derivatives accordingly. Put it another way: they may get high returns or they may lose their shirts.

The cause of America's financial crisis lies in the over-inflation of fictitious capital resulting from excessive liabilities, generally referred to as a high rate of leverage. Putting it another way, leverage rate can be interpreted as the number of coins that can be earned with 1 coin. Data on leverage rates for America in 2007 are, 8 to 12 for commercial banks and 25 to 40 for investing banks. In respect of the two Fs (Freddie Mac and Fannie Mae, American government sponsored enterprises), their leverage rate once attained 62.5 at its highest level, which means that they issued USD 5.2 trillion from only USD 83.2 billion. In addition, for a very few AAA-rated bonds, their leverage rate could be as much as a hundredfold.

A high leverage rate is, for one thing, conducive to high efficiency in the operation of capital. Let us assume that the leverage rate is 40 times, and the return on investment is one percentage point higher than borrowing rate, then the real rate of return could reach 40 percent or more. For another thing, however, it increases risks as well, because although one might do 1 million coins worth of business with only 25 000 coins provided that the leverage rate is 40 times, in case of any market disturbance - say the borrowing rate goes higher than return on investment - then the 25,000 coins will not be able to handle it, and the investor must make up the deficit by means of incurring new debts or selling his or her stock rights.

Reasons for the rapid development of the subprime mortgage market under the effect of high rates of leverage are as follows. Firstly, the American government enacted some unwise policies as they over-intervened in housing markets. Specifically, the American government forced their sponsored Freddie Mac and Fannie Mae to loan to buyers who lacked the capacity to pay their mortgages. In the second place, regulatory authorities neglected their duties by slackening or simplifying conditions and procedures of mortgage investigation, being acquiescent to concealed entities and implementing a loose supervision of derivatives. Thirdly, rating agencies made misguided ratings as they gave extremely high ratings to "toxic assets" that included subprime mortgages. Lastly, many executives and employees of American financial institutions betrayed their professional ethics out of human greed and desire, thus encouraging the growth of the subprime mortgage.

Amplification of inflation risk of fictitious capital

The balance of the American subprime market was estimated at USD1.3 trillion by the end of February 2007.[2] How could only USD1.3 trillion trigger the global financial crisis? No one so far has been able to come up with a complete explanation, as the process is extremely complicated and a long period of intensive study will be required before it can be done. Based upon initial analysis, however, the author will illustrate a general explanation as follows.

By means of financial innovation, two industrial chains are formed. The first is, Borrower—Housing loan institutions such as commercial banks—Housing loan issuer—Investment banks—Insurers; the other is Mortgage debt creditor's rights—MBS—CDO—CDS. By following these two chains, fictitious capital gradually inflates with increasing risks, causing a debt crisis developing into a liquidity crisis and eventually becoming a credit crisis.

The Debt crisis

A borrower is required to pay a loan facilitator (such as a bank or other financial institution) in time as stated in the contract to repay the mortgage debt signed soon after he or she has purchased housing property with a loan from a commercial bank or other loan institution. If a contract break or default occurs, then the borrower must pay default interest. If the default goes beyond the deadline and the borrower is still unable to repay the outstanding money, the lender may take ownership of the property in line with the law and the procedures of the loan. Then the property will be retaken, in accordance with the law for auction. Hence we can understand that risk in the first-mortgage market mainly come from default and this is usually assumed by the financial institution. When the estate price goes down while interest rate rises, default will begin with subprime mortgages, since those who accept subprime mortgages badly lack anti-risk capacities. The default rate of subprime mortgages was approximately 16%[3] in October 2007 and this figure rose to 21%[4] and then on to 25%[5] in January and May of 2008 respectively.

With real estate prices go down further, some prime loans also default as they are unable to repay the interest, and still others deliberately default in that price of estate is lower than the difference between its buying price and capital interest being paid, which results in rapid growth of default rate and the house property for auction. In 2007, 1.286 million houses lost their right of redemption, an increase of 79%[6] compared with 2006. In 2008, this number rose to 2.335 million, an increase of 81% compared with that of 2007[7]. Values of dead account for housing loan defaults by American families reached to USD 9.9 trillion in 2006, yet this figure increased to USD 10.6 trillion[8] by the middle of 2008. Worse, debt crisis occurs as a result of losses for loan institutions such as heavy decline in stock price or even bankruptcy triggered by the declining price of house property for auction and the sluggishness of marketing in this regard.

As a result of the impact of the subprime mortgage crisis, a general debt crisis, which expanded from defaults on housing mortgage to defaults on automobile loans and other amortizations, even defaults on credit cards, dealt a fatal blow to commercial banks.

Liquidity crisis

With the development of financial innovations, several financial derivative products came on to the market.

MBS(Mortgage-Based Securities)

With the fast growth of first mortgage markets, secondary markets, which focus upon mortgage sale and resale, gradually formed with MBS via asset securitization. MBS, more often than not, are bonds that take a creditor's right of mortgage as pledge and issued with fixed monthly payments and with coupon rate as well as repayment of the loan on its due date. People who purchased MBS could earn a profit, provided there was an increasing house price and a relatively low loan interest rate, and also provided that their income could meet the capital and interest repayment of the mortgages, since the interest on MBS is much higher than that of deposit.

At the beginning of the growth of secondary markets, MBS was issued by some Government Sponsored Enterprises (GSE), among whom Fannie Mae and Freddie Mac were the two largest with major business in purchasing loans in the American mortgage secondary market as well as issuing bonds or MBS. Guaranteed by Fannie Mae and Freddie Mac under the aegis of the American government, these MBS enjoyed very high credibility. From 1989, MBS issued by Fannie Mae and Freddie Mac attracted many legal investors as their interest rates, on average, were 137 basic points higher than those of 10-year American public bonds.

Private sectors or institutions were also involved in issuing MBS as the secondary markets grew. Commercial banks might sell packaged mortgages to a Special Purpose Vehicle (SPV), which was established for separating the risk of bankruptcy, and then allow the SPV to issue MBS. Risk separation meant that the creditor of the originator could not conduct recovery of pledged assets truly sold to the SPV after the originator had been bankrupted.

In fact, SPVs are shell companies with no links to commercial banks. Usually registered in places enjoying tax preferences such as the Cayman Islands, these companies do not have any fixed staff or office as all of their functions are outsourced to other professional institutions. The SPV purchases (on credit) mortgage assets from commercial banks, finances in its own name by issuing MBS, and then uses the newly raised funds to repay the cost of mortgage assets purchased before. With almost equal assets and liabilities, the SPV entrusts facilitators to collect receivable capital and interest from borrowers and consigns trustee banks to repay capital and interest to MBS holders in line with the contract.

The emergence of secondary markets changed the traditional ways in which commercial banks alone undertook risks, for these were now distributed to investors in MBS, while the commercial bank no longer had to hold its mortgage till the due date. MBS enabled many financial institutions and investors around the world to invest in the American real estate market yet distributed risks across borders. The value of MBS mainly depended upon the repayment rate of mortgage and house price.

During the periods of rapidly rising house prices, as the interest rate of MBS was much higher than that on borrowing, with a spread of 2 to 3 percentage point, financial institutions such as prime banks and investment banks invested heavily in MBS by means of borrowing in great amounts. By the end of March 2007, there was a USD 6.3 trillion balance of MBS including USD 900 billion in subprime mortgage. The proportion of securitization in subprime mortgages increased from 54% in 2001 to 75% in 2006.

America issued three provisions on issuing MBS for the purpose of guarding against risks and increasing investors' confidence. Firstly, it was necessary to retain a certain margin, i.e., quantities of financial claim for supporting MBS should be maintained above or beyond that of bonds issued for the purpose of guarding against decrease of remainder capital resulting from speedier payment of interest or repayment of capital by borrowers. Secondly, if borrowers were unable to repay in time during the initial repayment period, investors might force issuers to buy back those securities. Thirdly, SPVs had to invite credit rating agencies to assess their proposed issuance of MBS before they conducted credit ratings. If the rating process itself failed to meet the desired standard, then it was necessary to invite financial bonding companies or other institutions to raise their credit by means of excess warranty or other effective methods, and this process was defined as credit enhancement.

However, the above measures were unable to deal with problems caused by a sharp fall of house prices as well. When the debt crisis occurred, institutions issuing MBS were unable to collect the receivable capital and interest on mortgage, and thus did not have enough cash to pay back contracted interest to investors nor could they pay capital to those who demanded a pay-back, a situation which, eventually brought about liquidity issues. To increase their liquidity, what issuers generally did to obtain cash in these cases was either borrow money from other financial institutions or sell their own assets such as stocks or bonds. However, the credit rating of issuers was lowered greatly as people became pessimistic about the prospects of real estate, which resulted in other financial institutions being reluctant to lend. At such a time, investors' capital would shrink greatly, while the price of MBS would decline more steeply with rises in default rate. Moreover, because MBS is one type of constant income security, the price of MBS could decline once the interest rate rose, which in turn would result in a decline of the stock price of MBS issuers, hence making it difficult to rely upon new borrowing or selling assets for obtaining the money in question. If liquidity issues originating in this way could not be eased or settled, financial institutions would eventually go into bankruptcy.

CDO(Collateralized Debt Obligations)

Financial institutions such as investment banks or funds further re-securitized MBS via financial innovation to create a variety of derivatives with methods of financial engineering such as estimation, portfolio and packages. Then they sold them in the secondary financial market with high interest to attract other financial markets or hedging funds. As one of the best-known derivatives among them, CDO was a structuring Asset-Based Securities (ABS for short) whose issuers collected various mortgages including housing mortgages, student loans and commercial loans into an asset pool and then divided it into different tranches according to their risks and rewards for the purpose of selling them to different investors based upon their risk preferences. Usually a typical CDO might be classified as senior tranche, middle tranche and rights and interests tranche bonds. As far as risk exposure was concerned, rights and interests tranche bonds did not generally have credit ratings, and were therefore the most vulnerable tranche as it had to undertake responsibility in the very first place if there were any default losses occurring in the basic asset pool. Yet accordingly it enjoyed higher returns than the others. The repayment of capital and interest of the senior tranche, more often than not, with AAA ratings, enjoyed priority over the other two tranches while it had less return because of a lower credit risk exposure. The features of risk and gain of the middle tranche came between the previous two with a rating range of between AA and BB.

Similar to MBS, initiators of CDO (usually investment banks) packaged their own diversified mortgage assets into assets pool (basic assets) and then conducted a "true" sell to SPV. After this process of risk separation, CDO holders were not entitled to pursue recovery from initiators for the reason that the mortgage assets could not meet its return. As the titular issuer of CDO, the SPV supported the issuing CDO by taking basic assets as guarantee, and then paying out consideration of initiators' assets with the money obtained from CDO issuance.

Assets regulators of CDO (usually investment banks) tended to be holders in the rights and interests tranche, and often attracted investors by displaying their past performance and holding large numbers of rights and interests of CDO. Regulators not only earned commissions during the period of issuance, they could earn fees of management within the duration of the CDO as well. Credit rating institutions were charged with examining and assessing the affordable risk intensity of basic assets as well as defining the scale and proportion of allocation for different tranches for the purpose of ensuring that rating requirements could be met by them. In addition, rating institutions might continue their follow-up ratings of the CDO afterwards.

Purchasers of CDO tended to be insurance companies, banks, pension funds, investment corporations, investment banks and hedging funds,. They were trying to earn a high cost of carry (as the return rate of CDO, under normal circumstances, was higher by 2 to 3 percentage points than that of company debentures with the same ratings). With regard to those who played a more active role in investment, they conducted arbitrage by means of CDO transactions. And hedging funds usually put their purchased CDO in pledge and then obtained loans from commercial bank with a high leverage rate of 5 to 15 times.

Moreover, the introduction of CDOs of CDOs, CDO-Squared and CDO-Tripled made the process of securitization more complicated even for the élites in financial circles. By the end of 2007, American CDO scaled up to USD 19.8 trillion compared with the USD 25 trillion globally accumulated circulations.

Essentially, a SPV was a form of Off-Balance Sheet Entity in a "blank space" that was free of regulation because bank regulators and stockholders did not know of its existence at all. Securitization of mortgage assets enabled financial institutions to transfer their issued mortgages to SPV, which being outside the balance sheet for the purpose of avoiding capital requirements, thus increased profits but with a corresponding increase in risk [9].

When the debt crisis was triggered by the collapse of housing prices, a great many mortgage loans, as basic assets of the CDO, then defaulted, and investment banks or other financial institutions had to undersell their numerous CDO as they were facing great pressure from creditors dunning for debt, thus resulting in a further decline of price of the CDO. According to the newly issued accounting standard of Market to Market (MTM for short), financial institutions should, quarterly, adjust their held financial assets in line with market price. However, the price of these assets was far less than that value during normal periods in that price then was determined by the recent status of transactions of similar assets. As the price of demand was quite high while the price provided was very low in CDO markets, financial institutions had to lower the price of their bonds to a market standard, which resulted in a significant decrease in their rights and interests, thus intensifying investors' panic for they had to undersell more CDO till their face value in terms of USD 1 declined to 7 to 11 cents. Furthermore, if their income from selling assets could not meet their financial obligations, they would eventually have to go bankrupt as a result of the emerging liquidity problems.

In order to reduce risk, investors might insure with insurance companies for credit protection. Generally, MBS and CDO were underwritten by institutions of monoline insurance mostly with a credit rating of AAA. Yet if the credit rating of their warranted housing mortgage went down rapidly, the amount of claim would rise dramatically, thus leading to a reduction in the credit rating of institutions of monoline insurance and this would affect their warranted municipal bonds as well as other products in question. A number of insurance companies would go bankrupt as a result of emerging liquidity problems.

CDS (Credit Default Swap)

CDS was a recent financial innovation based upon CDO. Investors of MBS and CDO could purchase CDS to guard against credit risks. In fact, CDS was a type of credit production with features of insurance. The buy-side of CDS were creditors who were anxious about defaults of debtors with warranties, so the sell-side promised that the opposite party might exchange their warranties for deserved arrearages if credit events such as bankruptcies or defaults occurred to debtors. Usually lasting for 5 years, contracts of this kind featured curb exchange with free assignments. All of the transactions were conducted in an anonymous way with secret transaction records and prices, thus making effective supervision and regulation harder for the regulators.

Like other derivatives, CDS could be used as hedges for the purpose of safeguarding creditors against losses from debtors' default and could also serve as instruments for speculation. Prices of CDS relied heavily upon debtors' capacity for repayment including default probabilities, probable time of default, value of recovery and fundraising cost, etc. The default rate of housing loan was relatively low as the price of real estate went up, thus leading to a low price for CDS. As a result, many investors purchased CDS in great numbers for the purpose of gaining credit protection at a lower price. Apart from investors, some speculators would do the same as they were planning to earn a profit by means of selling these CDS at the time of good price, or expecting to get significant compensation when credit events occurred. On the other hand, financial institutions such as insurance companies also seized the opportunity to sell massive CDS because they wanted to increase their premium income during the period of a relatively low risk. Furthermore, some speculators acquired premium easily through selling CDS although they did not have any loan transactions at all. CDS markets inflated rapidly in the financial markets of developed economies like America and Europe as they could be used to speculate via free assignment. It was estimated that the total value of open interest in the world was as much as USD 33 to 62 trillion by the end of 2007.

As one kind of instrument for speculation, CDS could affect stock markets as well. If speculators considered that a certain over-indebted company was becoming insolvent, they would purchase CDS of that company in large numbers meanwhile overselling its stocks for the purpose of raising the price of the CDS and then selling out immediately. As the price of the CDS went up, the company would find it hard to obtain loans from banks, and thus they would sink into crisis. In fact, CDS had become a gambling instrument at this moment as it was played like an unrestrained game between speculators of the buy-side and sell-side.

Credit events occurred massively right after the breakout of the subprime crisis. The number of dead accounts increased 100 times from 1998 to 2008. As the sell-side of CDS had to pay significant compensation while recovered guarantees were difficult to realize, this triggered issues of liquidity. For instance, AIG held a total value of USD 440 billion while being lucky to escape from bankruptcy due to an urgent rescue by the American government.

In summary, it was the sharp decline in the price of real estate, by means of derivatives such as MBS, CDO and CDS in American mortgage secondary markets, which results in tremendous liquidity risk for American financial markets, thereby, eventually enabling the subprime crisis to become a liquidity crisis.

Credit crisis

With the development of the liquidity crisis, a series of credit events occurred in the first half month of September 2008, including Freddie Mac and Fannie Mae being taken over by government, Lehman Brothers going into bankruptcy, Merrill Lynch being purchased and AIG accepting bailout from the government, all of which triggered a serious credit crisis, thus resulting in the Wall Street financial storm in September and bringing about the emergence of a global financial crisis.

The credit system functions as a cornerstone of the modern market economy and a necessary support of the fictitious economy. In recent years, fictitious capital, supported by the credit system, had inflated rapidly, thus promoting the fictitious economy, which developed rapidly and generated fabulous wealth for American-led western developed countries.

As stated before, just as the debt crisis was activated by the loss of personal credibility of numerous borrowers, so the liquidity crisis had to be caused by the loss of credibility of many financial institutions. The credit crisis, however, could only derive from the loss of creditability of individuals, financial institutions, enterprises and even governments. If the credit system broke down, it would be difficult for owners of actual capital to withdraw their right of use of their capital, which might have disappeared by then. Worrying about their counterparts' credit deficiency, the increasingly panic-stricken investors might, albeit reluctantly, undersell their holding at a lower price. Moreover, they would strive to withdraw their deposits from banks for the purpose of repaying their debts to avoid bankruptcy as well as preparing for future difficulties. However, banks would suffer a crisis in that they could neither recover their due loans through borrowers' default, nor would they have sufficient reserves due to depositors' large money withdrawal. Financial institutions would heavily impact bond markets as they might undersell their MBS and CDO holdings with a drastic decline in price. Hence the stock market would plunge as it would be dragged down by investors underselling and the devastating decline in value of financial institutions.

There was USD150 billion-worth of withdrawal for the first 2 days immediately after the credit crisis broke out and a further USD 5 billion outflow on average every 2 days during the following period.[10] On September 16, the per unit assets net value of the Reserve Primary Fund declined to less than USD 1 as it held bonds from Lehman Brothers. Such being the case, investors demanded to buy it back one after another. On the morning of the 18th of the same month, before the money market opened its doors, panic-stricken investors, worried about a credit squeeze caused by a slump in net value of monetary fund and commercial paper, demanded a USD 500 billion transaction order of "sale" compared with the approximately USD 400 billion aggregate market value. Thanks to the USD 105 billion liquidity bailout from the American Federal Reserve Committee, the market, however, was saved from collapse at this time.[11]

On September 21, Goldman Sachs and Morgan Stanley, the two surviving investment banks, applied to make a transition to bank holding corporations, which indicated that American investment banks had collapsed. Furthermore, on the morning of the 25th of the same month, Washington Mutual, the largest American deposit and loan bank, was taken over by the American Federal Deposit Insurance Corporation. A majority of the assets of Washington Mutual were transferred to J. P. Morgan Chase at a price of USD 1.9 billion [12]. Consequently on September 29, the Dow Jones Industrial Index dropped to a record low with the loss of 778 points in one day. [13]

The American financial crisis spreads to the rest of the world

With the development of economic globalization, ties between financial markets are increasingly close among the nations of the world. Cross-border financial transactions, particularly among developed countries, are conducted frequently. For instance, the transfer quantities of euro-dollars in the Chicago Mercantile Exchange are over USD 2 trillion per day. Contacts between financial markets and financial institutions among developed countries are so inextricably linked that one cannot be separated from the other.

The American financial crisis, first and foremost, spread to the developed world by means of "toxic assets" such as MBS, CDO and CDS. European investors would also be influenced by the same panic if these assets were undersold in America. As a result, derivatives issued by American financial institutions shrank dramatically because of the speedy undersell. Moreover, European financial institutions would also be impacted as prices of their derivatives and stocks slumped through being undersold by panic-stricken investors. Hence European financial institutions were increasingly being impacted as some of them even became incapable holding themselves together.

The crisis spread rapidly immediately after the Wall Street financial storm, first and foremost over-running the big banks of the developed countries of Europe. During the short period between September 18 and 30, a number of banks, including Germany's Hypo Real Estate and Belgium's FORTIS, delivered applications to their government for bailout or acquisition as they were in deep trouble. From then on, a money squeeze appeared in banking sectors with a rise of the London overnight dollar LIBOR from 4.7% to 6.88% on September 30.[14]

The financial markets of developing countries were also feeling the effects during the spread of the American financial crisis into Europe. Stock markets, housing markets and debt markets in several developing countries slumped as a result of rapid withdrawal of capital from developed countries. Some financial institutions of developing countries had made a loss from the purchase of toxic assets.

America and European countries, facing serious financial crisis, poured liquidity into banks in combination with other bailout measures, yet still failed to curb the globally spreading crisis. It is my view that a credit crisis is essentially a crisis of confidence and credence, and thus the permanent cure for that is to regain the public's confidence and credence in financial institutions and systems as well as their government rather than a temporary treatment by pouring in liquidity.

The sovereign debt crisis

Sovereign debt refers to the debts of one country, vouched for by its sovereignty, borrowed from international organizations such as the IMF and the World Bank, or from other countries, and financial institutions, as well as individual investors by means of signing debit and credit agreements or issuing public debt. If this debt cannot be refunded by its due date, then a sovereign debt crisis will occur. In addition to government over-indebtedness, the weight of excessive debt in large government banks and sponsored investing platforms may also trigger sovereign debt.

Government over-indebtedness

Under the "smart operation" of Goldman Sachs, Greece joined EU in 2001 without a hitch. With the growing economy of the eurozone, Greece maintained a strong economic growth rate of over 7% between 2001 and 2007, which enabled the Greek government to launch an expansionary fiscal policy of incurring a great number of debts from the European Central Bank and issuing massive public debts. However, the Greek government witnessed an increasing growth in its financial deficits and public debts, which went far beyond the standards stipulated by the EU, as a result of a series of economic problems, including low efficiency in investment, growing labor wages and high social welfare expenditures, unreasonable industrial structure (with only 20% manufacturing industry in its total GDP) and low taxation rates with many loopholes. With the American financial crisis spreading further into Europe, Greek extra-oriented industries such as tourism and shipping were heavily impacted with a drastic decline in agricultural export and overseas remittance. In 2009, the Greek government urgently lunched an economic stimulus plan including a massive issuance of short-term bonds with a 5-year-period or below and borrowing numerous short-term bailout funds, which resulted in a surge in its financial deficits and public debts. What was even worse for Greece was that there was a negative growth in its economy, in combination with investors' panic concerning its debt paying ability, which eventually triggered the sovereign debt crisis. On June 14, 2010, Moody's Investors Service, one of the three largest international rating agencies, downgraded by four consecutive levels for Greek sovereign debt from A3 to Bl, i.e., rubbish level. This was another disaster for the Greek sovereign debt crisis as their government credit was seriously damaged. Under such circumstances, some other countries in the eurozone with heavy sovereign debt started to feel insecure as well. Moreover, panic-stricken investors, worrying about the debt issue of the whole European economy, led to substantial tremors in the capital markets of many countries, thus making financing more difficult for enterprises in default countries and eventually being problematic obstacles for European economic recovery.

Similar to Greece, Portugal, for a period of almost 40 years between 1974 and 2010, had been encouraging over-expenditure and the creation of an investment bubble, including complicated partnerships between government and private sectors, substantial payment of unnecessary and inefficient consulting or advising fees, permission for over-expenditure in public projects regulated by government, increasing improvement of bonus and salary for senior executives of enterprises and senior government officials as well as expanding government staff members, which, in combination with mismanagement of funds and surges in public debts and credit risks, caused the Portuguese government to become heavily indebted to maintain its economy by means of continually taking on new debts to repay the old ones. Although the Portuguese economy, on average, developed faster than that of the EU during the 1990s, it had been declining since the beginning of the 21st century with a per capita GDP of only 2/3rds that of the EU as it had been impacted by cost-low countries in Central Europe and Asia. After the American financial crisis broke out, the Portuguese government experienced both a drastic decline in its fiscal revenue and a difficult time for making new loans, thus becoming incapable of repaying its due debts and eventually triggering its sovereign debt crisis. According to one report, Portuguese public indebtedness was as much as 83.3% of its GDP by the end of 2010. In April 2011, Portugal's debt maturity reached €4.23 billion, yet this number became €4.9 billion in June in the same year. However, Portugal only had a cash reserve of approximately €4 billion, so they had to plead the EU for help.

Over-indebtedness of big banks

Iceland, as the very first country to fall in the crisis, has its mode of economic development to blame, since its sovereign credit crisis resulted from the over-indebtedness of its banks. In the previous years, Iceland had accelerated the opening-up of their financial system with high interest rates and loose regulation for the purpose of attracting offshore funds, thus gaining a profit in the value-added chain of global capital flow. Following the lead of other international investment banks, the banks of Iceland borrowed substantial low-interest and short-term funds from international capital markets to invest in long-term or subprime-related assets with high returns. For the few years before the subprime crisis, when the global economy was bright, Icelandic banks incurred excessive debts with a shocking financial leverage. The total external debt was as much as €100 billion on a scale of 12 times its GDP. However, there were only €4 billion of current assets in the Central Bank of Iceland[15]. As the author has stated before, this mode of development, namely, relying upon international credit markets with a high leverage rate, though profitable, has great risk of an emerging debt crisis because of a small economic aggregate and inadequate foreign exchange reserve, at a time of credit squeeze in the international market, impacted by the American financial crisis, and facing difficulty in taking on new debts for the old ones.

Ireland benefitted greatly from its EU entry, as it became the second richest country after Luxemburg in the EU from having been one of the poorest countries in Europe. For many years, the Irish government budget maintained a surplus with a public debt of only about 30% of its GDP. Nevertheless, Irish banks, encouraged by its thriving economy, invested substantially in domestic and overseas real estate as well as in other industries, thus taking on potential risks. As early as December 2008, the scandal of a secret loan by the Anglo Irish Bank was exposed, which led to the resignation of their three senior executives and an investigation into their ten shareholders in business circles. On January 20, 2009, a bill nationalizing the Anglo Irish Bank was passed by the Irish Parliament, thus throwing a heavy burden on to the Irish government. Under the impact of the American financial crisis, the real estate bubble burst, and this resulted in an increase in the growth of bad debts in Irish banks. The Irish government injected a total value of USD 24.4 billion capital over seven different occasions into the Anglo Irish Bank during the period between December 2008 and August 2010. However, it still failed to make up for their dozens of billions of deficits. This case reveals that the Irish government's gigantic public funds bailout to rescue their banks led to a soaring rise in public debt and eventually brought about a sovereign debt crisis.

People started to worry about the next country that might have a sovereign debt crisis--Spain, the fourth economy in the EU. Before 2008, the economy of Spain was sound with a large number of investments. Spanish Banks also invested in the real estate industry, whose building sector contributed 16% of the country's GDP and employed 12% of its total labor force. Although its public debt in 2008 was below that of other eurozone countries and there was a surplus in their government budget, Spain underwent a sharp deterioration in its financial conditions. During the fast growth period between 2006 and 2007, the credit of the Spanish Savings Bank expanded 5 times, accounting for 50% of the total credit of the country. However, regional small savings banks (Caja for short) were the first to be damaged and Spain's real estate bubble burst dramatically under the devastating impact of the American financial crisis. It is estimated that Spain had bad debts of €3.5 billion as CCM (Caja Castilla la Mancha) Bank was squeezed by its depositors and the Central Bank of Spain had to implement a take-over policy to guard against bankruptcy. On May 20, 2010, the Central Bank of Spain had to take over the defective bank CajaSur, damaged by its errors in speculation, by injecting a €500 million bailout and replacing its senior executives. Although the assets of CajaSur only accounted for 0.6% of those of the Bank of Spain, it initiated a decline of stock markets in America and Europe as well as in the euro because of investors' fears about the sovereign debt problems of Spain.

Over-indebtedness of government sponsored investment platforms

The sovereign debt crisis of Dubai was caused by the over-indebtedness of their government-affiliated Dubai World. In recent years, Dubai World, sponsored by their government, made substantial borrowings up to a total financial obligation of USD 59 billion, and then invested it in real estate for urban construction. Subsequently, various high-rise buildings and mansions sprang up like mushrooms, leading to the observation that "one could find one-third of world tower cranes in China and see one fifth in Dubai." After the American financial crisis broke out, Dubai had to declare its incapability of repaying some of its debts as the mode of management of Dubai World, that is, the cycle of borrowing—construction—selling—repaying—re-borrowing, could no longer be maintained. Faced with demands for repayment by creditors, they found it impossible to make new loans, thus triggering a debt crisis.

Although the world economy is regaining its strength, prospects for sovereign credit risks are rising in some countries, particularly those in Europe, as a result of the relative slow economic recovery in the region. Compensations for credit risks in these countries are improving, as can be seen from credit risk default premiums in the following table 2.

Table 2-1 CDS Premium of Different Countries

	Jan 2008	Jun 2009	Dec 2009	Jun 2010
UK	9	87	70	93
America	8	45	32	43
France	10	38	24	95
Germany	7	34	23	50
Greece	22	155	182	762
Ireland	13	220	150	285
Italy	20	105	85	245
Portugal	18	77	70	358
Spain	18	98	86	269

(Data Source—Thomson Reuters DataStream)

According to historical experience, a financial crisis is usually followed by government default. Statistics from the IMF show that 257 default events of sovereign debt occurred between 1824 and 2007, namely, default events resulting from inability or reluctance of a certain government to timely repay their obligations at debt maturity. Although Greek GDP accounts for only 2.5% of that in the eurozone, its sovereign debt crisis may result in the loss of investor confidence in countries in that area as Greece is a member of the special monetary system of the eurozone, or it may even lead to the disintegration of the eurozone itself, and that explains well the reason why the eurozone countries have had to bail out those with a sovereign debt crisis like Greece.

However, countries cannot be truly "bankrupt", and methods of solving sovereign debt crisis are nothing more than international relief, debt restructuring, national assets sale, and domestic expenditure restriction. Generally, international relief, including extension of loans and purchase of its bonds, is the most effective measure adopted for small economies such as Greece, Ireland and Portugal. Debt restructuring, after consulting with creditors for their satisfactory compensation or promise, and moratorium on the part of capital and interest may increase the cost of debit and debt, yet recovery to normal levels may be achieved after 2 or 3 years. With regard to demands like interest suspension or reduction or even repayment of a certain proportion of the principal of creditor's debt due, such solutions are unwillingly consented to by creditors because of their worries about consuming a large economic loss. Selling national assets may ease urgent needs; however, on the one hand, it is difficult to find buyers at the proper price in the short term. On the other hand, such sales may meet internal resistance. For instance, in December 2010, dispatchers at Spanish airports went on strike immediately after the news of the government's intention to privatize their airports was released, which resulted in the government taking military control over the nation's airport. Another important means of getting through a crisis, a restriction on domestic expenditure, might, however, bring about political risks for the government or even jeopardize the ruling party as it would impact the advanced social welfare system of Europe. Furthermore, it might discourage consumer enthusiasm for spending, thus reducing the dynamic force of economic recovery.

The most worrying thing, however, is the rapid increase in American public debt arising from the need to stimulate the economy and increase employment since the outbreak of the American financial crisis, which shifts commercial risk in markets into sovereign risk rapidly. If America, the issuer of the global major reserve currency, outsources its inflation to the world in order to mitigate the pressure of its own indebtedness, it will bring about a disaster to the world economy.

The financial crisis spreads into the real economy

Three phenomena appeared after the occurrence of the credit crisis.

The first one lay in the reluctance of banks to lend money as they perceived increasing risk in loans, thus making conditions of loan more difficult and raising the inter-bank offered rate even higher. In this situation, it became more difficult for enterprises and individuals to obtain loans from banks.

The second was investors' reluctance to invest as people started to consider that at this time the safest way of guarding against loss was to keep their money in their own pockets. Under the circumstance of declining American stock markets, the price per share for some listed companies has been less than that of their net assets value or has even been less than that of its net present value. Investors should be very sure about the success of buying stocks in these companies, yet still no one buys in case they are being fooled by fake information in this regard.

The third phenomenon is consumers' reluctance to purchase as they are pessimistic about the economic prospect. People's property values shrank dramatically as a result of losses in the stock markets, and they have had to cut down their expenditure and consumption in case of economic deterioration in the future.

Finance is the heart and capital is the blood of modern economies. The real economy is driven by bank accommodations, investment and consumptions. If reluctance to loan, invest and purchase grows in banks, investors and consumers respectively, the real economy will be directly affected. And so it is that the real economies of countries in the world have been sliding downwards since 2008. Many countries, witnessed a negative growth in 2009. However, by 2010, most countries had rebounded as figures show in the following table 2-2.

Table 2-2 Economic Growth Rate of Major Countries(2008~2010)

	2008	2009	2010
Australia	3.73	1.29	
Canada	0.52	-2.46	3.07
France	-0.08	-2.73	1.48
Germany	0.99	-4.72	3.63
Italy	-1.32	-5.22	1.30
Japan	-1.17	-6.29	5.12
South Korea	2.30	0.32	6.16
Mexico	1.50	-6.08	5.50
Turkey	0.66	-4.83	8.95
UK	-0.07	-4.87	1.25
America	-0.02	-2.67	2.85
Brazil	5.16	-0.64	7.49
India	4.93	9.10	9.72
Indonesia	6.01	4.58	6.10
Russia	5.25	-7.81	4.03
South Africa	3.58	-1.68	2.84
China	9.60	9.20	10.30
Argentina	6.76	0.85	9.16
Spain	0.86	-3.72	-0.14
Singapore	1.49	-0.77	14.47

(Data Source: World Bank Database)

According to data from the IMF, the global economy only increased by 2.8% and -0.6% in 2008 and 2009 respectively; comparable figures in 2008 and 2009 for the eurozone were 0.32% and -4.04% respectively, which indicates that recession in this area was more serious than that in America.

In order to analyze relations between the real and the fictitious economy further during the process of crisis spread, we studied the relevant mode and degree of correlation between them during the financial crisis by applying tail correlation of SJC-Copula-based matrix and time-variation correlation of DCC t-Copula-based matrix. Results of our study show that the crisis had a notable impact upon the correlation structure of the fictitious and the real economy. Specifically, tail correlation, compared with that of pre-crisis, increased after the outbreak of the crisis, which indicates that the financial crisis increased the probability of co-occurrence of extremum between the real economy and fictitious economy; parameters of time-variation show that the real and the fictitious economy maintained a relatively high level of correlation during the stationary phase of the pre-crisis, but that the correlativity of the two economies declined with the further development of the financial crisis.

The following table 2-1 shows the time-variation of relevant parameters between fictitious economic indicators and the U.S. Coincident Index (USCI). Deriving from the American Economic Cycle Research Institute (ECRI), the USCI is an index integrated with the real economic indicators which change synchronously with the American economic cycle. From the figure below one can see parameter changes in a similar trend, although they are different in numbers. Before 2008, parameters between fictitious economic indicators and the USCI maintained a relatively high correlation. However, characteristics of correlativity have been declining dynamically since the financial crisis developed further in 2008.

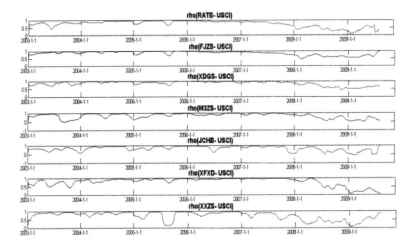

Figure 2-1 Time-varying Correlation of the Real Economy and Fictitious Economy

(Note: In the above figure, USCI refers to U.S Coincident Index; RATE refers to the effective Interest Rate of U.S Federal Funds; FJZS stands for House Price Composite Index; XDGS means the Total Credit Number of American Domestic Financial Credit Companies; M3ZS refers to American M3 Index; JCHB means Circulation of American Monetary Base; XFXD stands for the Total Number of Consumption Credit Held and Securitized.)

From the perspective of historical developments, the fictitious economy both originates from and adheres to the real economy in the context of the market economy. However, on the very eve of the financial crisis, the American fictitious economy expanded excessively, thus, to some extent enabling its separation from the real economy like a horse free of its reins and eventually becoming a great scourge to the whole of society. It was this serious deviation of the fictitious economy from the real economy that led to the American financial crisis.

Summary

1. Fictitious capital is a trust-based resource that produces profits and has indefinite prices rather than being in real forms or sharing monetary features. One main characteristic of fictitious capital is its expandabil-

ity, based upon the credit systems of banks, and including features of overvaluation, over-indebtedness, small investment for large deals and multiplier effects. The main cause of this financial crisis was the over-inflation of fictitious capital from speculative over-indebtedness, generally being referred to as an over-high leverage rate, which, on the one hand, is conducive to efficiently operating capital, but on the other, increases risk as well.

2. The reasons for the rapid development of subprime mortgages under the effect of highly leveraged rates are as follows. Firstly, the American government pursued some unwise polices as they over-intervened in the housing markets. Specifically, the American government forced their sponsored Freddie Mac and Fannie Mae to make loans to buyers lacking the capacity to pay their mortgage. In the second place, regulatory authorities neglected their duties by slackening or simplifying the conditions and procedures of mortgage investigation, being acquiescent to concealed entities and implementing a loose supervision of derivatives. Thirdly, rating agencies made misguided ratings as they gave extremely high ratings to "toxic products" that included subprime mortgages. Lastly, many executives and employees of American financial institutions lost their professional ethics out of the greed and rapacity of human nature, thus resulting in the growth of subprime mortgages.

3. By means of financial innovation, the following two industrial chains were formed. The first was, Borrower---Housing loan institutions such as commercial banks---Housing loan issuer---Investing banks---Insurers; the other was Mortgage debt creditor's rights---MBS--CDO---CDS. By following these two chains, fictitious capital gradually inflated with increasing risks until there was a debt crisis, which then developed into a liquidity crisis and eventually into a credit crisis. After the financial crisis broke out, banks were reluctant to loan, investors did not want to invest and consumers were unwilling to purchase, which enabled the crisis to spread from the fictitious economy to the real economy, and eventually led to a serious economic crisis. In 2008, the world economic

growth rate slumped to 2.8% and then fell into recession with a growth rate of -0.6% in 2009.

4. Sovereign debt refers to the debts of one country, vouched for by its sovereignty, incurred from international organizations such as the IMF and the World Bank, or other countries, financial institutions as well as individual investors by means of signing debit and credit agreements or issuing public debt bonds. If this debt cannot be refunded by its due date, a sovereign debt crisis will occur. This kind of debt crisis may occur not only as a result of over-indebtedness by governments (such as Greece and Portugal) or governments being dragged down by their overly indebted banks (such as Iceland and Ireland) but also by being dragged under by government- sponsored investment banks burdened with over-indebtedness(such as Dubai in the United Arab Emirates).

5. The crisis had a notable impact upon the correlation structure of the fictitious economy and the real economy. Specifically, tail correlation increased after the outbreak of the crisis, compared with its value pre-crisis, which indicates that the financial crisis increased the probability of co-occurrence of extremum between the real and the fictitious economy; Parameters of time-variation show that the real and the fictitious economy maintained a relatively high level of correlation during the stationary pre-crisis phase, but that correlativity between the two economies declined with the further development of the financial crisis.

3.

The Impact of the U.S. Financial Crisis on the Global Economy

If we apply the principle of dialectical materialism in analyzing the impact of the U.S. financial crisis on the global economy, two points call for our attention. First, the influence of the U.S. financial crisis must be seen as the external factor, while the economy of each country itself should be viewed as the intrinsic cause. The former manifests itself only through the latter. Therefore we analyze the economic conditions of various countries and categorize them. For this purpose, the 36 sample countries are summarized into five categories: seven major developed nations(the United States, Japan, Germany, the United Kingdom, France, Canada and Italy), fourteen other developed countries(Australia, Austria, Belgium, Denmark, Finland, the Netherlands, New Zealand, Norway, Sweden, Switzerland, Spain, Greece, Ireland and Portugal), four emerging Asian economies(India, Indonesia, Republic of Korea and Malaysia), six emerging European economies(Poland, the Czech Republic, Hungary, Slovakia, Slovenia and Turkey) and five other emerging economies(Mexico, Brazil, Chile, South Africa and Russia).

Second, although the U.S. Subprime Crisis exposed itself completely at the beginning of 2007, it did show some symptoms early in the middle of 2006, when the fictitious economic indicators of the second and third quarters of 2006 (including the federal funds effective rate, the House Price Index, real estate mortgage loan defaults of all commercial banks, the credit increase rate of domestic U.S. finance companies, total financial assets issuing ABS, and the U.S. Consumer Confidence Index) reached their peak and started to fall back. As the real estate market cooled down and oil prices surged ahead, demand for consumption and investment reduced their pace. By the fourth quarter, the growth rate of gross fixed capital formation had dropped to -0.4%. However, the sustained growth of employment and the gradual slide of oil prices managed to increase total U.S. consumption in the fourth quarter. After the second quarter of 2006, the United States and many other countries kept raising their interest rates to cope with excessive liquidity. On August 8, 2006, however, the Federal Reserve announced that it would maintain the 5.25% federal funds rate, ending the run of 17 consecutive interest rate rises, by 25 base points each time, since June 2004. Subsequently on September 20, October 25, and December 12, the Federal Open Market Committee decided to keep the interest rate unchanged. Such decisions and monetary policies mark the modulation of the U.S. economic expansion cycle, drawing extensive and close attention from all over the world. As oil prices fell back and the United States stopped raising interest rates, countries such as Canada, the Republic of Korea, Thailand and Indonesia adopted the same measure or even started to reduce interest rates. Such a series of adjustments indicated that fluctuations had emerged in the global economy, which can be seen as the prelude to the financial crisis. Therefore we selected the period of 2006-2009 for our research and analyzed the economic conditions of the 36 sample countries from the five aspects of stock market, industrial production, domestic demand, foreign trade and economic growth.

The impact of the U.S. financial crisis on global stock markets

This report collected the stock price index of 36 sample countries from 2006 to 2009 and the quarterly data of their year-on-year growth rates to analyze the stock markets of these countries at the build-up, outbreak, growth and recovery stages of the financial crisis. Data resources came from the Organization for Economic Co-operation and Development(OECD). Figure 3-1 shows the average growth rate of the stock price index 2006-2009 for developed countries and emerging economies.

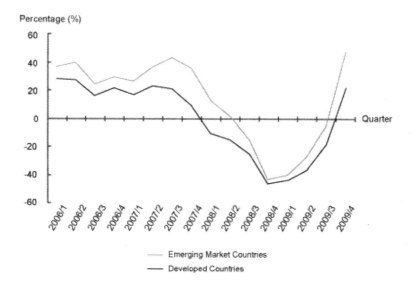

Figure 3-1 Average Growth Rate of Stock Price Index 2006-2009 for Two Categories of Countries

We can see from Figure 3-1 a similar situation in the average growth rate of the stock price index for the two categories of countries, with a correlation coefficient reaching 0.974. In the first half of 2006, the economic and financial recovery somewhat helped the global stock market to remain buoyant but accumulating a bubble. From June to July 2006, global inflation was exacerbated and the Federal Reserve and other central banks raised their interest rates. The year-on-year growth rate of the stock price index, as a result, slid downwards dramatically. At the beginning of 2007, the U.S. subprime crisis became visible, followed by global inflation pressure and the prospect of interest rate hikes, leaving investor optimism gravely damaged. The subprime crisis grew and the stock market of developed countries kept sliding backward from the second quarter. As the crisis got even worse from the third, stock price index growth for emerging economies also started to decline. Though the central banks joined hands to inject capital into the financial system, such remedies failed to relieve investor panic, leading to a continuous downslide of the stock market. The Wall Street Storm of September 15, 2008 spread the crisis to the world. By the fourth quarter of 2008, the stock price of developed countries and emerging economies dropped by 46.0% and 43.8% respectively, almost reaching the bottom.

In 2009, countermeasures by various countries started to function. Though the stock price of developed countries and emerging economies kept falling by a large margin, the extent was decreasing. By the fourth quarter, the average growth rate of stock price for the two categories of country turned positive. On the whole, the year-on-year growth rate of stock price index 2006-2009 for emerging economies had always been higher than for developed countries, indicating that the stock market of emerging economies were less affected by the U.S. financial crisis when compared with developed countries.

Figure 3-2 represents the average growth rate of the stock price index 2006-2009 for five categories of countries.

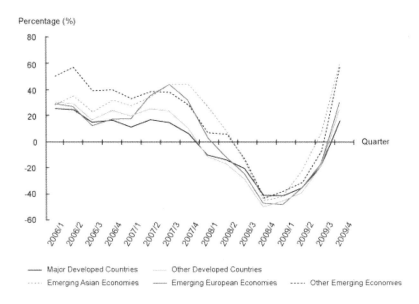

Percentage (%)

— Major Developed Countries · · · · Other Developed Countries
· · · · · Emerging Asian Economies — Emerging European Economies · · · · · Other Emerging Economies

Figure 3-2 Average Growth Rate of Stock Price Index 2006-2009 for Five Categories of Countries

We can see from Figure 3-2 a similar trend in the average growth rate of the stock price index in 2006~2009 for the five categories. "Other emerging economies" showed the fastest average growth rate while the emerging European economies performed worse than the other two categories of emerging economies. Major developed countries grew more slowly than "other developed countries", showing that the stock markets of the former were most hit by the financial crisis.

Figure 3-3 is a box plot showing the year-on-year growth rate of the stock price index from 2006 - 2009 for 36 sample countries. The black line in the middle is the median of the data while the short lines at the top and bottom are the upper quartile and lower quartile. This means that half of the data lies within the box whereas the other half is distributed outside it. The vertical segments at the upper and lower side of the box symbolize such distribution outside the box. According to the SPSS default, if all samples lie within 1.5 times the box length from the quartile, then the two ends of the line are the "maximum" and "minimum". For distance longer than 1.5 times the box length, the points are defined by the SPSS software as the "outliers". The two ends are called the "extremes" if the distance is longer than 3 times the box length[1].

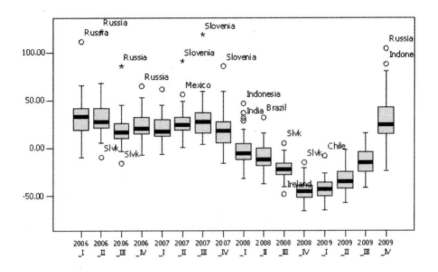

Figure 3-3 Year-on-Year Growth Rate of Stock Price Index 2006-2009 for 36 Sample Countries

Figure 3-3 shows that the third quarter of 2008 to the second quarter of 2009 was the gravest period of the crisis, witnessing the smallest degree of dispersion for growth rate distribution. This degree increased gradually from the first quarter to the fourth of 2009, reaching its highest figure since 2006 in the fourth quarter. This indicates that the recovery extent of the stock market for each country varied at the last stage of the crisis.

Figure 3-4 represents the year-on-year growth rate of stock price for 36 sample countries in the fourth quarter of 2009.

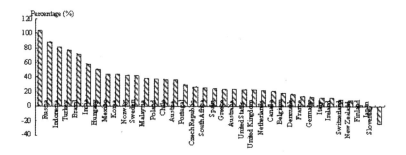

Figure 3-4 Year-on-Year Growth Rate of Stock Price for 36 Sample Countries in the Fourth Quarter of 2009

A comparison of the 36 sample countries shows that the stock price of Russia and Indonesia grew faster than all others. Emerging economies such as Turkey, Brazil and India also enjoyed a comparatively rapid growth rate. In addition, the stock market of most countries realized positive growth except those of Slovakia and Slovenia. Japan's stock price index regained growth but its growth rate turned out to be remarkably lower than others.

The impact of the U.S. financial crisis on global industrial production

Global industrial production can be reflected by the Industrial Production Index (IPI), an economic indicator that represents the status of the industrial economy of the report period by measuring the ratio of output in this period against that in the base period. However, the algorithm used by one country differs from that of another. For the sake of data comparability, we adopted the data published by the OECD based on a normative approach to represent the year-on-year growth of the Industrial Production Index for various countries.

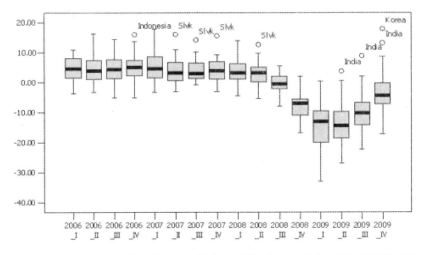

Figure 3-5 Year-on-Year Growth Rate of Industrial Production Index 2006-2009 for 36 Sample Countries

Figure 3-5 represents the year-on-year growth rate of IPI 2006-2009 for 36 sample countries. We can see that from the first quarter of 2006 to the second quarter of 2008 all sample countries grew steadily by around 4% in industrial production. In the third quarter of 2008, their average growth rate started to fall dramatically and this trend continued until the second quarter of 2009. In the third and fourth quarter of 2009 things got a little better. After the financial crisis broke out, the degree of dispersion for industrial production growth increased, indicating that the impact of the financial crisis on industrial production varied according to country, and their industrial growth rates differed greatly. At the later stage of the financial crisis, India and South Korea grew observably faster than others.

We group the 36 countries into two categories: developed countries and emerging economies. Figure 3-6 represents the average growth rate of their Industrial Production Index 2006-2009.

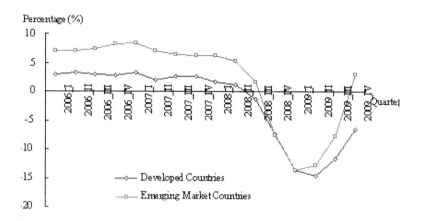

Figure 3-6 Average Growth Rate of Industrial Production Index 2006-2009 for Two Categories of Countries

We can see that the industrial production of emerging economies from the first quarter of 2006 to the first quarter of 2008 grew steadily at an average 6%, and fell to some extent in the second quarter of 2008. It dropped dramatically from the third quarter of 2008 to the first quarter of 2009, and started to turn for the better in the second quarter of 2009 until reaching positive growth in the fourth quarter. The situation for developed countries from 2006 to 2007 was not bad, either, though with a lower growth rate than emerging economies. Growth speed started to fall in the first quarter of 2008, and continued down to negative in the third quarter of 2008. It decreased further thereafter until the second quarter of 2009. In the third and fourth quarters, industrial production recovered to some extent, but the rate remained negative. As Figure 3-1 illustrates, the stock market of all sample countries started a downslide in the third quarter of 2007. We can see that the U.S. financial crisis took 6 to 12 months to transmit to the real economy, faster to developed countries than to developing countries. It is thus clear that the crisis struck a serious blow to the industrial production of both developed countries and emerging economies. After the first quarter of

2009, however, the latter performed obviously better than the former. By the fourth quarter, the industrial production of emerging economies returned to a positive growth of 3.0% on average whereas the figure for developed countries stood at -6.5%.

Figure 3-7 represents a detailed categorization of the sample countries.

The industrial production of major developed countries got hurt first and worst. From the fourth quarter of 2007, its growth rate gradually declined and reached -17.8% in the first quarter of 2009. Things got better afterwards but still stayed negative by the fourth quarter. In comparison, emerging Asian economies were less hit by the crisis. Their average growth rate in 2009 stood clearly higher than the other categories, turning positive in the third quarter of 2009 and reaching 9.09% by the fourth.

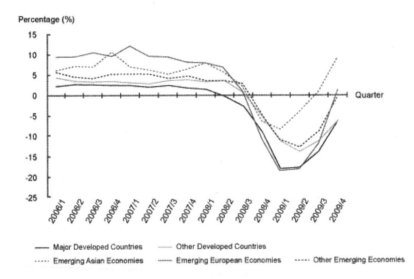

Figure 3-7 Average Growth Rate of Industrial Production Index 2006-2009 for Five Categories of Countries

The impact of the U.S. financial crisis on other countries' domestic demand

Domestic demand includes consumption demand and investment demand, which is an important driver for economic growth.

Consumption demand consists of individual consumption demand and government consumption demand. Investment demand consists of fixed asset investment demand and inventory increase, the former being the major component. Therefore, this report collects quarterly statistics of total consumption and gross fixed capital formation 2006-2009 for 36 sample countries and makes an in-depth analysis of the development of their domestic demands to provide a better understanding of country consumption demand and investment demand. The statistics are from the Organization for Economic Cooperation and Development (OECD).

Figure 3-8 shows the average growth rate of consumption and investment 2006-2009 in developed and emerging economies.

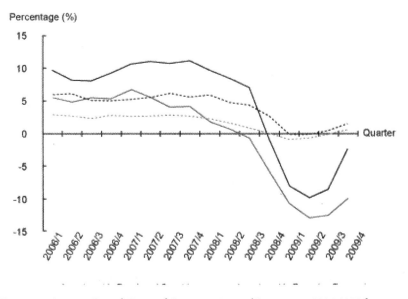

Figure 3-8 Average Growth Rates of Consumption and Investment 2006-2009 for Developed and Emerging Economies

The above figure shows that in 2006 all developed and emerging economies achieved favorable average growth rates, but that the growth rate of different countries' domestic demand varied greatly. Domestic demand in developed European countries increased steadily, while Japan's domestic demand increased slowly with fluctuations. All emerging economies experienced strong growth in their domestic demand, except for Hungary and Turkey, which were influenced by their governments' tight policies. Foreign direct investment contributed to rapid growth in the investment demands of emerging European economies and Russia, and the strong and constant capital inflow also stimulated the fast growth of their consumption.

In 2007, all developed and emerging economies maintained a stable average growth rate of consumption demand. The gross fixed capital formation in the first and second quarters of 2007 was almost the same as that in 2006, but started to drop in the third quarter, with Japan and Ireland even experiencing negative growth. At the same time, consumption demand and gross fixed capital formation in emerging economies maintained rapid and stable growth.

In 2008, under the influence of the U.S. financial crisis, the growth rate of domestic demand started to drop in developed and emerging economies. After the Wall Street financial turmoil of September, the financial crisis started to spread across the globe. Figure 3-8 shows that the growth rate of consumption demand in emerging markets started to fall dramatically in the second quarter and dropped to 2.68% in the fourth; the growth rate of consumption demand in developed countries started to fall gradually in the first quarter and turned negative in the fourth, standing at -0.06%. The growth rates of gross fixed capital formation in developed and emerging economies decreased dramatically and were negative in the fourth quarter, reaching -5.92% and -1.04 respectively.

Figure 3-9 shows countries' average growth rates of fixed capital formation in further division.

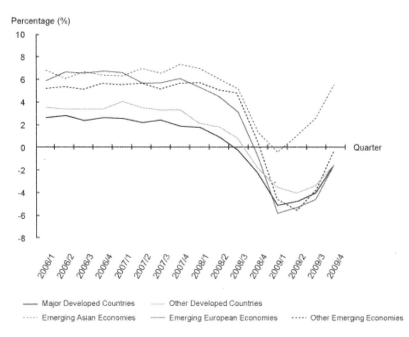

Percentage (%)

Quarter

—— Major Developed Countries ········ Other Developed Countries
····· Emerging Asian Economies ——— Emerging European Economies ····· Other Emerging Economies

Figure 3-9 Average Growth Rate of Fixed Capital Formation 2006-2009 for Five Categories of Countries

The growth rate of investment demand for the two types of developed country seemed similar in trend and level, while the emerging economies differed to a large extent. The growth rate of investment demand in other emerging economies increased in the second and third quarters of 2008, a rise mainly contributed by Chile and Brazil. The growth rate of fixed capital formation in Chile was 23.00% and 28.09% in the second and third quarters respectively, and for Brazil, 17.9% and 18.3%. Compared with the other two types of emerging markets, the emerging European economies experienced a huge drop in the growth rate of fixed capital formation. This is because most of these European countries had huge current account deficits and had relied excessively on foreign capital inflow for financing. Amidst the global financial turmoil, investors were concerned about the huge deficits and thus cut or even withdrew their investment in those countries. The decrease in capital inflow curbed the growth in domestic demand.

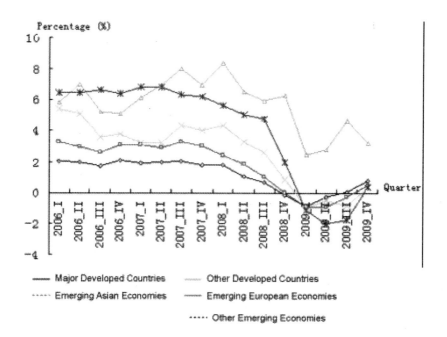

Figure 3-10 Average Growth Rate of Total Consumption 2006-2009 for Five Categories of Countries

In 2009, the growth rate of domestic demand in developed and emerging economies continued to drop. The two types of countries' growth rates of consumption demand were both higher than the bottom of the first quarter, -0.79% and -0.13% respectively; growth rates of investment demand were both higher than the bottom of the second quarter, -12.89% and -9.79% respectively. In the second half of 2009, the growth rates of country domestic demand started to rebound, and emerging economies had a higher rebound level than developed countries. In the fourth quarter of 2009, the average growth rate of gross fixed capital formation in developed countries was -9.96%, while growth rate of investment in emerging economies picked up to -2.50%. The average growth rate of total consumption in developed countries was 0.56% and 1.49% in emerging economies. Figure 3-9 and 3-10 show that in 2009, the growth rate of domestic demand in emerging Asian economies, in which neither investment demand nor consumption demand experienced negative growth, was higher than that in other countries, with India and Indonesia performing the best. In the second half of 2009 domestic demands in South Korea and Malaysia also recovered. In the fourth quarter of 2009, these four emerging Asian markets all achieved positive growth in their investment and consumption demands.

The impact of the U.S. financial crisis on other countries' foreign trade

Foreign trade is the exchange activity (import and export) of goods, labor, and technology between countries and regions. This report collects quarterly statistics of total import and export 2006-2009 for 36 sample countries, at constant price and weighing in quarterly change. It compares and analyses changes in countries' foreign trade during the period of the financial crisis. The statistics are from Organization for Economic Cooperation and Development (OECD).

Figure 3-11 shows the average growth rate of total import and export 2006-2009 in developed and emerging economies.

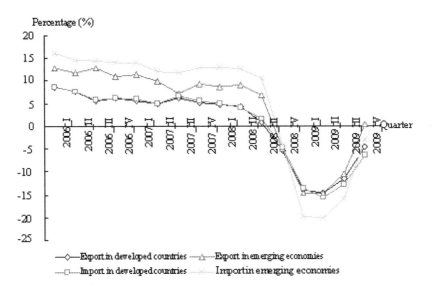

Figure 3-11 Average Growth Rates of Total Import and Export 2006-2009 for Developed and Emerging Economies

Figure 3-11 shows that in developed countries, the average growth rate of total export was close to the average growth rate of total import. In emerging economies, before the fourth quarter in 2008, the average growth rate of total export was much lower than that of total import, and afterwards, the growth rate of total export surpassed that of total import.

In 2006, stimulated by economic growth, international trade flourished. In the first and second quarter that year, the growth rate of total export in developed countries was 8.6% and 7.6% respectively, and for total import, 8.7% and 7.7%. In the third and fourth quarter, the number dropped to 3.0% and -0.6%. As for total import, the growth rate was 17.0% and 16.0% respectively in the first and second quarter and dropped to 2.7% and 0.8% in the third and fourth quarter. The growth rate of Japan's total import also decreased significantly in the third and fourth quarter. The growth rate was 6.0% and 6.2% in the first and second quarter, and only 2.2% and 2.6% in the third and fourth. With constant and moderate depreciation of the real effective exchange rate of the U.S. dollar, U.S. foreign trade was in good condition. The growth rate of total export in each quarter surpassed 8.0%, and the growth rate of total import also stayed at a high level in the first three quarters but decreased sharply in the fourth. The slowdown of the growth rate of countries' total import was closely related to the U.S. financial crisis from the second half of 2006. For the emerging markets, on one hand, the growth rates of total import and export all stayed at a relatively high level in each quarter, with the total exports of India, South Korea, Mexico, and some emerging economies in central Europe all keeping double-digit growth. Imports were even better; almost all countries achieved double-digit growth. On the other hand, the average growth rate of total export in emerging economies dropped in the fourth quarter. The four Emerging Asian economies all experienced decrease in the growth rate of total export, and India had the largest decline, from 33.0% in the third quarter to 14.1%. In addition, the growth rate of total export in Mexico, Chile, Poland, and Slovakia all fell sharply, this fall being related to the decrease in the growth rate of import in major trading nations including the U.S., the UK, and Japan. Thus it is clear that in the second half of 2006, the financial crisis had begun to exert its influence on world trade.

In 2007, the growth of foreign trade in developed and emerging economies was not as great as that in 2006, and countries varied in the extent of trading volume growth. For developed countries, due to the depreciation of the U.S. dollar, the United States achieved favorable growth in total export, and the growth rate in the second half of the year was higher than that in the first half. However, the growth rate of total import continued to fall after the sharp drop in the fourth quarter of 2006, and was only 0.92% in the fourth quarter of 2007. Thus we can see that the financial crisis influenced demand and supply in the United States. Furthermore, the growth rate of total import in Germany, Italy, Japan, and Denmark also decreased markedly. For emerging economies, Russia's growth rate of total import was 29.4%, 28.0%, 27.1%, and 23.0% in the four quarters respectively, much higher than the growth rate of any other country. In the second and third quarter, India's growth rate of total import and export decreased sharply, and the growth rate of its total export was 2.4% and -2.1%, import 2.0% and -0.2%. Thus the financial crisis also had serious impacts on India's foreign trade.

In 2008, foreign trade continued to go downhill, and conditions were similar in the second half of 2008. In the second and third quarter, India achieved a high year-on-year growth rate of total import and export, but this was due to the low growth rate in the second and third quarter in 2007. In September 2008, the investment bank Lehman Brothers in Wall Street closed down, and the financial crisis began to extend its influence. The disorder in the financial sector and the lack of credibility spread to the real economy, and trade was also seriously influenced by the decrease in credit of import and export financing.

An indicator for the decline in world trade is the decrease in international flight volume. According to International Air Transport Association (IATA), in December, 2008, air freight volume was down by 23% year on year. Relevant research indicates that the fall had reached a record low since September 2001. At that time, most flights were grounded, and only 14% were still in operation. Another indicator of public concern is the Baltic Dry Index which weighs the shipping cost of commodities and reflects the change in global demand for manufactured goods. From June to November 2008, the Baltic Dry Index dropped by 94%[2].

World trade in 2009 faced the most difficult situation since the Second World War, with the first and second quarters being the toughest[3]. In the first and second quarter, average growth rates of total export in developed and emerging economies were below -14%, and the growth rate of total import in developed countries was -13.7% and -15.7% respectively in the two quarters, in emerging economies -19.7% and -20.3%. In terms of export, Japan suffered the greatest decrease. In the first quarter, its year-on-year growth rate of total export dropped to -36.25%, much lower than the growth rate of any other country. In addition, Finland, Slovakia, Mexico, Italy, and Slovenia were also influenced, their exports all falling by more than 20%. In terms of import, Russia, Turkey, Mexico, and other emerging economies had the largest decrease. Russia's growth rate of total import dropped to -34.3% and -38.7% in the first two quarters, and Turkey's growth rate of total import also decreased to below -30% in the first quarter. From the third quarter of 2009, trade in these countries began to take on a positive look. The sharp decrease in trading volume was under control, and the decline was lower year on year. In the fourth quarter of 2009, the average year-on-year growth rate of total export in emerging economies was 0.4%, changing the situation of negative growth, and the average year-on-year growth rate of total import was -2.9%. As for developed countries, the average year-on-year growth rates of total import and export were negative, -4.6% and -6.5% respectively. It is evident that growth rates of import were much lower than those of export, a fact connected with the growing trade protectionism around the world. Although nations had made promises to abandon trade protectionism, they were still taking more policy measures to put limitations on import.

Figure 3-12 shows the quantity of anti-dumping investigations launched by WTO members from 2001 to October 2009. From 2001 to 2007, there were fewer and fewer cases, but in 2008, the number increased again, higher than that in 2005 and close to that in 2004. By the end of October 2009, WTO members had launched 171 anti-dumping investigations, more than all the cases in 2007.

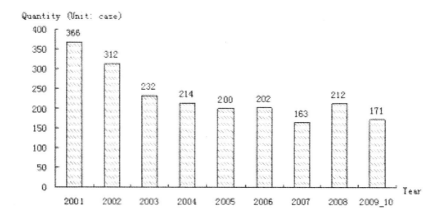

Figure 3-12 Anti-dumping investigations Launched by WTO Members from 2001 to October 2009

(Data Source: WTO, November 2009)

3.5 The impact of the U.S. financial crisis on other countries' economic growth

GDP (Gross Domestic Product) is an economic statistical indicator of major concern to the macro-economy. This report collects quarterly statistics of the year-on-year growth rate of real GDP (weighing in price fluctuation and quarterly change) in 36 sample countries from 2006 to 2009, and it analyses and compares changes in the growth rate of countries' real GDP. The statistics are from Organization for Economic Cooperation and Development (OECD).

Figure 3-13 shows the average growth rate of GDP 2006-2009 for developed and emerging economies.

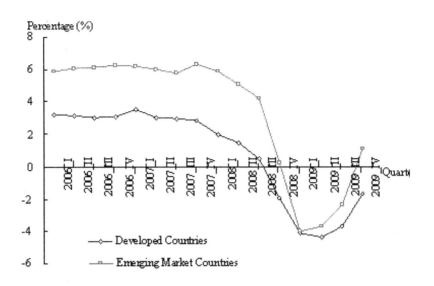

Figure 3-13 Average Growth Rate of GDP 2006-2009 for Two Categories of Countries

The above figure shows that the global economy sustained steady growth in 2006. From statistics of the 36 sample countries, we can see that the average growth rate of GDP in developed countries was all above 3% in each of the four quarters in 2006, and the average year-on-year growth rate of GDP in emerging economies was increasing steadily, 5.91% to 6.28%, from the first to the fourth quarter.

In 2007, the GDP in emerging economies sustained strong growth. Although the average year-on-year growth rate of GDP declined from the first to the third quarter, it was still at a relatively high level, and in the fourth quarter the average year-on-year growth rate of GDP in emerging economies reached 6.33%, the highest since 2006. However, the year-on-year growth of GDP in developed countries was relatively fast in the first quarter but then began to slow down, and in the fourth quarter, the average year-on-year growth rate dropped to 2.8%. Thus we can see that the financial crisis had begun to exert its influence on the macro-economy of developed countries.

From the first quarter of 2008 to the first quarter of 2009, the financial crisis had serious impacts on the world economy including both developed and emerging economies. The global economy slowed down and even fell into recession. From the fourth quarter in 2007 to the first quarter in 2009, the average growth rate of GDP in developed countries dropped from 2.8% to -4.1%, down by 6.9%. The average growth rate of GDP in emerging economies dropped from 6.3% to -4.0%, down by 10.3%.

In the second quarter of 2009, the average growth rate of GDP in developed countries further declined, but in emerging economies began to pick up. With the implementation of large-scale financial aid measures and the guidance of economic stimulus policies, in the second half of 2009, the growth rates of GDP in developed and emerging economies recovered to different extents, and countries' economic contraction lessened. The growth rate of GDP in developed countries increased from -4.3%, the lowest in the second quarter, to -1.7%, and the growth rate of GDP in emerging economies increased from -4.0%, the lowest in the first quarter, to 1.1%, a positive growth.

Figure 3-14 shows changes in the average growth rate of GDP 2006 -2009 for five categories of countries.

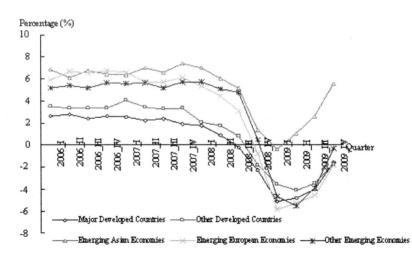

Figure 3-14 Average Growth Rate of GDP 2006- 2009 for Five Categories of Countries

The above figure shows that compared with countries in other categories, emerging Asian economies gave a better performance in the financial crisis. In 2009, the average growth rate of GDP of emerging Asian economies was much higher than that of countries in the other categories, and was negative only in the first quarter of 2009, thereafter picking up rapidly. At the same time, the growth rate of GDP in the other two types of emerging economies continued to decline to a level which, in the second quarter of 2009, was even lower than that of developed countries. Thus we can see that the real economies of these two types of countries were seriously influenced by the financial crisis, and their economies were fragile. Table 3-1 lists the time when the GDP for 36 sample countries started negative growth.

The table shows that the GDP of all countries, except Australia, India, Indonesia, and Poland, experienced negative growth in the financial crisis. Countries went into recession mainly in the fourth quarter of 2008 and the first quarter of 2009. It can be seen that the financial crisis had spread rapidly and influenced a wide area.

Table 3-1 Time When the GDP for 36 Sample Countries Started Negative Growth

Time	Country
Q1, 2008	Ireland
Q2, 2008	New Zealand, Italy, Japan
Q3, 2008	Denmark, Sweden
Q4, 2008	Austria, Belgium, Finland, the Netherlands, Norway, Swiss, Spain, Portugal, Canada, France, Germany, UK, U.S., South Korea, Mexico, Russia, Slovenia, Turkey, Hungary

Q1, 2009	Greek, Malaysia, Brazil, Chile, South Africa, Slovakia, Czech
No Negative Growth	Australia, India, Indonesia, Poland

3.6 A comprehensive analysis of the impact of the U.S. financial crisis on countries in different categories

To provide a comprehensive analysis of the impact of the U.S. financial crisis on countries in different categories, we choose seven indicators: year-on-year growth rate of stock price, GDP, the industrial production index, gross fixed capital formation, total consumption, total export, and total import. In addition, we adopt the Principal Component Analysis method for dimensional reduction in order to find representative points to describe the changes in countries' economies.

Principal Component Analysis (PCA) is a multivariate statistical analysis method recombining variables to a group of aggregate variables that are not interconnected through linear transformation, while at the same time, several aggregate variables are chosen to reflect the information of the original variables as clearly as possible. It is widely adopted in dimensional reduction[4].

Generally in math, p indicators are linearly combined to form a new aggregate indicator. The most widely adopted method uses the variance of the first aggregate indicator F_1. The larger the $\text{Var}(F_1)$ is, the more information F_1 contains. Thus F_1 should have the largest variance in linear combination and is thereafter called the first principal component. If it cannot fully contain the information of p indicators, we will choose F_2, the second linear combination. To effectively reflect the original information, what is contained in F_1 should not also be contained in F_2, i.e. $\text{Cov}(F_1, F_2)=0$. Thus F_2 is called the second principal component. In this way we can have the third, fourth, up to the *pth* principal components.

Table 3-2 shows PCA results of statistics in time sequence concerning the above indicators 2006- 2009 for 36 sample countries.

Table 3-2 PCA Results(The First Three Principal Components)

Principal component	Original Eigen Value		
	Total	Contribution Rate (%)	Accumulated Contribution Rate (%)
1	5.21	74.44	74.44
2	0.65	9.23	83.67
3	0.51	7.32	90.99

We can infer from the Table that the contribution rate of the first principal component has reached 74.44%, and thus can represent most of the information of the seven variables.

The factor loading matrix in Table 3-3 and the factor loading diagram in Figure 3-15 both reflect the connection between the first and second principal components and the seven original variables. We can see that the first principal component is positively correlated to the seven original variables, and the correlation is strong with the industrial production index, GDP, gross fixed capital formation, total export, and total import, while being medium with stock price and total consumption. The correlation coefficients all surpass 0.7. Therefore, the first principal component can comprehensively reflect the different countries' economic growth rates.

Table 3-3 Factor Loading Matrix of Principal Components

Number of Clustering	
9	0.908
8	0.898
7	0.188
6	0.175
5	0.091

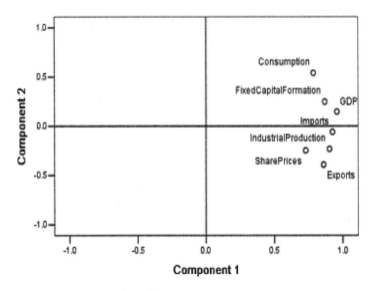

Figure 3-15 Factor Loading Plot

Furthermore, we also adopted the method of Functional Data Analysis (FDA)[5]. Based on the functional data of countries' economic growth rates we provide a variance analysis of the economic growth rates of countries in different categories.

Figure 3-16 shows the estimated results of influence functions on different countries($\alpha_j(t)$).

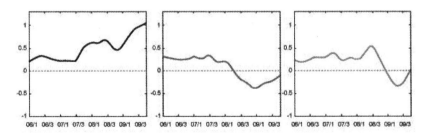

(a)Emerging Asian economies(b)Emerging European economies(c)Other emerging economies

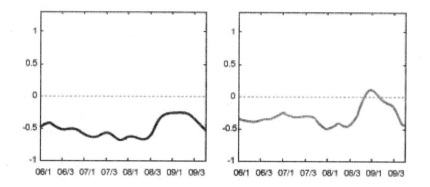

(d)Major developed countries　(e)Other developed countries

Figure 3-16 Influence Functions of Countries in Different Categories

Based on this, we can make the following analyses of the relationship between the economic growth rates of countries in different categories and the average economic growth rate of all countries.

(1) The economic growth rate of emerging Asian economies is higher than the average level. Specifically, from the first quarter of 2006 to the third quarter of 2007, the growth rate of these countries kept a stable leading position. From the fourth quarter of 2007 to the third quarter of 2008, the economic growth rate of emerging Asian economies had an even greater lead advantage over the average growth rate. In the fourth quarter of 2008, this lead became narrower, but then increased to a larger extent from the first to the fourth quarter of 2009. In the fourth quarter, the lead advantage was greater than ever before.

(2) For emerging European economies, from the first quarter of 2006 to the third quarter of 2007, their economic growth rate was higher than the average level of all countries with a stable leading position. In the fourth quarter of 2007, the lead began to narrow. In the second quarter of 2008, the economic growth rate of emerging European economies was close to the average level and then dropped below in the third quarter of 2008. Afterwards, the gap between these countries' economic growth rate and the average level became larger and larger, and reached

its peak in the first quarter of 2009. After the second quarter, the gap began to narrow, but in the fourth quarter, the growth rate of these countries was still below the average.

(3) For other emerging economies, from the first quarter of 2006 to the first quarter of 2008, their economic growth rate was higher than the average level of all countries with fluctuations in their lead advantage. This advantage became greater in the second and third quarter of 2008 and reached its peak level since 2006. From the fourth quarter of 2008, the lead declined sharply and in the first quarter of 2009 fell below the average level. In the second quarter, the gap became larger, and then began to narrow from the third quarter. In the fourth quarter of 2009, the economic growth rate of other emerging economies was close to the average growth rate of all countries.

(4) For developed countries, from the first quarter of 2006 to the first quarter of 2009, their economic growth rate was lower than the average level of all countries. Specifically, from the first quarter of 2006 to the third quarter of 2008, the gap between these countries' economic growth rate and the average level widened. From the fourth quarter of 2008 to the second quarter of 2009, the gap narrowed due to the fact that many emerging economies were seriously influenced by the financial crisis. But from the third quarter of 2009, with the economic recovery of some emerging economies, the gap became larger and larger again.

(5) For other developed countries, from the first quarter of 2006 to the third quarter of 2007, their economic growth rate was lower than the average level of all countries, and the gap between their economic growth rate and the average level in the first three quarters of 2007 was less than that in 2006. From the fourth quarter of 2007 to the third quarter of 2008, the gap widened to a large extent, and in the fourth quarter narrowed again. In the first quarter of 2009, the economic growth rate of other developed countries surpassed the average level of all countries for the first time, but in the second quarter dropped below the average level again, and the gap further widened in the third and fourth quarter.

Figure 3-17 shows the estimated value of economic growth rate functions of countries in five categories, represented by solid lines, and the estimated value of their average economic growth rate functions, represented by dashed lines.

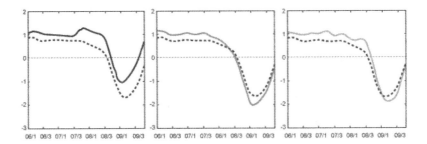

(a)Emerging Asian economies (b)Emerging European economies (c)Other emerging economies

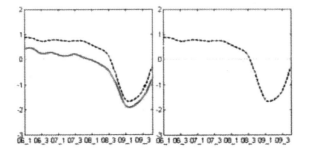

(d)Major developed countries   (e)Other developed countries

Figure 3-17 Comparison of the Economic Growth Rates for Five Categories of Countries with the Average Level

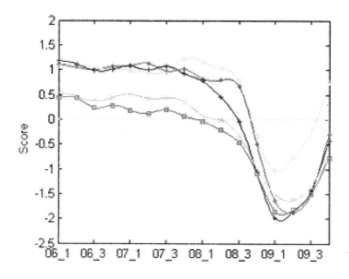

Figure 3-18 Estimated Value of Economic Growth Rate Functions for Five Categories of Countries

Figure 3-18 shows the estimated value of economic growth rate functions of countries in five categories. The curves with squares represent major developed countries; crosses, other developed countries; circles, emerging Asian economies; plus signs, emerging European economies; and diamonds, other emerging economies.

From the above figure, generally, the economic growth rates of countries in all categories declined and rebounded from 2006 to 2009. But specifically, there exist some differences among these countries.

In terms of the time when the economic growth rate started to decline, major developed countries started to fall in the fourth quarter of 2007. In fact, Figure 2-18 shows that from the second half of 2006, the economic growth rate of major developed countries had already gradually decreased with fluctuations. The economic growth rates of other developed countries and emerging European economies also started to fall in the fourth quarter of 2007, and other emerging economies and emerging Asian economies started to decline in the first quarter of 2008. However, compared with that of developed countries and emerging European economies, the decrease in the economic growth rate of other emerging economies and emerging Asian economies was relatively small. Furthermore, the economic growth rate of emerging Asian economies was still higher than the level from the first quarter of 2006 to the fourth quarter of 2007. The economic growth rates of other emerging economies and emerging Asian economies started to fall dramatically in the fourth quarter of 2008.

In terms of the time when the economic growth rate dropped to its lowest level, major developed countries, emerging Asian and European economies all decreased to their low points in the first quarter of 2009. Other developed countries and other emerging economies touched bottom in the second quarter of 2009.

In terms of the decrease in economic growth rate in the financial crisis, major developed countries and other developed countries were close to each other. Emerging European economies had the largest decrease. Before the fourth quarter of 2007, the economic growth rate of emerging European economies was close to that of the other two types of emerging economies, and much higher than that of developed countries. However, in the first quarter of 2009, the economic growth rate of these European countries dropped to the lowest among the five categories, with large gaps between them and the other four. It is evident that the emerging European economies were seriously affected by the financial crisis. Other emerging economies also had a considerable decline in their economic growth rate, and their low point was close to that of major developed countries and much lower than that of other developed countries. The decline of the economic growth rate of emerging Asian economies was smaller than that of the other two types of emerging economies. In addition, from the first quarter to the fourth in 2009, the economic growth rate of emerging Asian economies was higher than that of the other four types of countries.

In terms of the recovery of the economic growth rate, emerging economies performed better than developed countries. Major developed countries and emerging European economies all reached their lowest growth rates in the first quarter of 2009. In comparison, the economic growth rate of emerging European economies was much lower than that of major developed countries in the first quarter of 2009 but higher in the fourth. Similarly, other developed countries and other emerging economies all reached their lowest economic growth rates in the second quarter of 2009, and the economic growth rate of other emerging economies was much lower than that of other developed countries in the first quarter but also higher in the fourth. Emerging Asian economies only suffered a small decrease in their economic growth and had a strong capacity for recovery. In the fourth quarter of 2009, the economic growth rate of emerging Asian economies was the highest, followed in order by other emerging economies, emerging European economies, other developed countries, and major developed countries. Major developed countries and other developed countries had very similar economic growth rates.

The solid line in Figure 3-19 is the value function to make a variance analysis on the economic growth rate of the 36 sample countries. If we set the confidence coefficient at 95%, then the critical value of statistic F remaining to be verified is:

F0.05 (4, 31) = 2.6787. Thus the dashed line in the figure represents y=2.6787.

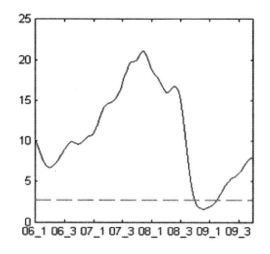

Figure 3-19 Function of Value F for Variance Analysis

According to the principles of variance analysis of functional data, whether F can pass the verification indicates whether country category has a significant impact on the economic growth rate. The higher the Value F, the greater the impact.

Figure 3-19 shows that from the first quarter of 2006 to the fourth quarter of 2007, Value F all passed the verification. Therefore, country category had a significant impact on the economic growth rate, which is to say that the economic growth rates of countries in the different categories also differed to a large extent. From the third quarter in 2006, the impact became even greater, and gaps between the economic growth rates of countries in different categories further widened, while from the first quarter in 2008, the impact became less and the gap narrowed. In the fourth quarter of 2008 and the first quarter of 2009 when the economy of all countries suffered a sharp decline, F could not pass the verification, which means that country category did not have a significant impact on the economic growth rate during that time, i.e. the economic growth rates of countries in different categories were influenced by the financial crisis to the same extent. The gap between the economic growth rates of countries in different categories was the smallest in history. From the second quarter of 2009, country category again began to have an increasingly significant impact on the economic growth rate. Thus we can see that in the process of economic recovery, the gaps between the economic growth rates of countries in different categories became larger and larger.

A comparative analysis of the economic development process of the sample countries

In the above section, we discussed the differences in the process of economic development among countries in different categories. However, in each category, different countries have different processes of economic development, especially during the financial crisis when the gap between different categories became smaller. Consequently, this section adopts Functional Principal Component Analysis to make an in-depth investigation of the changes in the economic growth rate for each country. In addition, it analyses and compares the economic growth rate and the decrease level of those countries, and, based on this, carries out quantity clustering to identify countries with similar economic development processes.

Functional Principal Component Analysis (FPCA) is a key technology in functional data analysis. With a group of functional data, we need to further study the features of those functions and find the internal change law. The purpose of FPCA is to find a group of indicators to reflect the internal change law.

We now apply FPCA to some functional data of the economic growth rate of the 36 countries. Figure 3-20 shows the weighting functions of the first and second principal components. Numbers in the brackets represent the variance contribution rate, i.e. the percentage of variation information.

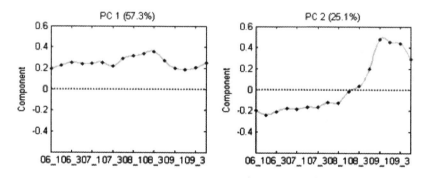

Figure 3-20 Weighting Functions of the First and Second Principal Components

In the above figure, the variance contribution rate of the first principal component is 57.3%, which means that its variation accounts for 57.3% of the total. The weighting function of the first principal component was of positive value from 2006 to 2009, with a larger weight from the fourth quarter of 2007 to the fourth quarter of 2008 than that of any other time period. That is to say, during that time, the gap between national economic growth rates was the largest. In conclusion, those scoring higher in terms of the first principal component were countries with a higher economic growth rate than the average level from the fourth quarter of 2007 to the fourth quarter of 2008 and also with relatively high economic growth rates in other periods. The first principal component measures national economic growth rate from the first quarter of 2006 to the fourth quarter of 2009.

The variance contribution rate of the second principal component is 25.1%. From the first quarter of 2006 to the third quarter of 2008, the weighting function of the second principal component was negative, but turned positive after that. This means that the contribution of the second principal component to economic growth rate was negative before the breakout of the financial crisis and positive after that. Therefore, the second principal component reflects the consistency of national economic growth rates from 2006 to 2009. Countries whose economic growth rate did not change much before and after the crisis scored higher.

After calculation, the contribution rates of the third and fourth principal components are 6.8% and 4.6% respectively, while the aggregate contribution rate of the first and second principal components is 82.4%. Thus, we can use the first and second principal components to study the functional data variation of the economic growth rates of the 36 sample countries.

As the weighting function of the first principal component was positive and did not change much, we can refer to each country's score in terms of the first principal component to make an overall evaluation of their economic growth rate from 2006 to 2009. The higher the score, the higher the rate. Figure 3-21 shows the 36 scores in terms of the first principal component, with India achieving the highest. That is to say, the economic growth rate of India was much higher than that of any other country from 2006 to 2009. Furthermore, the emerging economies of Russia, Poland, Indonesia, and Brazil also had relatively high economic growth rates, while the economic growth rate was at a medium level in some small developed countries like Norway, the Netherlands, Greece, Finland, and Austria. Major developed countries like the UK, the U.S.,

Japan, and Italy, had relatively low economic growth, with Japan and Italy growing much more slowly than any other country.

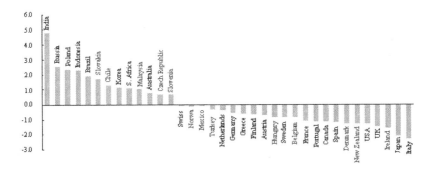

. Figure 3-21 Countries' First Principal Component Scores

From the above analysis, the second principal component is the measurement of the consistency of a country's economic growth rate at different time periods from 2006 to 2009. It can reflect the degree to which economic growth rates were affected by the financial crisis. Countries whose economic growth rate did not change much before and after the crisis scored higher in terms of the second principal component. Figure 3-22 shows 36 countries' scores from the highest to the lowest. We can see that the scores of Australia and Indonesia are the highest, which means that their economic growth rate did not change much before or after the crisis. At the same time, the scores of Turkey, Slovakia, Finland, Slovenia, and Russia are relatively low, especially Slovenia and Russia. This indicates that these countries' economic growth rates declined sharply during the financial crisis and their economic development was seriously affected.

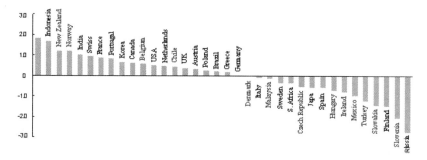

Figure 3-22 Countries' Second Principal Component Scores

Based on FPCA results, we can use two variants — scores of the first and second principal components - to describe each sample and categorize these 36 countries.

From the R^2 shown in statistics Table 3-4 we may understand that when we set seven categories instead of eight, statistics will decline dramatically. Therefore, it is appropriate to divide these countries into eight categories.

Table 3-4 R^2 Statistics

Number of Clustering	
9	0.908
8	0.898
7	0.188
6	0.175
5	0.091

Figure 3-23 shows the clustering results of dividing the countries into eight categories.

Category 1: India
Category 2: Russia

Category 3: Australia, Indonesia

Category 4: Slovakia, Slovenia

Category 5: South Korea, Poland, Chile, Malaysia, South Africa, Brazil, Czech Republic

Category 6: Austria, Belgium, Canada, Denmark, France, Germany, Greece, New Zealand, Norway, Portugal, Switzerland, UK, U.S.

Category 7: Finland, Hungary, Ireland, Mexico, Spain, Sweden, Turkey

Category 8: Italy, Japan

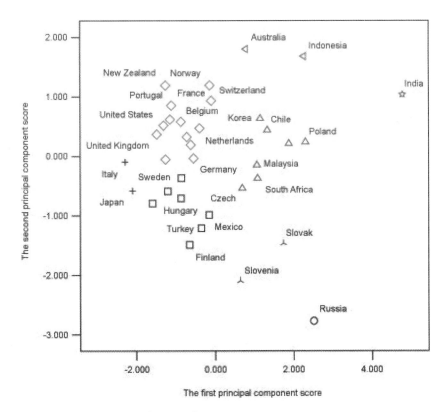

Figure 3-23 Clustering Analysis Results

According to the meaning of the first and second principal component, countries in each category had a close overall economic growth rate from 2006 to 2009, and their economic growth rate did not change much before and after the financial crisis (degree to which economic growth rate was influenced by the financial crisis).

Figure 3-23 shows that India and Russia each represent one category with a typical process of economic growth rate change. India's overall economic growth rate was higher than that of any other country from 2006 to 2009, and the rate did not change much before and after the financial crisis. Russia's overall economic growth rate from 2006 to 2009 was also very high, only second to India. However, after the financial crisis, its economic growth rate suffered a huge decline, much greater than that of any other country.

Australia and Indonesia are in the same category, both sustaining high overall economic growth rates. After the crisis, their economic growth rate only decreased by a relatively small margin.

Slovakia and Slovenia are in the same category, both sustaining high overall economic growth rates. However, after the crisis, their economic growth rate decreased markedly.

Emerging economies including South Korea, Poland, and Chile are in the same category. Their overall economic growth rate was relatively high from 2006 to 2009 and declined to a medium degree after the crisis.

Developed countries including Belgium, Canada, Denmark, France, Germany, Greece, New Zealand, Norway, Portugal, Switzerland, UK and U.S. are in the same category. Their overall economic growth rate was relatively low from 2006 to 2009 and declined only a little after the financial crisis.

Finland, Hungary, Ireland, Mexico, Spain, Sweden and Turkey share the same category. Their overall economic growth rate was relatively low from 2006 to 2009 and declined sharply after the financial crisis.

Italy and Japan are in the last category. Their overall economic growth rate was the lowest from 2006 to 2009 and also declined steeply after the financial crisis.

Summary

1. We chose 36 sample countries and divided them into five categories. Their industrial production, GDP growth, stock market, domestic demand and foreign trade were affected by the financial crisis to different degrees. In the second and third quarter of 2009, most countries started to recover, especially in terms of the stock price.

2. PCA was adopted to combine the above indicators into a comprehensive indicator reflecting the economic growth rate of a country. Then the discrete data representing countries' economic growth rate was turned into functional data, and we adopted functional data analysis methods to analyze the differences among the sample countries in terms of their economic growth rate, the time of the beginning of economic recession, degree of recession, and economic recovery. As regards the time when the economy began to decline, major developed countries, other developed countries, and emerging European economies were all earlier, in the fourth quarter of 2007. Emerging Asian economies and other emerging economies started their decline in the first quarter of 2008 and continued afterwards, but their sharpest decline began in the fourth quarter of that year. The economic growth rates of major developed countries, emerging Asian and European economies all hit bottom in the first quarter of 2009 with other developed and emerging economies reaching their lowest point in the second. Emerging European economies suffered the greatest economic decline, and other emerging economies also had a sharp decline in their economies. At the same time, the decrease in the economic growth rate of emerging Asian economies was much smaller. Generally, the three types of emerging economies performed better than the two types of developed countries in economic recovery.

3. In terms of the overall economic growth rate from 2006 to 2009, India grew much faster than any other country. Japan and Italy, however, had a much lower growth rate than others. In terms of the degree of

economic decline, Russia's was the highest, and Australia and Indonesia had the best performances. We adopted the hierarchical clustering method to divide the 36 sample countries into eight categories.

4.

The Performance of Different Countries in the Financial Crisis

Performance of Britain

Economic overview

Britain is one of the leading economic powers in the world. The ratio of manufacturing industry in the British economy is declining while the share of service and energy industry is increasing. In particular, its business, financial sector and insurance industries are growing fast.

Britain's GDP ranks the fifth and the size of its economy takes the fourth place in the world. It is also the second largest overseas investor. Private companies form the main part of the British economy, accounting for 60% of GDP. Its service industry is one of the criteria for measuring how developed a state is. In 2008, people working in the British service industry made up 77% of the entire workforce, producing 63% of GDP.

Chart 4-1 shows the share of different industries in Britain. Financial intermediaries, property, renting and other business activities take the largest share. Education, health and social work; other entities, social and individual service as well as bulk and retail trade; automobile and private and family repairmen; and hotels and restaurants took the second and third place. Clearly, the financial sector is the pillar industry of Britain. If it does not function well, the British economy will fail.

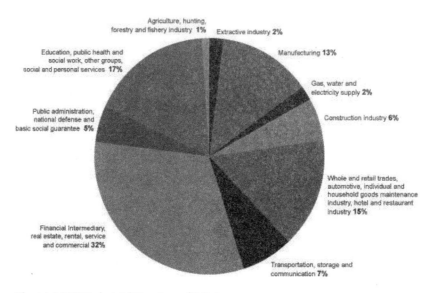

Chart 4-1 2008 Industrial Structure of Britain

Britain has the most abundant energy resources in the EU. It is one of the major producers of oil and natural gas in the world. Its energy resources include coal, oil, natural gas, nuclear energy and hydraulic power. Iron ore reserve is 2.7 billion tons. Recoverable coal reserve is 4.6 billion tons. There are also 7 billion tons of oil reserve and 1.226~3.8 trillion m³ of natural gas reserve. Britain is the first country in the world to be able to satisfy its own demand of 26 million users for power and natural gas.

Tourism is another important economic sector in Britain with an annual output of more than £70 billion. The revenue from tourism in UK accounts for 5% of the total tourism income of the world. Unlike countries famous for their beautiful scenery, Britain's royal culture and museums are its biggest attractions. The main tourist spots include London, Edinburgh, Cardiff, Brighton, Greenwich, Stratford, Oxford, and Cambridge.

Britain is the fourth largest trading country. Its trade volume is 5% of the world total. The export of commodities and labor takes the third place and accounts for 29% of its GDP (Chart 4-2). The main export products are machinery, automobiles, aeronautical equipment, electrical and electronic products, chemical products and oil. Import products include raw materials and food. Britain is the sixth largest overseas investor and the sixth largest aid provider. London is a world financial and trade center.

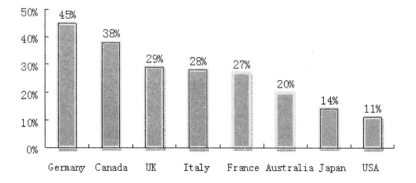

Chart 4-2 2006 Ratio of Commodity and Service Export to GDP in Major Developed Countries

Financial overview

Credit risks faced by the British banking system

The credit risks of British banks came from their debts to domestic and foreign non-bank clients as well as the effects of domestic and foreign banks on British clients. As the world economy began recovering, the credit risks of some borrowers was therefore reduced; however, some other borrowers in particular countries still suffer increasing risk.

Chart 4-3 shows the sources of credit risks (domestic and foreign economic entities and borrowers) in most British banks.

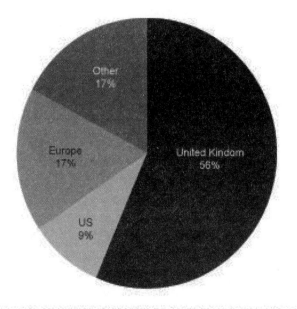

Source: Bank of Englian, Federal Deposit Insurance Corporation (FDIC), published accounts and Bank calculations.

(a) Aggregate balance sheet at end-2009, except for National Australia Bank and Nationwide which are as of March 2010 and April 2010 respectively
(b) Includes exposures to households, non-financial companies, banks and other financial corporations, and holding of sovereign debt.
(c) Total assets come from consolidated accounts. UK-owned banks' foreign exposures reflect consolidated claims of their banking operation. Non-UK owned banks' foreign exporsures are sourced from consolidated global group accounts.
(d) The percentage do not sum to 100% due to rounding.

Chart 4-3 Sources of Credit Risks in Britain

While the international economy is recovering, the expectation of risk in sovereign debt of some countries is rising, especially some European countries, because recovery there has been at a relatively slower speed. According to Chart 4-1 CDS Premium of Different Countries, the credit risk compensation for such countries is increasing.

Chart 4-1 CDS Premium of Different Countries

	January 2008	June 2008 Report	December 2009 Report	June 2010 Report
United Kingdom	9	87	70	93
United States	8	45	32	43
France	10	38	24	95
Germany	7	34	23	50
Greece	22	155	182	762
Ireland	12	220	150	285
Italy	20	105	85	245
Portugal	18	77	70	358
Spain	18	98	86	269

Source: Thomson Reuters Datastream.

(a) Senior five-year credit default swap premia in basis points.

At the same time, some European banks increased their estimate of the credit risks of Britain's creditors with a consequent effect on the British banking system. In fact, Britain only provided minor loans to Greece and some small European countries and so did its creditors. However, the relevance of financial system increases the credit risk faced by a single banking system. In 2010, the credit risk of creditors increased sharply, which indirectly increased the credit risk of British banks to their debtors. Chart 4-4 shows the credit risk faced by France and Germany who lent a quarter of British debt.

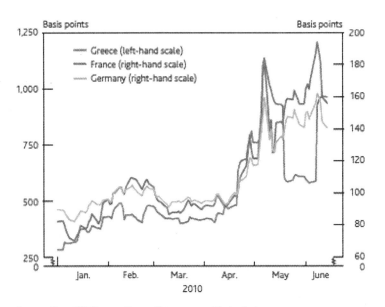

Basis points (left axis label, 1,250 / 1,000 / 750 / 500 / 250 / 0)

Basis points (right axis label, 200 / 180 / 160 / 140 / 120 / 100 / 80 / 60 / 0)

— Greece (left-hand scale)
— France (right-hand scale)
— Germany (right-hand scale)

Jan.   Feb.   Mar.   Apr.   May   June

2010

Sources: Capital IQ, Thomson Reuters Datastream and Bank calculations.

(a) Average five-year senior credit default swap premia, weighted by assets, for banks with assets of more than US$100 billion.
(b) Data to close of business on 14 June 2010.

Chart 4-4 Credit Risks of Debtors to European Banks

Furthermore, the recession in the American property market was affecting the banking sector and increased the credit risk of American banks for Britain. Chart 4-5 shows the rate of loss of American bank loans.

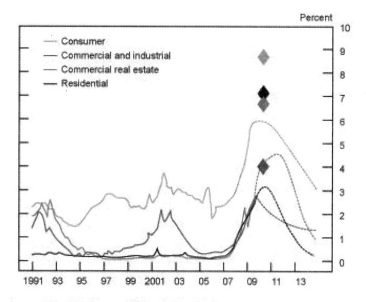

Percent

- Consumer
- Commercial and industrial
- Commercial real estate
- Residential

1991 93 95 97 99 2001 03 05 07 09 11 13

Source: FDIC Federal Reserve, IMF and Bank calculations.

(a) Diamonds represent implied 2010 adverse scenaio loss estimates from the Federal Reserve's Supervisory Capital Asessment Program. These are calculated by deducting 2009 loss rates from the mid-points of the 2009-10 range of loss estimates published in the overview of results on 7 May 2009. Dashed lines represent the IMF's central forecast of the future path of US loss rates.

Chart 4-5 Rate of American Loan Loss

In the domestic market, the mortgage loans of British banks to domestic residents accounted for two thirds of the total. In the past two decades, the fast growing safe loans led to a high capital debt ratio (Chart 4-6). Since there was no plan for reducing the loans, if the interest rate rose or fluctuated upwards from the current historical low point, the British banking sector would experience a higher risk of default.

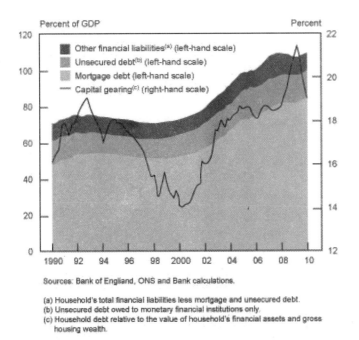

Percent of GDP   Percent

- Other financial liabilities[a] (left-hand scale)
- Unsecured debt[b] (left-hand scale)
- Mortgage debt (left-hand scale)
- Capital gearing[c] (right-hand scale)

1990 92 94 96 98 2000 02 04 06 08 10

Sources: Bank of England, ONS and Bank calculations.

(a) Household's total financial liabilities less mortgage and unsecured debt.
(b) Unsecured debt owed to monetary financial institutions only.
(c) Household debt relative to the value of household's financial assets and gross housing wealth.

Chart 4-6 Debt Capital Ratio of British Residents

At the same time, non-mortgage loans have always been the source of credit risk in British banks. Such loans take a small share of all loans. However, since 2007, the amount of mortgage loans that was cut accounted for two thirds of all reduced or exempted loans.

Recovery capacity of British banks

Since December 2009, the recovery capacity of British banks has been enhanced and debts are reducing (Chart 4-7) while the quantity and quality of asset and capital flow are improving. The capacity of banks to make a profit is still limited (Chart 4-8), because the loss from loans continued at a high level and credit quality is very sensitive to the general situation of the economy. At the same time, trade revenue in 2009 was restored with a large margin (Chart 4-9), while its growth potential may be reduced in the future. Banks optimistically estimated an increase in deposits and a decrease in loan with bad credit. Nevertheless, risks still exist. When profits rise, the banks have to be cautious and limit the dividends for share-holders and employees. Only in this way can banks recover.

Maintaining financial stability

The international community has agreed that if we want to restore the economy through balancing and encouraging loans, enhance the recovery capacity of banks and ensure sufficient capital and liquidity in the banking sector, a stricter administration is necessary in the current situation. However, viewing from a more macro and cautious perspective, it is necessary to allow banks to borrow money from real economy.

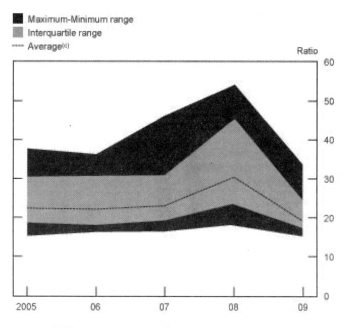

Sources: Published accounts and Bank calculations.

(a) Gross leverage is caculated as total assets divided by total equity. Total reserves are used as total equity where appropriate.
(b) Excludes Northern Rock.
(c) Asset weighted.

Chart 4-7 Debt Ratio of British Major Banks

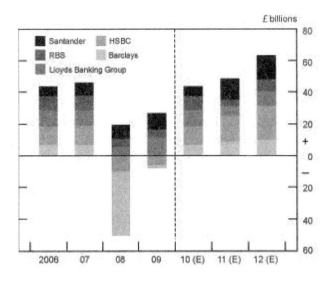

Chart 4-8 Revenue of Most British Banks and Uniform Estimation of Revenues

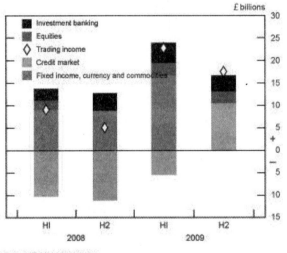

Source: Published accounts

(a) Chart shows data for a subset of the major UK banks peer group-Banco Santander, Barclays, HSBC and RBS

Chart 4-9 Trade Revenue of Major British Banks

In order to ensure a more stable service from the financial sector to the real economy, reform of administration should be an important part of policy measures. The policy framework should prevent the increase of risks and provide radical solutions to banking problems to guarantee an effective implementation. The British government is considering regulations for bank behaviors. The increasing demand for capital has accelerated the attempts to find solutions to the problems. A stricter market regulation and a healthier market infrastructure are of prime importance [1-2].

Influence of financial crisis on Britain

Along with the development of the financial crisis, both the fictitious economy and the real economy of Britain were severely affected. The nation is facing its greatest difficulties of the last half century. On the one hand, major British banks need capital to improve their balance sheets. On the other hand, they are worried about the default risk of borrowers. In this context, there is a severe problem of credit crunch. All kinds of economic activities have decreased for this reason. Production capacity has weakened and GDP has had negative growth (Chart 4-10).

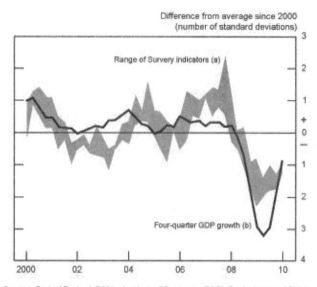

Difference from average since 2000
(number of standard deviations)

Range of Survery indicators (a)

Four-quarter GDP growth (b)

2000   02   04   06   08   10

Sources: Bank of England, British chambers of Commerce (BCC). Conferderaton of British Industry (CBI). CBI/Pricewaterhouse Coopers and ONS.

(a) Three measures are produced by weighting together surveys from the Bank's Agents (manufacturing and services), the BCC (manufacturing and services) and the CBI (manufacturing, financial services, business/consumer services, distributive trades) using shares in nominal value added. The BBC data are non seasonally adjusted.
(b) Chained-volume measure at market prices.

Chart 4-10 British GDP Growth Rate

Labor market

A fast growing unemployment rate is a prominent sign of economic recession. If the laid-off cannot find a new job for a long time, they will gradually lose their skills. As a result, they have to give up looking for the job that they are good at and that will cause an increase in mismatch of labor. In other words, this is a waste of labor. Moreover, the unemployed may live far away from potential employment. Their choice of job will be confined by regional mobility. At the same time, in order to avoid risks, entrepreneurs will move away from certain industries (e.g.,those relating to assets) in favor of others (e.g., those relating to export). The result will be an even worse mismatch. The unemployed workers cannot find a position in the new, fast growing industries because they are not qualified for the jobs.

Many economists used mismatch of labor to explain the increasing unemployment rate in Europe in the 80s of the 20th century. The temporary occurrence of labor force mismatch had a long lasting influence on the labor market. Cyclical unemployment has a lag effect, so that people are unemployed for a longer time. After a period of time, a higher unemployment rate will be reached.

As Chart 4-11 shows, the current long-term unemployment rate of Britain has been growing in recent months, but compared with the mid 80s and early 90s of the 20th century it is still low. A long low unemployment rate means the lag effect may be smaller than has been reported in previous research. There are many uncertainties as to how the labor market is going to develop, and the current unemployment rate has reached 8%. Therefore, the danger of an increasing long term unemployment rate still exists.

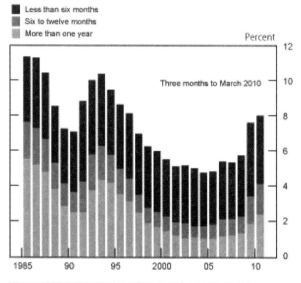

Sources: ONS (including the Labor Force Survey) and Bank calculations

(a) Annual data. Data prior to 1992 are based on LFS microdata. These annual observations correspond to the March-May quarter.

Chart 4-11 British Unemployment Rate

Capital market

The supply capacity of an economy partially relies on the quantity of available assets. In theory, assets mean all sorts of investment, including tangible assets: plant, machinery, building, information systems etc; and intangible assets: copyright, patent, trade mark etc. In fact, the official statistics may not include all the assets. In long term economic activities, the balance of capital service is decided by such basic factors as technology, the size of population and global interest rates. After a relatively long period of time, business activities will adjust their real capital toward this balance. The total investment, reutilization and the life of assets may be the factors influencing the total amount of capital.

In recession, capital is impacted through low level business channels. When companies think that demand will shrink, they will reduce their investment in the uncertain economic environment. The result will be the sharp reduction of business investment. (Chart 4-12)

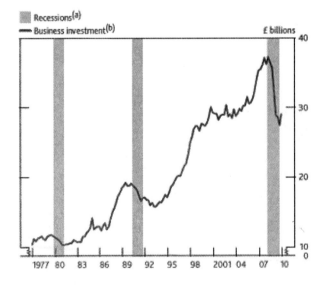

Chart 4-12 Business Investment and Economic Recession

The second aspect of the capital market that was influenced was its life expectancy. Economic recession led to more and more bankruptcy

(Chart 4-13). The capital of some bankrupted companies became worthless and could not be traded in the second-hand market. Such waste appeared in the 1980s, especially in the manufacturing industry. Plant and facilities were abandoned before they had completed their lifespan. In the current recession, the number of bankrupted companies has been soaring. Nevertheless, the reduction of production and the seriousness of the financial crisis are better than estimated (Chart 4-13). The reason might be the healthy state maintained by enterprises before the crisis, or the enhanced cooperation among enterprises, banks and taxation institutions. This is also the effective result of British monetary and financial policies against the crisis. The smaller number of collapsed companies reflected a smaller influence from wasted assets.

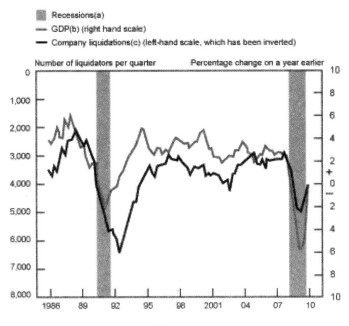

Sources: The Insolvency Service and ONS.

Chart 4-13 Failed Companies in England and Wales

Productivity market

The fluctuation of output indicates company's capacity for integrating labor and capital, or Total Factor Productivity (TFP). TFP is influenced by the following factors:

First, the reduction of new business operations will have a negative influence on TFP, for example, promising businesses cannot find capital to support their development. Such an effect has been even more severe during the current financial crisis. By adopting new technology, new business operations may be a crucial source of increased productivity which will ultimately improve efficiency. However, after the decrease in 2008, there were more and more mergers among companies (Chart 4-14). This shows that in the current context, the reduction in the number of new business operations had a relatively small influence on TFP.

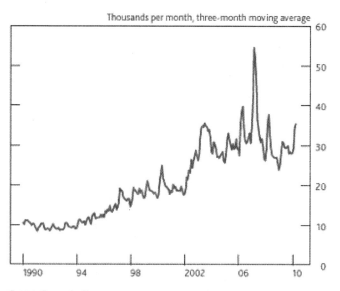

Source: Companies House.

(a) Data are for Great Britain and are non seasonally adjusted.

Chart 4-14 The Number of Merged Companies

Second, recession will harm productivity, especially in an area that enjoys a high GDP. For example, the recent recession reduced the productivity in some financial areas, because the low demand for financial products hindered financial innovation. According to UK National Statistics, the revenue of the British financial sector grew rapidly from the mid-90s (Chart 4-15). However, when recession came, the growth rate slowed down. Generally speaking, the depreciation of the pound weakened foreign competitors and lessened their incentives to develop business and improve efficiency in the UK.

Third, TFP may be different due to various ways of calculation. To be specific, intangible assets like patent and copyright are difficult to quantify. When working out TFP, such assets are usually neglected. So the result of TFP calculation may be higher. In economic recession, investment in intangible assets lessens. Even though such assets were not calculated when the economy was prosperous, their income is counted when working out TFP. This definitely lowers TFP.

Fourth, TFP is influenced by the amount of liquid assets. Daily business needs to be supported by liquid assets which come from internal cash flow, current liabilities and bank loans. A credit crunch brought about by a financial crisis sets up barriers against companies trying to get liquid assets. In this case also, the shortage of liquid assets will reduce TFP.

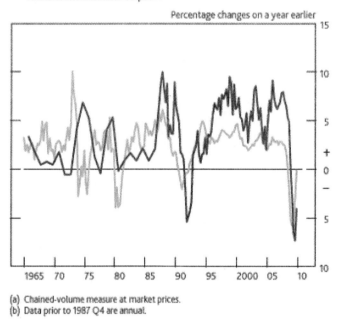

--- GDP(a)
— Financial intermediation output(b)

Percentage changes on a year earlier

(a) Chained-volume measure at market prices.
(b) Data prior to 1987 Q4 are annual.

Chart 4-15 Revenue in Financial Sector and GDP Growth Rate

Much evidence has proved that British companies are facing a shortage of liquid assets. The investigation of British Chambers of Commerce (BCC) and the investigation of Chief Finance Officer (CFO) conducted by Deloitte both have found out a severe shortage of liquid capitals in business activities. BCC's evaluation of liquid capitals dropped to a historical low point (Chart 4-16). Deloitte's investigation of CFO pointed out that increasing the flow of capital would be the most important issue in 2010 (Chart 4-17).

For some companies, the lack of assets will limit output, but such influence will not last long because of the deregulation of assets [3-4].

Sources: BBC and Bank calculations

(a) Companies are asked "During the last three months how has your cash flow changed: improved/same/worsened?"
(b) Average since 1992

Chart 4-16 Flow of Capital in Business Activities

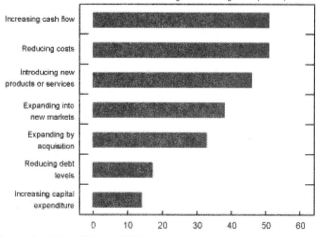

Sources: The Deloitte CFO Survey 2009 Q4

(a) Deloitte asked CFOs to select their top three priorities for 2010 from a list of ten. The score for each factor above is the percentage of CFOs that have included the factor in their top three priorities. The chart shows the top seven factors the CFOs selected.

Chart 4-17 Deloitte's Investigation of CFO: the Most Important Topic in 2010

While the financial crisis was easing, the British economic recovery did not develop smoothly. When the coalition government took office, it cut public expenditure to reduce the huge deficit, most of the cuts coming from investment in education. A large-scale students' demonstration broke out, protesting against the reduction in educational expenditure and the raised ceiling for college tuition.

According to the UK National Statistics, in the second quarter of 2011, the British economic growth rate was 0.2%, which is lower than the 0.5% in the First Quarter. From March to May, the unemployment rate remained as high as 7.7%. The inflation rate that year was expected to be 5%. A recent report from the IMF shows that the British economy is still facing risks, including high inflation rate, high unemployment rate, and low growth rate. In 2011, the estimated growth rate was only 1.5%, lower than the government's expectation of 1.7%. American debt rating was downgraded. The global economy was expected to touch bottom for the second time, and the European debt crisis might develop further. In this context, British trade and investment suffered increasing risk in the external market. In August 2011, the riots in the northern part of London quickly spread to Birmingham, Liverpool and other cities, showing that the British economic crisis was gradually evolving into a social crisis [5]. Even though the riots cooled down, the exposed problems, such as the non-integration of immigrants, a low employment rate, great disparity in wealth, look set to worsen British chances of economic recovery.

Performance of Germany

Economic overview

Germany is a highly developed industrial country. Its economy is the strongest in Europe. Between 2007 and 2009, German GDP was the fourth largest, right after the U.S., Japan and China.

The pillar of the economy in Germany is its industry, which plays a crucial role in its economic development. It is similar to Japan in that its ratio of industrial revenue to total GDP is much higher than that of the U.S., Britain and France, and a little higher than Australia and Italy (Chart 4-18). The features of German industry include the following points: 1. Emphasis on heavy industry. There are four pillar industries in Germany, namely the automobile and auxiliary industry, machinery and manufacturing, the electronic and electrical industry and the chemical industry. These are also the main areas for German exports. 2. Foreign-oriented strategy. More than half of the products in the major industries aim at export. 3. A large percentage of small-and-medium-sized enterprises. SMEs play a significant role in national economic development. The government attaches great importance to SMEs and provides great support.

Germany is a large export country. Its total export volume ranked the first in the world for the six successive years between 2003 and 2008. In 2009, influenced by the world financial crisis, German export shrank and was surpassed by China to become second in the world. From 2003 to 2010, the ratio of export volume to GDP was maintained at above 35%. From 2003 to the third quarter of 2008, this ratio showed a rising trend. After the outbreak of the Wall Street financial storm, the ratio dropped, but the lowest point was still as high as 39.56% and showed a fast growth momentum (Chart 4-19). Compared with other developed countries, Germany has a higher share of export in its GDP. It is four times that of the U.S. and three times that of Japan (Chart 4-20). Clearly, therefore, exports are crucial to the German national economy and have been a driving force for economic growth.

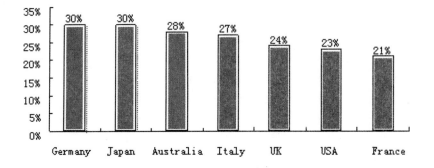

Chart 4-18 2006 Percentage of Industrial Revenue in GDP in Major Developed Countries

(Statistics from: 2006 World Development Indicator)

Percentage %

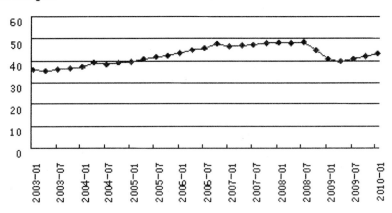

Chart 4-19 2003~2010 Ratio of Export Volume to GDP in Germany
(Statistics from: Deutsche Bundesbank)

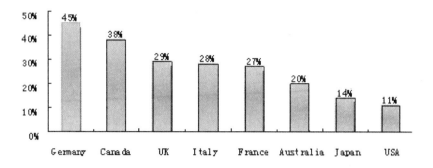

Chart 4-20 2006 Ratio of Commodity and Service Export to GDP in Major Developed Countries

    (Statistics from: 2006 World Development Indicator)

Major export commodities include finished products, machinery and transportation equipment, automobiles and chemical products. These four categories account for 80% of export (Chart 4-21). The target countries are developed countries, such as the U.S., the UK, France etc.

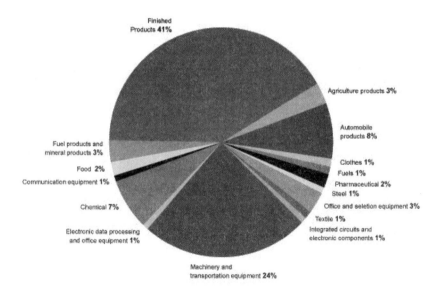

Chart 4-21 Mix of German Export Products
    (Statistics from: WTO)

Germany suffers a shortage of natural resources. Except for the abundant resources of hard coal, lignite and salt, its raw materials and energy requirements rely heavily on import. Two thirds of the primary energy needs to be imported. The production of natural gas can satisfy only a quarter of domestic demand. In the southeast, there is small amount of uranium reserve. Forest cover accounts for 1/3 of Germany's total area [6].

The German government follows the economic policies of national fiscal adjustment, cutting budget deficit, reforming the taxation system, encouraging private investment, furthering denationalization, reducing national interference and allowing free play in the market. Through these policies the German economy has achieved sustained and steady growth. Meanwhile, active measures have been taken to promote information technology and adjust the economic structure.

Financial overview

The German financial sector has developed swiftly in recent years. Its financial system is centered on its banking sector. The business of the financial sector is very diversified and has become increasingly focused. Chart 4-22 shows the categories of banks in Germany. They are divided into two large categories, comprehensive and specialized banks. Comprehensive banks include commercial banks, state banks, savings banks, local institutions of credit cooperation, cooperative banks and mortgage banks. Commercial banks can be further categorized into large banks, regional commercial banks and branches of foreign banks. Comprehensive banks have mixed operations, such as deposit, loan and electronic banking services. They can also run securities, wealth management and insurance while specialized banks can only operate specific financial services which are defined in their business license.

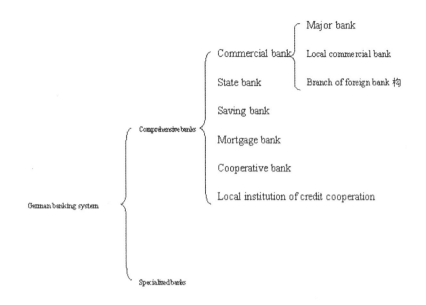

Chart 4-22 Categories of German Banks

Debt in the German financial system mainly occurs in the banking sector. The debt in the insurance sector remains stable at 18% of all financial sector debt while other sectors account for less than 10% [7].

Securities in Germany can be traded outside the stock exchange by telephone or in the secondary market through eight stock exchanges in Berlin, Bremen, Dusseldorf, Frankfurt / Main River, Hamburg, Hanover, Munich and Stuttgart. Among them, Frankfurt is the largest security market in Germany, ranking fourth in the world, behind New York, Tokyo and London.

The supervision system in Germany is comprehensive and effective. All activities of credit loan institutions are supervised by the Federal Credit Loan Supervision Bureau in Berlin. If a credit loan institution is trapped in financial difficulty, the deposit guarantee institution of the credit loan industry will provide partial protection for the account holders.

Influence of the financial crisis on Germany

Severe impact on some banks

In September 2009, Deutsche Bundesbank issued a report on the performance of German credit loan institutions in the financial year 2008. It pointed out that due to the financial crisis the institutions did not do well. Compared with the previous financial year, the total pre-tax revenue of all banks had dropped by €45.5 billion and bank losses were €25 billion. This was the lowest point in their history. Chart 4-23 shows the profits of German banks between 2000 and 2008.

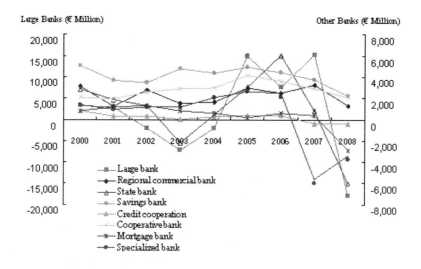

Chart 4-23 Profits of German Banks between 2000 and 2008 Financial Year
(Statistics from: Deutsche Bundesbank)

Large banks, state banks and mortgage banks were most seriously affected. In 2007 revenue had been €15.3 billion and in 2008 this turned into a loss of €17.8 billion. These banks suffered a large decline, and their total loss accounted for 71.2% of all bank losses. The second largest bank in Germany, CommerzBank, accepted a loan of €8.2 billion from the government in October 2008, as well as government mortgage bond of €15 billion, in the hope of having guarantee for liquidity. There was a clear reduction in state bank profits in the 2007 and 2008 financial years. The profit in 2006 had been €6 billion, in 2007 it was €790 million, and in 2008 it was once again €6 billion. The State Bank of Saxony and North Rhine Westphalia State Bank also fell into difficulties. There are two reasons explaining why state banks were hit more badly than others. First, they were deeply involved in the international capital investment market and had purchased large amounts of American subprime loan assets. Second, many state banks lacked a proper business structure and a clear direction of business. They had little resistance against risks. Mortgage banks, which have always made a profit had a major decline in 2008, from €380 million profit in 2007 to about €3 billion loss in 2008. This figure is larger than the sum of profits in the previous five years from 2003 to 2007. Specialized banks were affected too, and their losses appeared the earliest. In the financial year of 2007, their profits fell from €2.4 billion to minus €5.6 billion. In 2008, the loss was smaller, but remained as high as €3.4 billion. Comparatively speaking, savings banks, cooperative banks credit cooperation, and regional commercial banks suffered less damage from the crisis. Even though there was a clear decline in pre-tax revenue, profits could still be achieved.

Shrinking economy

The financial crisis had a negative effect on the German national economy. According to the GDP fluctuations (Chart 4-24), GDP growth rate started slowing down from 2007. In the third and fourth quarters of 2008 and the first quarter of 2009 it dropped dramatically. During the fourth quarter of 2008, the economy started to have negative growth, and the first quarter of 2009 saw a negative growth rate of -6.7%, hitting a historical low. In the second quarter of 2009, the negative GDP growth rate decreased to the point that in the first quarter of 2010, real GDP finally experienced positive growth of 1.5%.

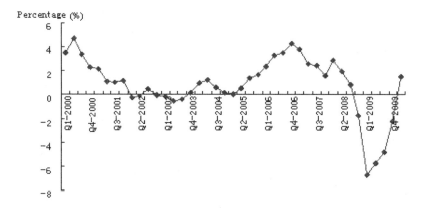

Chart 4-24 2000~2009 German Real GDP Growth Rate
(Statistics from: OECD)

Chart 4-25 demonstrates the change of German real GDP growth rate between 2000 and 2010. According to this chart, the major reason for German economic decline in the crisis was the reduction of exports and investment. In the fourth quarter of 2008, as the financial crisis spread around the world, the main trading partners of Germany, namely the U.S., the UK, France, Italy etc. were severely damaged. Ultimately, this caused the negative growth of German exports down to -6.3%. In the first three quarters of 2009, the situation was even worse, with per-centage declines of 17.2%, 18.2% and 15.5% respectively. There was no halt in this downward momentum until the fourth quarter of 2009 and the first quarter of 2010, when the growth rate rose to 7.15%. From the point of view of investment, the total volume of new fixed assets was decreasing as well. In all quarters of 2009, its growth rate had always been below -7%. It turned better in the first quarter of 2010, but was still a negative growth, namely -1.1%. In contrast, domestic consumption was more stable. Government procurement and individual consump-tion did not have a dramatic decline

Impacted industrial production

One of the features of this financial crisis has been the swift shrinking of world trade. Because of this, export-oriented industries were affected more seriously while those focused on domestic demands suffered much less. Since German industries are export-oriented, with half of their production sold to foreign countries, this financial crisis clearly had a huge negative effect on German industries.

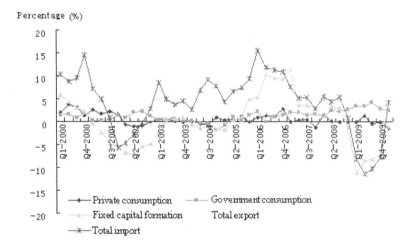

Chart 4-25 Growth Rate of German Consumption, Investment and Foreign Trade between 2000 and 2010
(Statistics from: OECD)

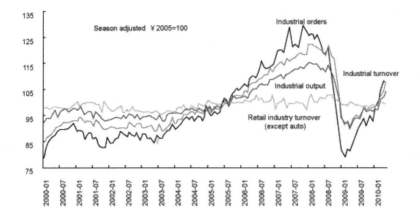

Chart 4-26 German Economic Indicators between 2000 and 2010
(Statistics from: Deutsche Bundesbank)

Chart 4-26 shows changes in industrial output, orders and industrial turnover, and retail industry turnover in Germany between 2000 and 2010. It takes 2005 as the basis and seasonal adjustment has been made. It is easy to see that industrial development maintained a strong momentum before the financial crisis, with all statistics showing healthy growth. By the end of 2007, in parallel with the development of the financial crisis, the output volume of production, industrial orders and industrial turnover all began to decline. By early 2009, the decline touched bottom and began to recover. Before that, all three statistics had fallen, with industrial orders registering the largest decrease. Between November 2007 and February 2009, the figure fell from 129.2 to 79, a 38.9% decline that went back to the level of January 2000. The decrease in orders and turnover led to a cut in investment and damaged the economy. Consumption demand in Germany remained comparatively stable. The retail industry, which had little dependence on export, was less affected by the financial crisis. The turnover in retail industry declined after September 2008, but the change was quite small. From September 2008 to January 2010, the turnover index dropped from 103 to 97.5, or by 5.3%, much smaller than the damage to industrial production.

Crisis in the automobile industry

Germany is the third largest producer of automobiles in the world. This industry is the largest sector of the German national economy, as well as its driving force, its innovation base and the guarantee for employment. In Germany, one out of every seven people works in the automobile industry. A quarter of all tax derives from this industry or related areas [8], and it was hit badly by the financial crisis. The German Automobile Association indicated that the industry had suffered its greatest crisis since the 1990s.

The association's statistics show that automobile industry as a whole had a decrease in sales in 2009, from €330.881 billion in 2008 to €263.194 billion, a decline rate of 20.5%. Domestic sales dropped by 15.3% while overseas sales fell by 23.9%. The total capital investment in the industry declined from €13.1 billion to €10 billion, or by 23.7%. In terms of numbers, manufacturers reduced their production because of the decline in demand. In 2009, automobile production declined by 13.4% compared with 2008, of which passenger cars dropped by 9.2% and commercial vehicles by 50.5%.

In 2009, newly registered passenger cars increased by 23.2% and commercial vehicles by 27.7%. In terms of brands, three middle class brands, namely Ford, Opal and Volkswagen, maintained fast growth. Respectively, their growth rate was 37%, 31.1% and 30.9%. High end brands, such as Porsche, Audi, BMW and Mercedes-Benz, saw their newly registered cars fall by 5.4%, 6.6%, 9.4% and 13.9% respectively (Chart 4-27).

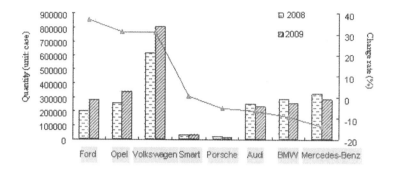

Chart 4-27 Comparison of Newly Registered Automobiles with Different Brands in 2009

(Statistics From: Verband der Automobilindustrie)

The export of automobiles worldwide shrank seriously. With the exception of China and Korea, all other passenger car exports declined. Commercial vehicles export fared even worse. The apparently large increase rate of commercial vehicle export to Japan depends on scale effect. Compared with export to other countries, export to Japan was almost nothing in quantity, though high when expressed as growth rate. The U.S. was the largest overseas market for German automobiles. The export of passenger cars dropped by 31.3% in 2009 while commercial vehicles decreased by 77.7%. Elsewhere, east European countries were impacted even more by the financial crisis, and the export of the two types of vehicles from Germany to east Europe dropped by 49.8% and 78% respectively (Chart 4-28).

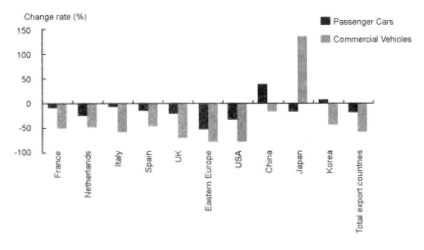

Chart 4-28 2009 Passenger Cars and Commercial Vehicles Export Quantity
(Statistics from: Verband der Automobilindustrie)

Between 1999 and 2006, passenger car exports grew steadily with a small increase every year. In 2007, there was a significant improvement with a growth rate of 10.6%. In 2008, influenced by the financial crisis, this export dropped by 4%, but was still much higher than the export volume between 2001 and 2006. In 2009, the financial crisis finally hit the German automobile industry. Passenger car exports dropped by 17.1% compared with 2008, hitting a ten year low (Chart 4-29).

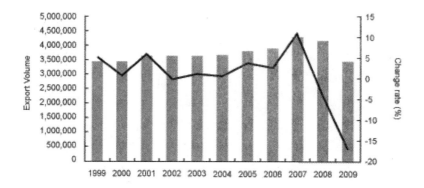

Chart 4-29 Export Volume of German Passenger Cars between 1999 and 2006
(Statistics from: Verband der Automobilindustrie)

Performance of Russia

Economic overview

Russia is a world economic power. During the time of the Soviet Union, it was the second largest economic power in the world. After the collapse of the Soviet Union, there was severe recession. However, after 2000, the Russian economy recovered gradually. In 2006, its economy had surpassed its pre-1990 level, when the Soviet Union collapsed. Its 2007 GDP was $1135.6 billion, ranking tenth in the world. Affected by the financial crisis, Russian GDP growth began to drop, from 8.06% in 2007 to 5.62% in 2008 (Chart 4-30).

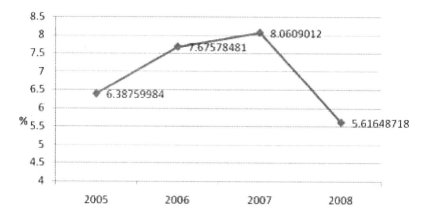

Chart 4-30 Russian GDP Growth Rate between 2003 and 2008

Russia enjoys abundant resources of many kinds and large reserves, so its self-sufficiency rate is very high. Forest coverage is 50.7% with a total area of 867 million hectares, ranking first in the world, and providing a timber volume of 80.7 billion m³. The ascertained natural gas reserve is 48 trillion m³, accounting for 1/3 of the world total and taking the first place in the world. Ascertained oil reserves are 6.5 billion tons, accounting for 12~13% of the world total. Iron ore reserves are the largest. Hydraulic power is 4270 km³/year and the second largest. Uranium reserves rank seventh and gold reserves between fourth and fifth.

Rich resources have provided strong support for Russian industrial and agricultural development. The foundations of heavy industry are very solid and there are comprehensive departments. Machinery, iron and steel, metallurgy, oil, natural gas, coal, forestry and the chemical industry are especially strong. In recent years, Russia has seen the emergence of its electronic computer industry, aerospace aviation industry and high-tech industry. In particular, the defense industry in Russia is very strong and plays a unique role in the world. The weapons it produces have been sold all over the world. Agriculture and farming are equally important in Russia. Major agricultural products include wheat, barley, oats, corn, rice and beans, and farming mainly focuses on the rearing of cows, sheep and pigs.

Major Russian export products are fuels such as oil and natural gas, chemical products, mineral ores, metal products, gems and their products, and agricultural raw materials such as timber and pulp (Chart 4-31). The export services are mainly computers, information, communication and other commercial services, as well as finished products such as machinery and transportation vehicles (Chart 4-32). Import products include machinery, transportation vehicles, food and agricultural raw materials, chemical products, rubber, metal and its products, and textiles. Affected by the international financial crisis, Russian foreign trade volume decreased greatly. In 2009, the trade in goods was $38.915 billion, a decrease of 37.55% compared with the previous year, of which exports dropped by $23.394 billion or 36.36% and imports by $15.521 billion or 39.27%. Trade surplus was $7.873 billion, 29.71% lower (Chart 4-33) [9-10].

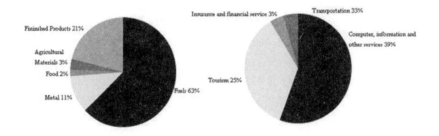

Chart 4-31 Commodity Export Mix Chart 4-32 Service Export Mix

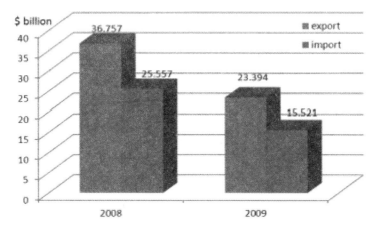

Chart 4-33 Russian Foreign Trade Volume in 2008 and 2009

Financial overview

The Russian banking sector started early and has always been a leader in the financial world. After the 1998 financial crisis, the Russian economy was on a downturn and he banking sector was seriously hurt. The ruble depreciated quickly and the inflation rate soared. Russia immediately launched reforms in its financial system. It shut down some low-credit banks, and after three years, with the joint efforts of the central bank and commercial banks, the Russian banking sector has overcome the negative effects of the financial crisis and recovered to its pre-crisis level. The development of banking is an important factor for economic growth. Recently, the capital of the Russian banking system has increased and investment for production has therefore grown. Currently, 90% of the 1300 Russian banks run well and public trust in banks has recovered.

Securities developed as early as the banking sector. After the crisis in 1998, the security industry was damaged and even today it does not have a large share in the market. There is therefore little room for its development. Capital in the Russian market was very limited. In

1997, capital volume reached its peak, about $120 billion, but that is still much lower than that in other developed countries such as the U.S. and European countries, and is even no larger than some large companies. The securities market plays the role of adjusting national debt, ensuring capital investment in the economy and redistributing wealth. Of these roles, the best fulfilled task of the securities market is adjusting national debt. Recently, the Russian securities market has shown the following features: 1) the Russian securities market is a single market. In other words, it is the only market for securities in the country. 2) It is an isolated market. Issuers, investors and professional participants comprise the foundation of the securities market, but they are independent from each other and fulfill their own responsibilities. There is no real coordination. In terms of function, the market can be divided into three models: an issuer securities market, an investor securities market and a professional participant securities market. In general, the Russian securities market did not attract investment for the national economy. The major reason is that the structure of the market is not complete and shows the features of single and isolated operation.

After the Soviet Union collapsed, the Russian banking and security sector developed very fast. In contrast, the insurance industry started late, only beginning to develop from 1997. In that year, the capital it attracted increased by 40%. After 1998, it accelerated its development and doubled its capital. However, the insurance market was still in an early stage of development. In 2000, there were only 400 thousand people who had bought life insurance. One third of the public were not willing to buy insurance. The trust in domestic insurance companies was very low. In other words, Russian insurance industry was an emerging industry with huge market potential and room for development [11].

The effect of the financial crisis on Russia

A drop in oil price and the growth of fiscal deficit

After the Financial Tsunami, the global demand for commodities fell sharply. The international oil price decreased from $147 per barrel in 2008 to $40 (Chart 4-43). For Russia, which relies heavily on the revenue from the energy sector to support and promote its economic development, this was a heavy blow.

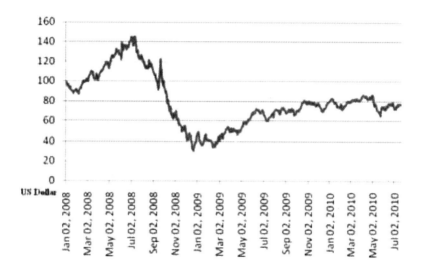

Chart 4-34 International Crude Oil Price

Because of the constant decline of the price of oil, Russia's foreign reserves, which depend on the exchange of oil for U.S. dollars, shrank. In the third quarter of 2008, $26 billion had fled from Russia. By December 1, 2008, Russian foreign reserves had been reduced from $484.6 billion in the previous month to $455.7 billion.

The financial crisis extended to the deeper levels of the Russian economy, and Russia could not expect foreign capital to flow in to encourage its economic growth as had happened in 1998, because Europe, the U.S. and Japan were also in economic recession. Therefore, the Russian government had to adopt systematic measures, including tax reduction, national loan assistance, favorable loan interest rates, unsecured guarantees for loans from financial institutions to enterprises, guarantees for national procurement and restructuring of taxation. In this way, it was expected to overcome the crisis by supporting enterprise production and easing the tension on capital chains [12-13].

A blow to the property market

Before October 2008, property prices had increased continuously, because of the rich returns from the oil trade and the sharp increase in the population's income. Foreign capital flooded into the Russian property market. Moscow became a city with some of the most expensive property prices in the world. With the effects of the Financial Tsunami, global commodity demands decreased, the international oil price dropped and public income therefore decreased. As a result, house purchasers could not get loans and foreign capital fled. The property market in Russia experienced a sharp decline of 25%.

By the end of 2008, large projects had been reduced by 90%. Many companies did not receive new orders for months and 90% of employees were laid off. Banks almost halted new mortgage loans, and nationwide house sales were affected. In order to help purchasers, the government decided to allocate 20 billion rubles, from January 1, 2009, to tide over mortgage loan borrowers who were unemployed or had had their income reduced.

The Russian property market and stock market were brothers in trouble. The major index of Russia's stock market dropped by 70% in 2008, topping the list of world stock market collapses. Stock holders suffered severe losses. The main listed companies all issued American Depositary Receipt (ADR) and Global Depository Receipts (GDR) to trade in major European and American stock markets. In other words, foreign capital could buy Russian shares directly. As a result, 30% of the Russian stock exchange was controlled by foreign capital, and domestic investors declined to less than a million, demonstrating how sensitive the Russian stock market was to the international financial crisis and how strong is its relationship with the world market. According to estimates, by November 2008, share value had decreased from $1.3 trillion to $459.5 billion, compared with early 2008. This was a 73% reduction compared with the highest point in June (Chart 4-35). The price-earnings ratio was only 5.6, which was the lowest around the world. Rich people in Russia had their wealth reduced by $300 billion [14].

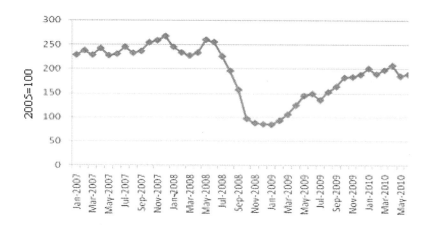

Chart 4-35 Russian Stock Index

Decline in ruble exchange rate

Dragged down by oil prices and impacted by the financial tsunami, the Russian ruble exchange rate with the U.S. dollar rose from 23.13 in July 2008 to 35.76 in February 2009, with a depreciation rate of 55% (Chart 4-36). This was its lowest point since 2001. The exchange rate of ruble is closely related to the international oil price. When the oil price dropped, the ruble exchange rate also decreased.

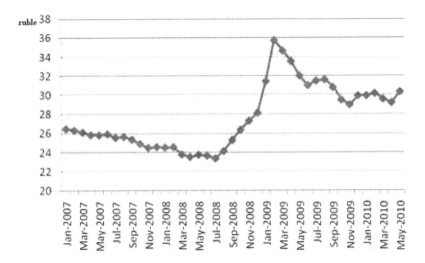

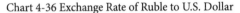

Chart 4-36 Exchange Rate of Ruble to U.S. Dollar

If oil price had dropped to 30 dollars per barrel, the exchange rate would have been 42:1. The Russian central bank would have had to inject large sums of U.S. dollars to maintain the stability of its exchange rate. This would have led to further reduction of gold and foreign currency reserves and weakened Russia's capacity to resist the effects of the financial tsunami.

The fast depreciation of the ruble led to an increase in the price of imported goods. The inflation rate therefore rose and assembly production which relied on parts and raw materials import was hurt. Lower imports also damaged the transportation industry. Railway companies had to increase their fees for transporting goods, which ultimately increased the expenses of manufacturers.

Shrinking industry and severe unemployment

In November 2008, production by Russian industrial enterprises quickly declined and the national industrial output value fell. Compared with October, it decreased by 9.7% and compared with the same period of the previous year, it decreased by 9.1% (Chart 4-37). Similar decrease occurred in every area of Russian industrial production. The margin of decrease in iron ore mining, tar coal, black metal products was more than 1/3. In December, the situation was even worse. In January 2009, it touched bottom. Many Russian media thought that the 1998 economic crisis had reappeared, because the industrial added value of Russia had only fallen by 8.9% at that time.

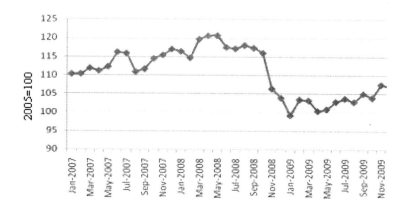

Chart 4-37 Russian Industrial Output Value

The downturn of Russian industries caused a cut in the workforce, a decrease in production, and even the closing of companies. The unemployed population increased continuously in November 2008, 10.5% more compared with October. By September 2009, it reached its peak, which was a 63.9% year on year increase (Chart 4-38).

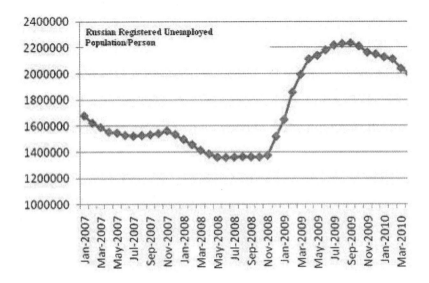

Chart 4-38 Russian Registered Unemployed Population

Government countermeasures to combat large-scale unemployment were to first help those enterprises which had large workforces and had received government orders for 2009. The Russian government planned to raise the highest unemployment subsidy from 1275 to 4900 rubles, with the lowest level at 850 rubles. Apart from that, the government took no other comprehensive or effective measure to encourage employment, and thus the unemployment issue could not be completely resolved. The swift degradation of the Russian economy together with a high inflation rate led to great difficulties in people's lives and therefore general dissatisfaction. Demonstrations occurred in Moscow, St. Petersburg and other cities.

Performance of Australia

Economic overview

Australia is located in the South Pacific and Indian Oceans. It is the most economically developed country in the southern hemisphere.

Since the 1990s, Australian economy maintained a sustainable growth. In the fourteen years between 1996 and 2009, its GDP grew swiftly, except for the effects of the Asian financial crisis and the current crisis (Chart 4-39). At the same time, both the inflation rate and the unemployment rate remained low. It is now one of the countries with the strongest economic growth and was listed by the OECD as the most dynamic economy. According to Chart 4-40, from 2002 to this financial crisis, the unemployment rate was decreasing steadily and from 2002 to 2004, the inflation rate was low. After 2005, inflation started to rise, but it was always lower than 4%. From the second half of 2006 to the third quarter of 2007, the inflation rate dropped sharply (Chart 4-41).

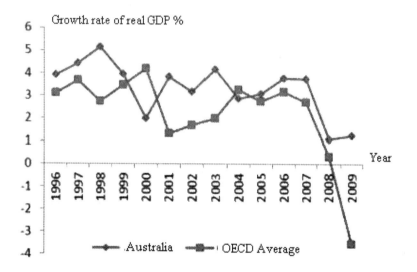

Chart 4-39 1996~2009 Australian Real GDP Growth Rate
    (Statistics from: OECD)

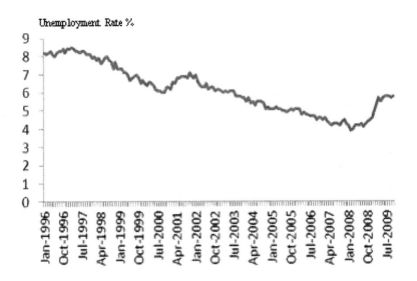

Chart 4-40 1996~2009 Australian Unemployment Rate
(Statistics from: OECD)

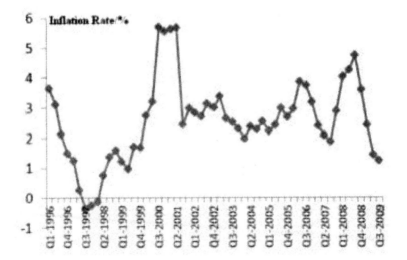

Chart 4-41 1996~2009 Australian Inflation Rate
(Statistics from: OECD)

Australia is an industrial country which developed later than other nations. Its agriculture and animal husbandry are very advanced. It is known as "the nation riding on the sheep's back", and is the largest exporter of wool and beef. Australia has abundant mines and is a large producer and exporter of mineral resources. There are more than 70 kinds of ascertained mineral resources, among which the reserves of lead, nickel, silver, tantalum, uranium and zinc top the rest of the world. This country also is the largest producer of Bauxite, alumina, diamonds, lead and tantalum; the largest exporter of bituminous coal, bauxite, lead, diamonds, zinc, and mineral concentrates; the second largest exporter of alumina, iron ore and uranium; and the third largest exporter of aluminum and gold [15]. Service, manufacturing, mining and agriculture are the four leading industries in Australia. According to official statistics, in the financial year between 2006 and 2007, the service industry (A$782.6 billion), manufacturing (A$97.98 billion), mining (A$48.75 billion) and agriculture (A$23.37 billion) account for 82.1%, 10.3%, 5.1% and 2.5% of GDP respectively [16]. The service industry is a strong area of the Australian economy. Recently, emerging powers have produced a strong demand for raw materials which drives the fast growth of the mining industry. The share of Australian agriculture in its economy is decreasing. However, the quantity of production, output and profits are increasing. The export of agricultural products is growing dramatically too.

Foreign trade is an important component of the Australian economy. 70% of agricultural production, 80% of resource products and 18% of manufacturing are exported. A large proportion of service industry product is exported, with a value of $48 billion. In 2007, the foreign trade volume of Australia was A$355.9 billion, which is an increase of A$16.1 billion or 4.7%. Overall, export growth was A$168.1 billion or 2.6% while import growth was A$187.8 billion or 6.7% [17] Australia has trading relation with more than 130 countries and areas. Major trade partners include China, Japan, the U.S., Singapore, UK, Korea, New Zealand, Thailand, Germany, and Malaysia. The Australian government constantly improves its international trading environment. Since 2004, it has signed free trade agreements with Singapore, the U.S. and Thailand.

Financial overview

In recent years, the financial service in Australia has been growing steadily. It is one of the fastest growing industries, and the value of the financial sector has always been high. According to Chart 4-42, between 2003 and 2006, the growth rate of the financial sector was much higher than the GDP growth rate, reaching 8.7% in 2006. The total value of all investment funds run by Australia was $777 billion which ranked fourth in the world. The stock exchange in Australia is the eighth largest in the world. The market has capital as high as $870 billion which is three times the Hong Kong market or five times the Singapore market. Personnel engaged in the financial sector number 350,000, which is more than the sum of those in Singapore and Hong Kong [18].

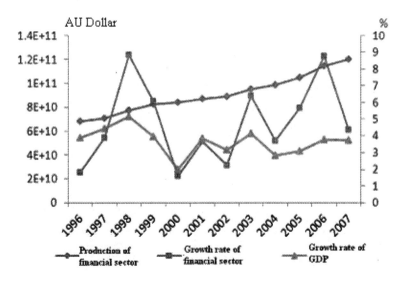

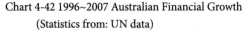

Chart 4-42 1996~2007 Australian Financial Growth
(Statistics from: UN data)

The Australian stock market is very advanced. About 54% of Australian adults own stocks. The stock market is run by ASX. There are three traditional indexes, namely All Ordinaries, All Industrials and All Resources. Since April 2000, the Australian stock exchange and S & P jointly launched new indexes to better reflect the new changes in the investment market. New indexes include the S&P/ASX100, S&P/ASX200 and S&P/ASX300. The S&P/ASX200 represents 88.2% of the capital in the local market, and is considered to be the most important of the indexes to measure the state of the stock market [15].

By June 2007, there were in total 55 commercial banks in Australia. The Reserve Bank of Australia is its central bank which is very independent. It shows in the following aspects: on one hand, the board of directors of the bank has independent power to stipulate and implement monetary policy; on the other hand, the bank has the capacity to implement monetary policy independently. The independence of the Australian Reserve Bank is above the medium level of all developed countries [19]. Furthermore, ANZ, Commonwealth Bank, National Bank and Westpac Bank are four major banks in Australia. Their assets in total account for 50% of all bank assets.

Financial supervision is in the charge of the Council of Financial Regulators. This is a cooperative entity, composed of the Reserve Bank of Australia, the Australian Prudential Regulation Authority (APRA) and the Australian Securities and Investment Commission (ASIC). APRA supervises deposit institutions, insurance companies and retirement funds. ASIC supervises the credibility of the market and protects consumers and enterprises. Each component has its own responsibilities. Together they reinforce the communication and coordination of different institutions, and maintain the high efficiency, competition, and stability of the financial system [20-21].

Effects of the financial crisis on Australia

Effects of the financial crisis on the Australian economy

Australia was affected by the global economic crisis triggered by the U.S. Unlike other countries, the Australian economy was the very first one to recover and its economic activities have shown a strong rebound.

Chart 4-43 shows the GDP growth of world major economies. The changes in their GDP growth rates are similar. From the end of 2007 to early 2008, the global economic crisis struck the whole world. Real GDP growth rate of all economies began to drop and started to rise only after the end of 2009 when it had touched bottom. However, there is a marked difference between the Australian economy and all others: while the financial crisis was deepening in 2009, the real GDP growth rate of Australia decreased more slowly than others. While other economies were experiencing negative GDP growth, the Australian economy always had positive growth. This means that Australia's real GDP was growing all the time, but it was the growth rate that was changing.

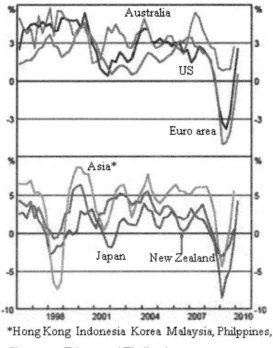

*Hong Kong Indonesia Korea Malaysia, Philippines, Singapore, Taiwan and Thailand
Sources: ABS, CEC, Thomson Reuters

Chart 4-43 Real GDP Growth Rate

The effect of the financial crisis on the Australian financial sector

Australia has a complete financial system and an active financial market. Its financial market has become one of the major capital markets in the Asia-Pacific region. Financial institutions in Australia are banks, professional financial institutions, and non-banking financial institutions. The financial sector has a mixed operation. Commercial banks can run all the financial businesses of investment banks, but have to be listed companies. There are four major banks, namely the Commonwealth Bank, ANZ, NAB and Westpac, which mainly operate the business of commercial banks.

In the context of global financial crisis and economic recession, the Australian financial sector was less influenced than that of other developed countries and maintained a very good capacity of recovery. As is indicated in Chart 4-44, the income of banks was stable and the loss from mortgage securities and loans was limited. The banking system is gradually making profits. Some signs show that the amount of bad debt is likely to have reached its peak, encourages good expectations for the future. The banking system can take advantage of the increase of capital and reduce the use of Australian government reserves[22].

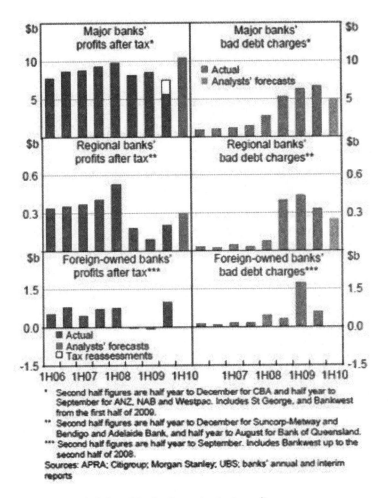

Chart 4-44 Profitability of Banks Operating in Australia

Analysis of reasons for recovery

The Australian economy has been recovering for more than a year while other countries are still in recession slowdown. The reasons for the Australian recovery are the following:

Enhanced trade with Asian countries

The economic features of Australia can be described as "riding on the back of sheep" and "riding on a mine car". There are abundant resources in Australia. This country is an important producer and exporter of mineral resources. It is the largest producer of Bauxite, alumina, diamonds, lead, and tantalum. It is also the largest exporter of bituminous coal, bauxite, lead, diamonds, zinc and refined minerals; the second largest exporter of Alumina, iron ore and uranium; and the third largest exporter of aluminum and gold. Moreover, Australia has advanced agriculture and animal husbandry. It is the largest exporter of wool and beef. Its agriculture is highly modernized and mechanized. The size of farms are usually large with a high output of animal products, most of which are exported. The production and export of wool is No. 1 in the world and that of meat and wheat are also the top in the world. Australia is one of the five major grain exporters.

Australia is the first country to have recovered from the economic crisis, and one of the main reasons is its trade with Asian countries. Of particular significance is the fact that during the crisis, Australia expanded its exports to Asian countries, and this accelerated the process of emerging from the crisis. As Chart 4-45 shows, when the world was trapped in economic crisis, business investment and export volumes of all other economies were in downturn, while in contrast, Australia maintained a high level of investment and export.

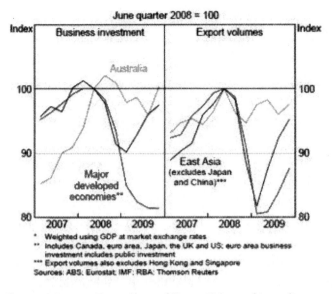

June quarter 2008 = 100

Index — Business investment — Export volumes — Index

Australia

100 — 100

90 — 90

East Asia (excludes Japan and China)***

Major developed economies**

80 — 80

2007   2008   2009   2007   2008   2009

*   Weighted using GDP at market exchange rates
** Includes Canada, euro area, Japan, the UK and US; euro area business
    investment includes public investment
*** Export volumes also excludes Hong Kong and Singapore
Sources: ABS; Eurostat; IMF; RBA; Thomson Reuters

Chart 4-45 Business Investment and Export Volume of Australia
(Statistics from: ABS; Eurostat; IMF; RBA; Thomson Reuters)

World economic recovery caused the sharp increase in demand for iron ore and coking coal which are two main raw materials of steel refinery. Since 2010, the prices of spot iron ore and coking coal have increased by almost 70% and 35% (counting in USD) and reached two to three times higher than its lowest level by the middle of 2009 (Chart 4-46). The price of spot goods was higher and Australian exporters raised the negotiated price, until, in the second quarter, the price made a new record.

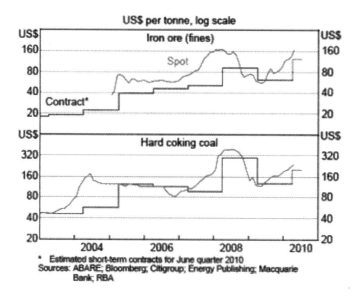

* Estimated short-term contracts for June quarter 2010
Sources: ABARE; Bloomberg; Citigroup; Energy Publishing; Macquarie
Bank; RBA

Chart 4-46 Price of Bulk Commodities

Global steel production seems to have returned to the prime time. It has had a stronger capacity of recovery than industrial production, and consequently, oil prices have begun to rise. What is more, the Chinese steel industry only slowed down at the end of 2008, but then started to grow strongly again. The current output volume is 20% higher than its level before the crisis. Steel industry in other countries had a serious recession and has only recently started to recover (Chart 4-47). The demands of the Chinese steel industry are increasing continuously, partly because domestic fiscal measures encourage investment in large infrastructure programs. Moreover, the Chinese government has reduced the purchase tax on automobiles which has led to the increase of production and ownership of automobiles.

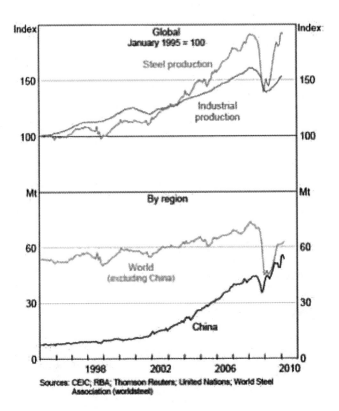

Chart 4-47 Steel Production

  (Statistics from: CEIC; RBA; Thomson Reuters; United Nations; World Steel
Association)

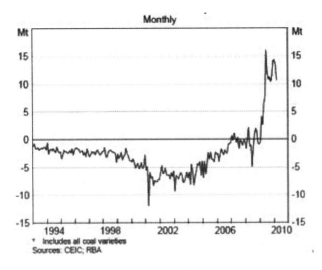

Chart 4-48 China's Net Import of Coal

Along with the recovery of steel refining, the supply of global iron ore and coking coal has become increasingly problematical. Australia and other major exporters have almost reached the saturation point and ships crowd the major ports. In China, due to the integration of the coal industry, limited resources of fine coals, and the emergence of new steel factories, domestic supply of coal has fallen far behind demand. This situation has changed China from being a pure exporter to being an important coal importer. Chinese iron ore is low grade and high cost. China has to turn to international markets and imports to satisfy its demands (Chart 4-48). The trade between Australia and China continues to develop and expand in this context [23-24].

Effective fiscal and monetary incentive policy

Since mid to late September 2008, the Australian government has launched many policies to stabilize the financial market and maintain economic growth. It has injected capital into the financial system and adjusted interest rates to prevent the negative influence of the financial crisis on Australia. On September 26, Australian Treasurer Swan announced that the government would provide 4 billion Australian dollars to purchase the supporting securities of Australian mortgage loans to alleviate the exhaustion of liquidity in RMBS caused by the financial crisis and enhance the financing and credit loan capacity of non-banking institutions. On October 2, according to the joint requirement of state leaders, the Australian Government Committee decided to accelerate the launching of a national infrastructure fund which worth A$20 billion. In early October, ANZ Bank, Westpac and National Australia Bank received long-term financing of A$4.2 billion from the sovereign fund, and futures fund, administrated by the government. In this way, banks expected to overcome the problem of insufficient liquidity. Meanwhile, the government has increased its fiscal expenditure by A$10 billion, targeting disadvantaged groups. It hopes to improve public living standard through increasing pensions, providing living necessities, subsidizing the expense of raising children for middle and low income families, aiding first house purchasers and paying for training. By creating these incentives, the government hopes to generate domestic demand.

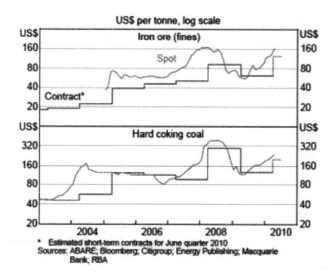

Chart 4-49 Policy Interest Rate of Major Countries

Worried that an increasingly prosperous mineral industry might bring about inflation, the Australian central bank decided to raise its base interest rate to "normal level" to contain the possibility. Asian trading partners, such as China, accelerated their economic recovery, which generated strong demands for Australian coal and iron ore. The price of iron ore export to China has increased. Australia has raised its base interest rate six times and is expecting to raise it again. After the economic crisis, the Australian central bank was the very first one among the G20 countries to raise its interest rate [25] (Chart 4-49).

Stable financial system

The financial system in Australia is highly developed. Financial institutions have sufficient capitals and high credit. Moreover, Australian financial institutions are different from those of Europe and the U.S.. They are conservative and held few American subprime loans and their related assets, so that there were smaller losses for Australia. At the same time, the mortgage loan business in Australia is conservative and the volume of issued loans is very small.

Australian banks have always had high credit ratings. According to the S & P credit rating for the 100 banks with the largest assets in the world, banks with AA are very few, but all of the four major Australian banks are rated as AA (Chart 4-50).

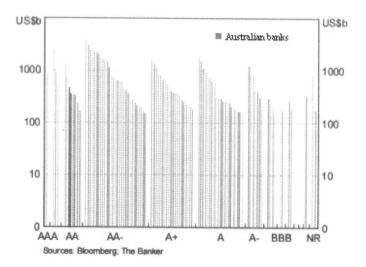

Chart 4-50 Credit Rating of 100 largest Banks in the World

	Outlook	Current	Last change	
			Direction	Date
Adelaide Bank	Stable	BBB+	↑	October 2004
AMP Bank	Stable	A	↑	April 2008
ANZ Banking Group	Stable	AA	↑	February 2007
Arab Bank Australia	Stable	A-	--	January 2007
Bank of Queensland	Stable	BBB+	↑	April 2005
BankWest	Developing	A+	↓	September 2008
Bendigo and Adelaide Bank	Stable	BBB+	↑	February 2005
Citigroup	Negative	AA	↓	January 2008
Commonwealth Bank of Australia	Stable	AA	↑	February 2007
Elders Rural Bank	Negative	BBB	↑	August 2007
HSBC Bank Australia	Stable	AA	↑	July 2006
ING Bank (Australia)	Stable	AA	↑	August 2005
Macquarie Bank	Negative	A	--	November 1994
Members Equity Bank	Negative	BBB	↑	August 2006
National Australia Bank	Negative	AA	↑	February 2007
Rabobank Australia	Stable	AAA	↑	December 1996
St George Bank	Watch Positive	A+	↑	January 2006
Suncorp-Metway	Stable	A+	↑	March 2007
Westpac Banking Corporation	Stable	AA	↑	February 2007

(a) Includes all Australian-owned banks, and foreign-owned banks operating in Australia that have a issuer rating from Standard & Poor's
Source: Standard & Poor's

Chart 4-51 Credit Rating of Australian Banks

After the financial crisis in 2008, only two out of 19 Australian banks were downgraded by S & P (Chart 4-51), and after 2009, Australian banks maintained a high credit rating.

Higher population growth rate.

The population growth rate in Australia is higher than that of housing (Chart 4-52). This leads to pressure on house supply and rising prices in the property market. When the economy maintains a good momentum, people have enough money to buy houses. According to the theory of demand and supply, the price of housing rises [26].

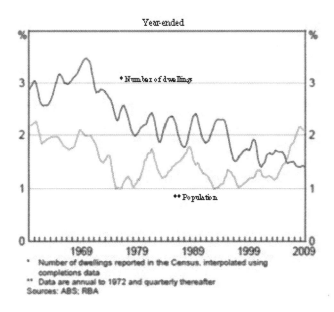

Chart 4-52 Growth Rate of Housing and Population

Performance of Greece

Economic overview

Greece is a geographically small country with a small population. Its area is 132,500 km² and the population 11 million. In January 2001, Greece officially joined the Eurozone and became the 12th member state. Greece is one of the economically least developed nations in the EU. The per capita GDP was among the lowest few member states. In recent years, especially after its accession to the Eurozone, the Greek economy developed very fast. Between 2001 and 2007, except for 2005, the real GDP growth rate of Greece was much higher than the average level of the EU. To be specific, the rate was consistently above 4% (Chart 4-53).

Chart 4-53 1997~2011 Real GDP Growth Rate of Greece and EU
   (Statistics from: Eurostat, 2010 and 2011 are estimation)

The economic foundation of Greece is weak. In particular, industry and manufacturing were backward and had lower productivity without international competence. Chart 4-54 shows the change of the index of unit labor cost in Greece and the EU between 2000 and 2010. From 2002 to today, unit labor cost in Greece grew rapidly and much higher than the average level of the EU. Higher labor cost reduced the international competitiveness of Greece in commodity and service export.

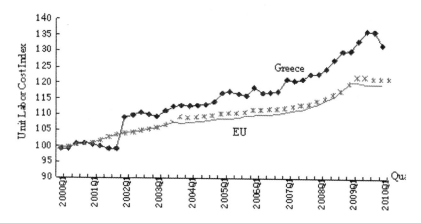

Chart 4-54 The Change of Unit Labor Cost of Greece and EU in 2000~2010
(Statistics from: European central bank)

Because domestic manufacturing is backward, the Greek economy relies heavily on foreign trade. Three foreign-oriented industries, including oceanic shipping, tourism, and overseas remittance are the pillars of the Greek economy. According to the mix of service export (Chart 4-55), tourism and transportation account for 40% and 51% of all service export. It means that the two industries play a very important role in the Greek economy.

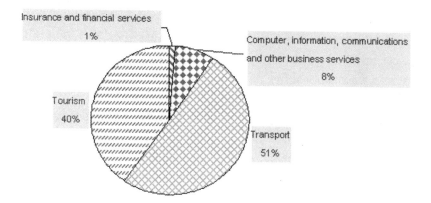

Chart 4-55 Mix of Greek Service Export
(Statistics from: 2006 World Development Indicator)

Tourism is a crucial economic sector for Greece to gain foreign currency and maintain its balance of international payments. From the 1960s, tourism began to develop very fast, and the number of inbound tourists grew continuously from the 70s. The revenue from tourism accounts for 20% of national income. It is an important source to compensate for the huge trade deficit. Greek shipping not only plays a crucial role in its own country, but also in the world. Both the quantity shipped and the number of commercial ships has been No. 1 in the world for many years. Currently, ship owners control 20.1% of world oil ships and 18.55% of world bulk carriers [27]. The major ports of Greece include Piraeus, Thessaloniki, Volos and Patras.

The main mineral reserves of Greece are bauxite (about 10 million tons), brown coal (5.6 billion tons), nickel, chromium, magnesium, asbestos, copper, uranium, gold, petroleum, and marble. Forest coverage is 20% [28].

Financial overview

In the mid-80s, the Greek financial system deregulated. Before that, ever since the 1950s, Greek government had over interfered in the distribution of loans. In other words, it practiced excessive supervision. After 1987, the Greek financial system started to change. Globalization and financial integration with the EU had led to the modernization of the Greek financial system, with measures such as the deregulation of interest rate, transnational free flow of capital between nations and cancellation of direct loan control.

Greece joined the EU in 1981. Greek banks therefore experienced substantial reform. Before 1981, the Greek central bank had compulsory limits for credit loan expansion and the ceiling of interest rate for commercial banks. Two national banks almost controlled the whole banking sector. In 1989, the second Bank Coordination Order allowed banks to have mixed operations and expand their traditional business to insurance, investment and other financial areas. Along with that, in 1992, the banking sector had to undergo cost reduction, merger and acquisition. While competition and earning capacity were increasing, Greek banks started to internationalize [29]. In the early 90s, the Greek securities and capital market developed fast. The quantity and frequency of exchange in the Athens Stock Exchange increased twofold.

The Greek banking sector is composed of three kinds of institution. The first is the central bank (Bank of Greece), which is in charge of administrating and controlling national currency supply and exchange rate. Its function is carried out by adjusting the liquidity of other banks and directly intervening in the foreign currency market. Furthermore, the Bank of Greece is also an important supervision institution for the quality of the commercial bank portfolio. According to the requirements of the 1992 Maastricht Treaty for the financial institutions of EU members, the Bank of Greece must be independent from government and must have strict control over government debt.

Commercial banks are the second category. They provide traditional services such as deposit, commercial and industrial loans. In the late 1990s, Greek commercial banks expanded their business, offering all kinds of bulk and retail banking services. Their loans included commerce, industry, consumption and mortgage loans. They issued credit cards, traveler's check and letters of credit, as well as trading in foreign exchange. In addition, commercial banks also engaged directly in the sales of securities. Through their subsidiaries, they provided brokerage services and mutual funds for Greek and foreign securities.

"Professional institutions of credit loan" is the third category, for example investment banks, the Agricultural Bank of Greece, the Mortgage Bank and the Postal Saving Bank. The traditional role of these banks is to provide credit loans in specific areas. However, the liberalization of banks and the unified policy of the EU for financial markets forced specialized banks to engage in diversified operations. In the 90s, the question of specialization in a certain area had to be decided by the market, not legislation. A typical example of such change is the Agricultural Bank of Greece. In 1991, the Agricultural Bank became a mature commercial bank. At the same time, other commercial banks were allowed to join the agricultural credit loan market. The same change can also be found in mortgage loans and investment banks [30].

Economic globalization generated the largest wave of merger and acquisition in the banking sector of Greek, which led to changes in the prospects of the sector. Between 1996 and 2008, a large number of mergers were completed and the competitiveness of the banking sector became more complicated. As a result, there were more open structures of administration, new financial intermediaries and new information technologies in the Greek banking sector.

Nowadays, Greece has 60 financial institutions of all kinds, among which 22 are domestic banks, 21 are foreign banks or branches and 15 are banks with joint capital. Local banks include: Ethniki, Agrotiki, Alpha Pisteos and Emboriki [31].

Effects of the financial crisis on Greece

Slowing down of economic growth and deterioration of fiscal deficit

Before the financial crisis, Greece maintained a relatively high pace of economic development. Chart 4-56 shows the changes of Greek GDP growth rate between 2006 and 2009. According to the chart, from 2006 to 2007 the growth rate was above 4%. Impacted by the financial crisis, in 2008, the economy of Greece slowed down. The growth rate for the four quarters were 2.74%, 2.67%, 1.94% and 0.72% respectively. Along with the global penetration of the crisis, the Greek economy continued to fall in 2009 and even suffered negative growth. The first and second quarters had growth rates of -0.96% and -1.87%. In the third and fourth quarters, economic recession was even worse, the growth rates dropping to -2.46% and -2.54%. In other words, economic recovery in Greece was much slower than that in other countries. Investors started to lose faith in the Greek economy. To a large extent, this sowed the seeds of a sovereign debt crisis.

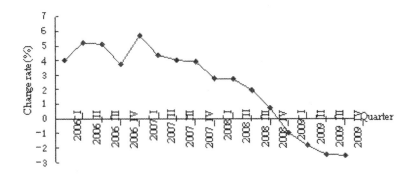

Chart 4-56 Changes of Greek GDP Growth Rate
(Statistics from: OECD)

In an attempt to cope with the financial crisis, the Greek government adopted a set of incentive measures, including offering funds to banks, tax relief, national debt assistance and providing unsecured guarantees to financial institutions giving loans to enterprises. However, the Greek government had improperly managed the fiscal budget for a long time and had adopted an economic growth pattern of high debt. As a result, the deficit deteriorated and the ratio of debt increased sharply. By 2009, Greek fiscal deficit accounted for 13.6% of GDP, and public debt 116.3% figures which were much higher than the 3% and 60% ceiling of the Eurozone.

Continuously rising unemployment rate

Unemployment has always been a serious problem in Greece. From 2001 to the first half of 2008, the unemployment rate in Greece was much higher than the average EU level. After October 2005, the rate began to decline. By June 2008, the rate was 7.5% which was almost equal to the EU average. However, after June 2008, hit by the financial crisis, the Greek unemployment rate rebounded. By October 2009, it went back up into double digits again. To be specific, it was 10.21%, which was higher than the EU average of 9.82%. Entering 2010, the Greek economy was on the downturn and enterprise production was impacted, because of the sovereign debt crisis. At the same time, Greek government put forward a fiscal austerity policy, raised taxes, reduced the cost of the public sector and cut the number of government employees. The unemployment rate therefore continued rising and reached 11% while the EU maintained an average level below 10% (Chart 4-57).

In 2010, the Greek National Chamber of Commerce carried out a sample survey among 1082 enterprises. Seven out of ten predicted a drop in their sales and revenue. 90% were not prepared to invest in any sector. 30% would cut their workforce, which meant about 100,000 employees would lose jobs [32]. The fiscal austerity policy and gloomy economy might lead to an even higher unemployment rate. The European Commission projected that the average unemployment rate of Greece would be 11.8% in 2010 and 13.2% in 2011. The IMF even estimated that it would rise to 14.8% in 2012 [33].

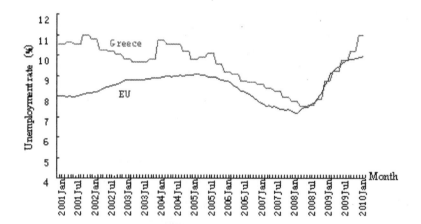

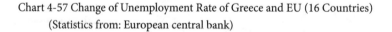

Chart 4-57 Change of Unemployment Rate of Greece and EU (16 Countries)
(Statistics from: European central bank)

Shrinking tourism

According to official statistics, Greek tourism makes a contribution of 18% to its GDP. It is a pillar industry and provides 850,000 jobs [34].

Tourists to Greece are mainly from Europe and the U.S. Therefore, when people in those areas lost their jobs or had reduction in their income, the number of tourists to Greece dropped dramatically. Many hotels had to close. After the outbreak of the sovereign debt crisis, strikes, demonstrations and protests were held frequently, which led to a further decrease in tourism. The Greek Tourism Enterprise Association reported that on May 1, 2010, when thousands of people protested on the street in opposition to government austerity measures, 5800 reservations in 28 hotels were cancelled [35].

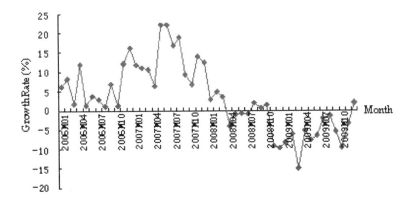

Chart 4-58 2006~2009 Increase Rate of Guests in All Greek Hotels
(Statistics from: Eurostat)

Chart 4-58 shows the growth rate of guests in all Greek hotels. From 2006 to March 2008, the number of hotel guests maintained positive growth. From April 2008, it experienced negative growth and was deteriorating further. In November and December 2008, the number decreased by 9.2% and 9.5%, and in 2009, it got even worse. It continued to drop in all months, except December. The 2009 national average growth rate was -5.7%.

Slump in the Shipping Industry

Shipping is a traditional and pillar industry in Greece. Its annual output is 7% of GDP. The shipping capacity of Greece and the number of commercial ships are No. 1 in the world. Its shipping capacity accounts for 20% of the world total and 50% of the EU's.

After the outbreak of the financial crisis, demand for oceanic shipping declined along with the cooling down of international trade. Estimations put the size of Greek shipping industry loans is over $600 billion. Because of the financial crisis, the price of commercial shipping had to be reduced. Bank credit loans became tighter, which broke the capital chain of many shipping companies in Greece [36]. The statistics of the Bank of Greece showed that in the first eight months of 2009 the income of Greek transportation (the majority from shipping) dropped by 31.2% compared with the same period of the previous year and ended up at €9.06 billion. The gloomy shipping industry caused a 0.7~0.8 percent drop in economic growth.

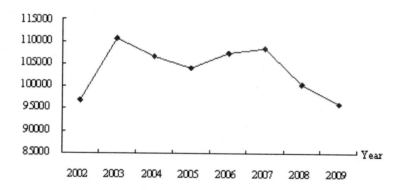

Chart 4-59 2002~2009 Total Amount of Shipped Goods in Greek Major Ports
(Statistics from: Eurostat)

This chart shows that from 2003 to 2007, major ports in Greece had shipped a total amount of more than 104 billion tons each year. In contrast, in 2008 the amount was only 100.488 billion tons which was 7.3 percent lower than that of 2007 and also the lowest level since 2003. In 2009, the volume of shipped goods continued to decline, 4.5% lower than the previous year and declining to 95.986 billion tons, lower than the 96.834 billion tons of 2002. In conclusion, the Greek shipping industry was in recession, because of the financial crisis.

Different businesses in the financial sector of Greece are supervised separately. The central bank is responsible for credit loan institutions and renting companies while the Greek Capital Markets Commission supervises brokers, investment companies, mutual funds, joint investment companies and exchange for securities and derivatives. The Insurance and Actuaries Commission is in charge of insurance companies. For credit loan institutions, the central bank only supervises general risks in the banking sector. Specific daily supervision is carried out by the Banking Association under the agreement between the association and the central bank [37].

Sovereign debt crisis of Greece

Sovereign debt means that a nation borrows money from IMF, World Bank or other countries with the guarantee of its sovereignty. When the nation cannot pay the debt or has to postpone the payment, a sovereign debt crisis will occur. According to past experience, there is usually a default of government after financial crisis. Greece experienced such a sovereign debt crisis.

Preface to the Greek sovereign debt crisis

Before the outbreak of the financial crisis, the Greek government had relied heavily on foreign debt to compensate for its huge deficit in budget and current account. From 2001, when Greece joined the EU, the total amount of Greek foreign debt was larger than GDP. The ratios of budget deficit and foreign debt to GDP have respectively surpassed the 3% and 60% requirements set in the Stability and Growth Pact of the eurozone.

From 2001 to 2004, the percentage of Greek fiscal deficit to GDP increased from 4.4% to 7.4%. In 2005 and 2006, it was controlled to some extent. After the American financial crisis impacted the world,

Greece adopted a set of economic incentive measures. Government expenditure increased, while tax revenue decreased. This caused a further rise of fiscal deficit. In 2007, the deficit accounted for 4% of GDP and it rose to 7.8% in 2008. The trend continued in 2009 to 13.6% which was much higher than the ceiling of 3% defined by the Stability and Growth Pact. From 2001 to 2008, the proportion of government debt to GDP was declining in general, but the total amount of debt had always been larger than GDP. In 2009, the percentage increased sharply, from 103.6% in 2008 to 116.3% in 2009, both of which are higher than the ceiling of 60% set by the Stability and Growth Pact (Chart 4-60).

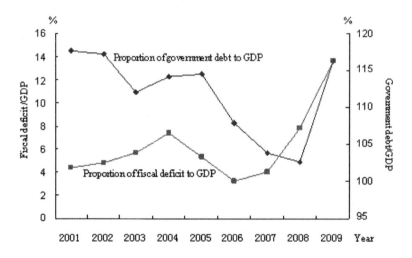

Chart 4-60 1999~2009 Greek Government Debt and Fiscal Deficit
(statistics from: OECD)

Greece hoped to borrow hugely from the international capital market. After its accession to the eurozone, Greece had borrowed money from the European Central Bank with an interest rate of 1%. With such funds, it bought government bonds with a high interest rate of 5%, in the hope of benefiting from the difference. This operation may be effective in prosperous times; but when economies fall into recession, it cannot work. On the one hand, liquidity shortage led to an insufficient supply of capital and an increase in the lending interest rate in the eurozone. On the other hand, the financial crisis caused a decline in the yields of government bonds and a smaller differential in interest rate. According to the statistics, borrowing from overseas to buy government bonds was alone responsible for raising Greek fiscal deficit by 5% [38].

In addition, after it joined the eurozone, Greece experienced sustained inflation. The rate had always been higher than the average level of the eurozone. It led to the degradation of competitiveness and the increase of deficit in current account. Chart 4-61 shows the percentage of the balance of Greek current account in GDP between 2001 and 2009.

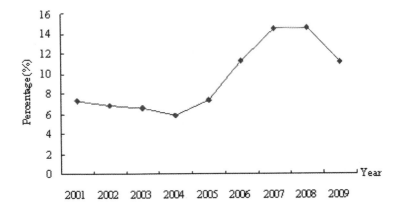

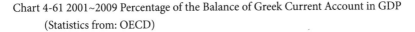

Chart 4-61 2001~2009 Percentage of the Balance of Greek Current Account in GDP (Statistics from: OECD)

It can be seen that between 2001 and 2004, the percentage of the deficit of the Greek current account compared to GDP decreased slightly, but was still high at more than 6%. From 2005, the percentage increased markedly, and reached 11.3% in 2006. After the financial crisis broke out, the world economy was on a downturn and Greek exports were badly affected. In 2007 and 2008, the deficit of current account was 14.5% of GDP. In the next year, the percentage decreased a little, but at 11.2%, was still higher than that of other EU members.

To sum up, the foundations of the Greek economy deteriorated between 2001 and 2009, and this paved the way for the sovereign debt crisis.

Outbreak of the Greek sovereign debt crisis

In October 2009, the new administration led by Papandreou decided to adjust the ratio of fiscal deficit to GDP from 6.7% to 12.7% which meant nearly doubling the ratio. This decision is now considered to be the focal point of the Greek sovereign debt crisis. Investors started to doubt the assurances of Greece to eurozone members. Investors' opinion of the Greek government changed from 'trustworthy' to 'unreliable'.

In the midst of this financial turmoil, on November 11, the Finance Department of the Dubai World Group suddenly announced that the group and its property branch Nakheel would postpone the payment of debt worth billions of dollars for at least six months to restructure their debt. The Dubai debt crisis generated thoughts about the possibility that many more countries might have to default on their sovereign debt in this severe financial crisis. Special attention was focused on countries like Greece which had huge foreign debt. In 2009, Greece borrowed €40 billion from the European Central Bank. In the second quarter of 2010, the debt of €18 billion would be due [39]. Along with the sharp increase of Greek fiscal deficit, the market, triggered by the Dubai crisis, reconsidered the financing problems of Greek national debt.

Very soon, the world's top three rating institutions downgraded Greek credit. On December 8, 2009, Fitch Rating was the very first one to adjust Greek credit rating from "A-" to "BBB+", a downgrade which led to a Greek stock market crash and the rise of risk-avoidance sentiment in the international market. This is the first time that Greek long-term national bond was reduced to below A-. Its mid-term outlook was downgraded to negative. Greece was also the first country among all eurozone states to have its sovereign credit rating below A-. Fitch Rating also reduced the credit rating of five Greek banks. The rating institution pointed out that such adjustment was based on the obvious deterioration of the Greek fiscal situation. The credibility of cutting deficit was reduced, which set up barriers for the Greek economy's capacity to reach balance and fulfill its debt in the future. The Greek government reported that by December 11 its debt was as much as €300 billion, making a new record. On December 15, Greece launched a 2 billion national bond to pay the old debt. On the next day, S & P downgraded Greek long-term sovereign credit from A- to BBB+. Another rating institution, Moody, also downgraded Greek sovereign rating from A1 to A2 with a negative outlook [41].

In addition to these problems, there were accusations concerning the falsification of statistics and the disguising of debt by complicated financial instruments. Even though no evidence was provided, the confidence of investors was further shaken. The Greek sovereign debt crisis had broken out in earnest.

In order to alleviate the debt crisis, Greek Prime Minister Papandreou stated several times that Greece would adopt a package of measures to cut the expanding fiscal deficit and invigorate the Greek economy. On December 14, 2009, the government launched its fiscal austerity policy. Papandreou claimed that in the following year government would reduce the cost of public departments, downsize the workforce and raise the tax rate. However, these measures were opposed by many ordinary employees. On December 17, thousands of people started to strike and demonstrated on the streets.

Even though there was public opposition, the Greek government adopted more measures of fiscal austerity policy. On December 23, 2009, the Greek parliament passed the 2010 Crisis Budget, aiming at alleviating public debt. It expected to reduce the ratio of fiscal budget to GDP from 12.7% in 2009 to 9.1% in 2010 [42]. On January 4, 2010, the Greek Ministry of Finance submitted its Stability and Growth Program (Draft) to the European Commission. It put forward the objective of cutting the ratio of fiscal deficit from 8.7% to 7.0% in 2010 and 2011 respectively and minimizing it within 3% by 2013. On January 14, 2010, the Greek government promised to reduce fiscal deficit by €10 billion (about $14.5 billion) through cutting expenditure and improving revenue. On February 2, Papandreou delivered a televised speech, announcing a series of more pragmatic measures to address the economic crisis that was plaguing Greece.

Deterioration of the Greek debt crisis

At the end of March 2010, member states of the eurozone reached a consensus with the IMF through negotiation, promising that they would provide assistance to Greece when it was necessary or when the Greek government applied for it. However, the amount of fund to be offered was still in discussion. In April 2010, investors were panicking, for Eurostat had estimated that the ratio of Greek fiscal budget to GDP was 13.6% which is one percent higher than the number released by Greek government. Thus, investors became worried about Greece's capacity to pay the €8.5 billion debt which would become due on May 19.

The yield of Greek national bond survived March and April (the bond was issued with an interest rate above 6%) and rose to 10% at the end of April. There was no choice for Greece. On April 23, the Greek government formally applied for financial rescue from the IMF and eurozone states. By the end of April 2010, the spread of interest rate between Greek 10-year government bond and German 10-year government bond reached 650 basis points which was the highest level in history. Moody adjusted the rating of Greek sovereign debt from A2 to A3 which is only four grades away from speculation or "junk" level. Moody also categorized Greece in the list of negative observation. Moody made its decision based on the understanding that Greece might have to pay more than expected to stabilize its national debt. On April 27, S & P downgraded Greek sovereign debt to junk level. On the same day, the Greek composite stock price index dropped sharply by 6.7%, ending up at its lowest point in 13 months. This added more difficulties to the financing of Greece and intensified the debt crisis.

On May 2, Greek Prime Minister Papandreou held a special Cabinet meeting, announcing that Greece had finished negotiations over assistance mechanisms with the EU and the IMF and had arrived at agreement for a rescue plan. In order to justify a huge loan to solve the financial crisis, Greece had to accept harsh requirements under the agreement to adopt further austerity measures. Greek Minister of Finance Papaconstantinou released details of the rescue plan on the same day. According to the plan, in the coming three years, Greek government had to further cut its fiscal budget by €30 billion. In terms of savings, the subsidies and bonuses for civil servants and retirees would be reduced. Specifically, the bonuses for civil servants would be cut by up to 8%. In terms of increasing revenue, VAT would be raised from the current 21% to 23% while the tax on alcohol, tobacco and fuel would be 10% higher.

In the early morning of May 10, the EU decided to raise €750 billion jointly with the IMF, who would provide €250 billion, to save small crisis-trapped countries in the eurozone and ensure the position of the euro in the international financial market. Without such a measure, there might be even more dangerous global financial and economic crisis. On May 19, EU members and the IMF offered aid to Greece of $14.5 billion to fulfill the €8.5 billion debt which was due. The spread of interest rate between Greek and German 10 year national bonds started to decline, risk expectation of the market turned better, international gold price dropped and euro rebounded.

Improvement in the Greek debt crisis

Greek Minister of Finance Papaconstantinou said, on May 30, that Greece didn't need to restructure its debt or adopt additional austerity plans. Moreover, it expected to move out of economic recession in 2010 and start to recover. On June 2, the Greek government announced the privatization of certain State-owned enterprises (SOEs) to cope with the serious debt crisis. Several Greek ministers jointly held a press conference on that day, explaining that in the following three years, the government would collect €3 billion by more rational use of public assets.

Moody said on June 14 that it would downgrade Greek national bond to junk level, because it believed the rescue plan of EU and IMF contained risk. The sovereign rating was reduced by four grades from A3 to Ba1 with a stable outlook. Moody also reduced the rating of Greek short-term issue from Prime-1 to not prime. This move was in line with the general expectation and did not have a great impact. Other markets were not influenced by Moody's decision.

On June 23, Minister of Finance Papaconstantinou said that economic recession in Greece was not as serious as expected. Some economic sectors had restored their confidence and might get out of recession in the middle of the following year. On June 27, the head of the negotiation team, Poul Thomsen, told the media that Greece would overcome the huge debt crisis through its austerity plan, and that Greek deficit cutting plans were making progress.

In fact, since Greece accepted the rescue plan of the IMF in May 2010 till now, its government has faithfully followed the strict austerity plan in spite of strong opposition. The measures include streamlining institutions, welfare cuts, and lower wages. However, this still has not helped Greece to shake off the crisis. The fiscal deficit remains 10.5% of GDP (at the time of writing) which means a failure in its deficit cutting objective.

Development of the Greek debt crisis

By the middle of 2011, the Greek debt crisis had deteriorated further. On May, S & P had downgraded Greece again, and the European debt crisis re-appeared. On June 13, S & P reduced Greek long-term sovereign rating from B to CCC which is four grades away from default. At the same time, S & P maintained its C rating for Greek short-term sovereign credit with a negative outlook. It made a statement on that day, saying that the risk of one or more default because of the financing gap had increased noticeably. The "negative outlook" meant that the sovereign credit rating of Greece might be further downgraded within 12 to 18 months. After that, the yield on Greek 10 year national bond rose for the second time in the year to above 17% which created additional pressure on Greek financing from the international market.

The Greek Parliament passed another package of economic austerity plans on June 29 to encourage the rescue loan from the EU and the IMF, in the hope of avoiding repayment difficulties and temporarily saving Greece from default.

On July 21, a eurozone summit agreed to provide Greece with a new aid plan worth €109 billion. Leaders in the eurozone also promised to prolong the term of Greek debt from the European Financial Stability Fund from 7.5 years to 15~30 years with a lower interest rate of 3.5% [43].

The Greek Congressional Budget Office announced on August 31, that Greek debt was getting out of control and it was hard to reach the objective of lowering fiscal deficit. The media released the news that Greece would withdraw from the eurozone which caused further depreciation of the euro [44]. Even though the news was simply rumor, it is true to say that Greece was on the verge of collapse. Greek Minister of Finance Venizelos stated that in 2011 the Greek economy would decline by 4.5%, leading Greece into the most serious recession cycle in 40 years. At the same time, the "snowball" of Greek debt had expanded to the size of €350 billion [43].

According to Bloomberg, by 18:00 of September 13, the yield on the 1-year national bond had rocketed to 114.4% while the 2-year bond and 10-year bond had reached 67.9% and 22.9% respectively. Five-year Greek government bonds hedging the risk of credit default swaps (CDS) rose by 11.63%, reaching a record high of 4038 points. It had become the most expensive CDS product. Based on the above statistics, the possibility of sovereign credit default in Greece now is as high as 98% [45]. Ministers of Finance from the eurozone states held a meeting in Poland on September 16 and decided to continue the second round of the assistance plan to Greece. American Treasury Secretary Geithner for the first time joined the meeting. Jean-Claude Juncker, Chairman of the Euro Group, said the next loan to Greece would be delivered in October with the premise that Greece maintains its fiscal austerity policy [46]. However, on October 3, the meeting of 17 Ministers of Finance from the eurozone failed to make any concrete decision about whether the sixth round of loans would be delivered to Greece or if the European financial stability instrument would be used to lever Greek capacity to borrow. It only agreed to postpone discussion on a new round of rescue loan of €8 billion for Greece [47]. The situation in Greece continues to change overnight, and meanwhile the whole world is paying close attention.

5.

Impact of the U.S. Financial Crisis on the Economy of China

Under the circumstances of widening economic globalization, the American financial crisis, has certainly had a noticeable impact on the economy of China for the simple reason that America is the strongest economic power in the world and a major trade partner of China.

Economically, China has also undergone a slowdown as a result of impacts from the American financial crisis. China, taking 10 years from 2001 as one economic period, maintained a double digit GDP growth rate between 2003 and 2007. Specifically China's GDP attained a growth rate of 10.0% in 2003, 10.1% in 2004, 10.4% in 2005, 11.6% in 2006 and 13% in 2007, a record high for that economic period. However, under the double effects from both the financial crisis and economic, the growth rate of China's economy declined sharply to 9.6% in 2008, a drop of 3.4 percentage points compared with the same period the previous year. The decline bottomed out during the period between the end of 2008 and early in 2009 with a growth rate of 9.2% in the whole year. As the following chart 5-1 depicts, in 2010, the economy of China maintained a growth rate of 10.4% as the financial crisis gradually faded away.

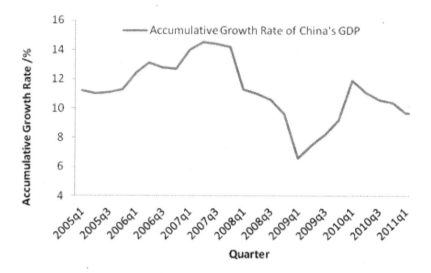

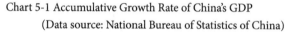

Quarter

Chart 5-1 Accumulative Growth Rate of China's GDP
(Data source: National Bureau of Statistics of China)

Chart 5-2 shows changes in GDP between China and America from the first quarter of 1993 to the second quarter of 2011. Taking China's WTO entry in December 2001 as a cut-off point, the correlation coefficient of economic growth rate between China and America is -0.13 from the first quarter of 1993 to the fourth quarter of 2001. Yet the above number becomes 0.52 from the first quarter of 2002 to the second quarter of 2011. If we just take the economic correlation between China and America in the period of financial crisis into our consideration, and then choose a sample section from the first quarter of 2007 to the second quarter of 2011, the correlation coefficient increases to 0.68, which indicates that there is an increasing synchronous enhancement, particularly notable during this financial crisis, between fluctuations in China's growth rate and those of the American economy.

Charter 5-2 Comparison of Economic Growth Rate between China and America
(Data Source: China Economic Net)

Spread mechanism of impacts from the financial crisis on the economy of China

From the second half of 2008, a financial storm, triggered by the American subprime crisis, swept rapidly through the international financial market, and eventually developed into a global financial and economic crisis, resulting in a notable decline for the world economy. Under the circumstances of global economic integration, China is increasingly being faced with a multi-angled and multi-leveled impact from external economies by means of international trade and financial markets as well as other channels, which can be summarized as follows. The very first and also the most direct impact lies in their influence on China's capital markets and financial industries as well as Chinese enterprises that had accessed into international capital markets through international financial markets. Specifically, it has brought about assets loss, not only to Chinese-funded banks and Chinese enterprises who purchased their subprime products, but to overseas-listed Chinese companies as a result of the decline of stock markets during the crisis. In the second place, Chinese export enterprises have been impacted, via international trade, by the declining consumer demand as a result of the crisis. In detail, a series of problems have appeared in Chinese export enterprises such as an increase of receivables and economic losses, a scale-down of recoveries, ratios and export orders. Furthermore, some export enterprises may even suffer bankruptcy as a result of these problems. Thirdly, the production operation of Chinese entity enterprises and domestic consumer demand may be impacted by the international financial crisis via channels such as exports, FDI and capital markets, in other words, the international financial crisis could exert secondary effects on the entity economy of China.

On the one hand, international risk capital flow has had a limited impact on China's financial markets as their capital account had not been opened up to the outside world. Furthermore, financial institutions in China only have a small number of toxic assets as the Chinese government maintains a strict control over its foreign investment, thus decreasing the impact from the crisis. On the other hand, the crisis led to a drastic shrinkage in China's overseas market demand because of the relatively high degree of dependence on foreign trade, thus exerting a negative impact upon Chinese exports, which, may be transmitted from the substantial shrinkage of FDI via the processing trade. Moreover, a decline in exports may have an indirect impact on China's entity economy.

In summary, I believe the crisis inserts impacts upon China's macro economy via the following channels.

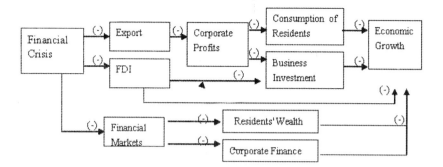

Chart 5-3. Spread Channel of Impacts of Financial Crisis on Economy of China
(+)stands for positive correlation, (-)refers to negative correlation.

> Spread route one (trade channel): Financial crisis→Export ↓ →Corporate Profits ↓ →Investment,Consumption ↓ →Economic Growth ↓ .

Crisis in one nation may affect the economic base of and then lead into crisis for another through trade connections. Specifically, if two countries are trade partners with each other, then the crisis-stricken country, as a result of their economic recession, will experience a decline in demand, thus exerting an impact on the exports and economic growth of the other. Alternatively, if the two are trade rivals, then, generally, the currency of the country in economic or monetary crisis may depreciate, thus weakening the export competitiveness of their opponent via a decline in export, which in turn brings about negative impact on their economic growth[1]. For this reason, we shall take trade channel as an important spread route for our study in question.

A financial crisis results in a recession in demand from major trade partners of China, which reduces China's exports and affects production in enterprises. On the one hand, the capacity for investment in export-oriented enterprises may become weak as their stocks increases while yield declines with lower profits, thus causing a slowdown in economic growth. On the other, enterprise profitability decreases as a result of export shrinkages, which may lead into a capital turnover crisis or even losses or bankruptcies for those enterprises. As a result, the unemployment rate will rise with a decreasing disposable income in the population, which reduces consumption and eventually creates a drag on economic growth.

> Spread route two:(Investment Channel): Financial Crisis→FDI ↓ →Economic Growth ↓ .

In addition to the trade channel, foreign investment is another important linkage to connect economic powers. From the perspective of investment, foreign investment includes Foreign Direct Investment (FDI) and Foreign Indirect Investment (FII). Indirect investment refers to investment in securities, which has close ties with relations of financial markets, and thus can be classified as having impact on financial linkages. However, sharing little connection with the relations of financial markets, direct investment, instead, has much closer connections with the entity economy rather than trade linkages.[2] Therefore, the author of this report believes that FDI is a basic spread mechanism that differs from trade linkages as well(newly-increased investment and additional investment).

The financial crisis decreases FDI in China as foreign investment institutions withdraw their funds to reduce direct investment in China, thus limiting China's usable foreign capital and, to a large extent, weakening the scale of investment, which decreases China's capacity to invest and eventually slows economic growth.

> Spread route three:(Financial Channel)Financial Crisis→Financial Markets ↓ →Economic Growth.

Two viewpoints are included in this spread route. The first one focuses on impacts on liquidity. In an interactive financial market, if the financial institutions of one country have their liquidity affected by investors' deposit withdrawal, then the country is obliged to respond to this by cutting down its cash position in the financial market of another country.[3] The second viewpoint is concerned with the adjustment of investment portfolios, which means investors' direct participation in financial markets instead of through financial institutions as they did before. In most cases, financial institutions themselves are investors, but they no longer function as intermediary agencies. Under normal conditions, the crisis may spread through financial markets more quickly although they have a faster response to impacts than the real economy. The financial crisis, by means of interactive effects of global financial markets, impacts China's financial markets with a drastic shrinkage in market value of stocks and a decrease in citizens' wealth as well as a slowdown of enterprise financing, thus indirectly affecting economic growth in China.

Impacts of the American financial crisis upon China's fictitious economy

Sources for the occurrence of the financial crisis are subordinated debt products whose huge but hidden risks disturbed Wall Street and many financial institutions across the world. Currently, China's domestic financial institutions and enterprises only hold a limited amount of subprime products as capital and financial projects are not open to the outside world. Moreover, insurance and securities companies in China do not obtained corresponding licenses as only a few large banks such as the Bank of China (BOC), the Industrial and Commercial Bank of China (ICBC) and the China Construction Bank (CCB), have the capacity for the relevant businesses connected with subordinated debt.

With core assets of USD 82.5 billion, Freddie Mac and Fannie Mae issued USD 5.2 trillion worth of securities. On April 21, 2008, Fitch Ratings released a report on Risks of Asian banks' Purchase of Subprime or Structural Credit Products, which pointed out that BOC held risk assets associated with subordinated debts of USD 9.6 billion as of mid-2007, ranking first among financial institutions in Asia in this regard. However, this figure dropped to USD 5.3 billion by the end of 2007 as the reserve assets of Bank of China could cover 30% of the risk. By the end of 2007, investments associated with subordinated debts for ICBC and CCB were USD 1.073 billion and USD 1 billion respectively, yet with corresponding risk coverage of 37% and 63%, revealing their very different strategies concerning risk, and indicating that CCB are very cautious about risk management of investments associated with subordinated debt. BOC were impacted more than others not only because of their huge risk positions but because the 46% of their CDO held in risk positions was far greater than their Residential Mortgage-Backed Securities (RMBS for short) and other low loss rate products. In respect of CCB, their positions associated with subordinated debts are all RMBS, which once again confirms their prudential attitude to risk management.

According to an annual report on American Securities Held by Foreign Institutions by the United States Department of Treasury in mid-2008, American Long-term Institution Asset-backed Bonds held by foreign institutions were as much as USD 1.5 trillion by 30th June 2008, including USD 527 billion held by China (accounting for 36% of the total). Among them, BOC, ICBC, CCB and Bank of Communications held a total value of USD 23.28 billion worth of bonds issued or warranted by Fannie Mae and Freddie Mac. By the end of June 2009, foreign institutions held a total of USD 1. 26 trillion worth of American Long-term Institution Asset-backed Bonds, a decline of 16% compared with the same period of the previous year, including USD 360 billion held by China (accounting for 28% of the total).

The quantity of American Long-term Institution Asset-backed Bonds held by China was reduced in 2009 compared with the same period in 2008. In order to bailout Freddie Mac and Fannie Mae, the American government poured in a huge financial allocation, which, however, produced little effect, causing China to cut down their American Long-term Institution Bonds for the purpose of guarding against risks brought about by future uncertainties. On June 16, 2010, Freddie Mac and Fannie Mae received an instruction from the U.S. Federal Housing Finance Agency, which declared that they would be delisted from New York. It is clear that the American government's reform policies towards Freddie Mac and Fannie Mae will, affect bonds held by China. Moreover, the indirect impact of the delisting of Freddie Mac and Fannie Mae is its negative effect on the possibility of expected debt service of bonds after the net value of shares had been hit in the very first place.

BOC holds the most subordinated debt products among China's several State-owned banks. Frank Gong, the Executive General Manager of JP Morgan, believes that, even so, the impact of this financial crisis on China is very limited as they hold the smallest proportion of subordinated debt products in the world. By the end of 2009, the book value of American sub-prime, Alt-A, Non-Agency and Mortgage-backed Securities held by BOC totaled USD 4.106 billion with a relevant devaluated reserve balance of USD 3.475 billion.

In summary, Chinese financial institutions are very cautious about holding subordinated debt products as they accounts for only a small proportion of assets held by banks and bring about a very limited impact to them. On this basis, a number of banks have shown good experience and preparations for risk coverage of subordinated debt products. Therefore, it is safe to believe that toxic assets, led by subordinated debt products, have had a very limited impact upon financial institutions in China since the outbreak of the financial crisis. To a large extent, it can be concluded that China's policies have been reasonable in terms of their prudence regarding capital projects and their steady progress in financial reforms. It can further be concluded that losses resulting from financial products, represented by subordinated debt products, are not a major channel of impact from this crisis on the economy of China.

However, the global spread of the subprime crisis also brought about heavy impacts on the fictitious economy of China.

China's stock markets, with the outbreak of the subprime crisis, underwent a decline both in quantities and prices. The CSI 300 Index dropped from 5688.54 points by the end of October 2007 to 1817.72 points by the end of November 2008, a decline of 68% or more. Monthly turnovers of the Shanghai and Shenzhen stock markets declined drastically from 902.77% in August 2007, with a long-term negative number, to a minimum value of -78.39% in August 2008. Thereafter, they began to recover and eventually turned the negative number into a positive one in February 2009.

Decline in quantities and prices also occurred in real estate markets, the price index of China's commercial residence market maintaining a continuous decline from the maximum point of 111.20 in January 2008 to the minimum points of 98.30 in March 2009, a drop close to 12%. Accumulative sales of China's commercial residences also underwent a drastic decline from 51.50% in October 2007, with a negative number, to a minimum of -19.50% during the initial stage of the financial crisis. Thereafter, it eventually turned the negative number into a positive one in January 2009.

China's bill financing markets maintained stability before the crisis, yet the balance of bill financing declined, with the full outbreak of the crisis, from RMB 1730.2 billion in August 2007 to RMB 1290.033 billion in June 2008, a drop of 25%. Through China's adoption of a new monetary policy in 2008, the scale of bill financing expanded gradually and eventually reached a peak of RMB 3638.5 billion in June 2009.

The outbreak of the financial crisis brought about impacts on trust markets as well. Taking the assembled trust as an example, there was no drastic decline in circulation of the trust nor did it suffer violent fluctuations in 2008. However, circulation of the trust, along with a series of economic stimulus plans, began to climb after 2009.

Meanwhile, China's futures market, its market of foreign exchange and the scale of government investment and financing were also impacted by the financial crisis. China changed direction on its monetary policies for the purpose of coping with these enormous economic impacts and adopted a moderately loose monetary policy instead of a tight one in the third quarter of 2008. Apart from actively cooperating with economic stimulus policies such as expanding domestic demand, the government also lowered the deposit-benchmark interest rate five times and the deposit-reserve ratio four times in the second half of 2008. Endeavors to enhance financial support for economic development eventually allowed China's financial markets to recover by the end of 2008 and the early part of 2009.

The overall impacts of the financial crisis on the real economy of China

It takes a period of time for the effects of a financial crisis, occurring in the system of the fictitious economy, to spread to the real economy. Therefore, the impacts from the American financial crisis on the real economy of China were felt relatively later than those on the fictitious economy.

The impact of the financial crisis on China's exports

Affected by the American financial crisis, world trade volumes shrank drastically in 2009. China's total export-import volumes of goods declined by 13.9% in that year, which was the first time for a offal in China's exports and imports since the 1998 Asian Financial Crisis. China's trade surplus, along with the decline in exports, decreased by large numbers as chart 5-4 depicts.

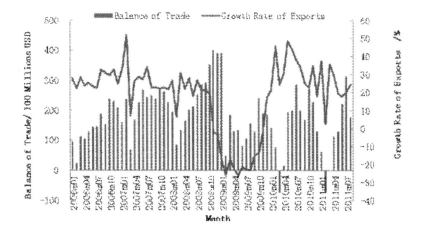

Chart 5-4 Year-on-Year Growth between Balance of Trade and Monthly Export
(Data Source: National Bureau of Statistics of China)

The significant decline in the total volume and year-on-year growth rate of China's exports occurred as a result of the following three

197

factors. Firstly, decline in external demand curbed the growth of China's exports. Major economies in the world such as America, the EU and Japan were heavily impacted by the financial crisis, and this brought about a sharp decline in import demand. Secondly, triggered by the financial crisis, trade protectionism regained ground, hence lowering exports from China. In the third place, exchange rate could also be a significant factor of the decline. After the crisis, the various appreciations of the RMB Yuan against the U.S. dollar, the euro, the Japanese yen, the pound and other currencies led to increases in the cost of China's exports as price advantages for many commodities were weakened.

Impacts of the financial crisis on China's investment in fixed assets

The following chart 5-5 depicts the changes in the accumulative growth rate of China's fixed assets investment, growth rate of investment in new fixed assets and growth rate of actual utilized foreign capitals between January 2006 and July 2011.

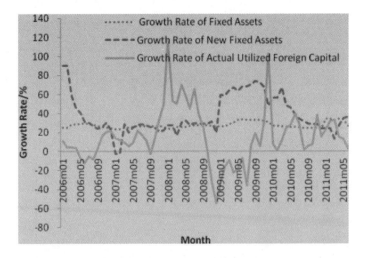

Chart 5-5 Changes of China's Investment
(Data Source: CEIC Database)

198

Chart 5-5 shows that the American financial crisis had only a limited impact on the accumulative growth rate of China's fixed assets investment, which is because of the relatively slow spread of the financial crisis to the investment field and the fact that willingness to invest in China by investors at home and abroad remained unchanged since before the Wall Street Financial Storm. However, the willingness of private investors declined as they became more cautious about investment in the real economy after the outbreak of the storm in September 2008. Furthermore, China's foreign capital began to outflow in great volume as a result of foreign institutions' deleveraging. Nevertheless, economic stimulus plans by the Chinese government made up for the deficiency of private investments and foreign investments. Therefore, the accumulative growth rate of China's fixed assets investment suffered only a limited change during the financial crisis.

Impacts of the financial crisis on China's consumption

As chart 5-6 shows, China's consumption declined clearly as a result of the impacts from the financial crisis.

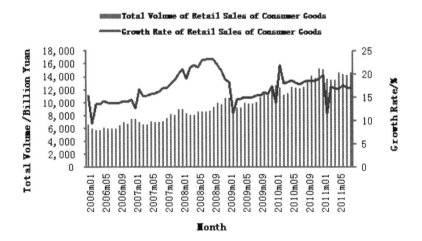

Chart 5-6 Changes in China's Total consumption
(Data Source: CEIC Database)

In the above chart 5-6, one could see a substantial decline in the growth rate of total volume of retail sales of consumer goods from January 2009, caused by the fact that China's economy underwent a downturn with losses and layoffs in many enterprises and a reduction in disposable incomes accompanied by decreasing purchase capacities. In addition, expectations of growth in the future incomes of Chinese citizens were lowered by the financial crisis, which forced them to tighten their current consumer expenditure to increase savings. The monthly Consumer Confidence Index maintained 110 or above on average in 2007, yet it dropped to the lowest point of 100.3 in March 2009. Furthermore, the monthly Consumer Expectation Index also dropped from the highest level of 115.2 in June 2007 to the minimum point of 99 in 2009.

5.3.4 Impacts of the Financial Crisis on China's Commodity Prices

The following chart 5-7 depicts the changes in China's CPI (Consumer Price Index) and PPI (Producer Price Index) in recent years.

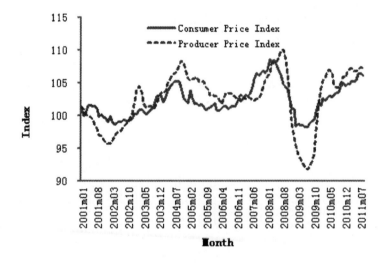

Chart 5-7 Monthly Year-on-Year Index of CPI and PPI
   (Data Source: National Bureau of Statistics of China)

In chart 5-7, one can see that China's CPI and PPI continued rising between 2006 and 2007. With a growth rate of 5% or more for a consecutive 12 months in their year-on-year index of consumer price from the second half of 2007 to the first six months in 2008, inflation apparently occurred in China as a result of inertia during China's years of rapid economic growth, a rise of food prices in international markets and a temporary short supply of farm produce on the market caused by domestic snow-bound conditions. In response to this situation, China issued a series of measures for the purpose of guarding against economic overheating. However, after the outbreak of the Wall Street Financial Storm in September 2008, China's CPI and PPI fell back drastically in November 2008 and the latter registered negative figures in the coming December. Furthermore, both China's CPI and PPI experienced negative growth in February 2009.

Meanwhile, the circulation of currency and credit of China's Central Bank also indicated that negative growth of the CPI and PPI at the same time was the result of a reduction in economic demand, a weakening of consumption and private investment in particular, rather than the reduced cost of production. Although Chinese RMB loans increased by 2.7 trillion Yuan between January and February 2009, their deposits rose by 3.1 trillion Yuan, which clearly signaled an increase in public and business expectations of economic downturn.

Impact of the financial crisis on China's employment

Chart 5-8 shows the changes of China's registered urban unemployment and overall unemployment rate in recent years.

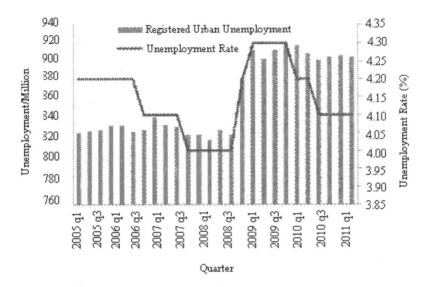

Chart 5-8 Changes of China's registered urban unemployment and overall unemployment rate

    (Data Source: National Bureau of Statistics of China)

One can see from chart 5-8 that China's unemployment reached a maximum point by the end of 2008 as a result of the American financial crisis. Estimations from the Chinese National Bureau of Statistics and the Ministry of Agriculture show that there were approximately 20 million off-farm workers returning home as a result of unemployment before the 2009 Spring Festival [5]. Moreover, the employment of university graduates remained lower than ever before the crisis.

Impacts of the financial crisis on China's different industries and regions

In recent years, the output value of China's primary and secondary industries and tertiary-industry has accounted for a relatively stable proportion of GDP with a respective ratio of 1: 5: 4. Basically, the growth of China's GDP depends heavily upon that of their secondary and tertiary industries as changes in their growth rate are almost identical. The following chart 5-9 depicts the value added growth rates of China's GDP and their primary, secondary, and tertiary industries.

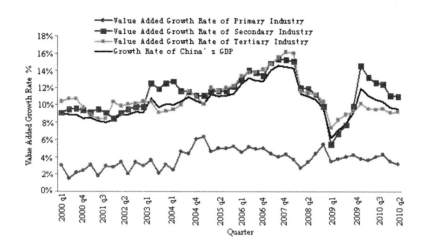

Chart 5-9 Growth rates of China's GDP and The Three Major Industries
(Data Source: CEIC Data Base)

Chart 5-9 shows that value added growth rates of China's GDP and their three major types of industry began to slow down from the fourth quarter of 2007 to the first quarter of 2009 with a minimum growth rate of 6.1%, 5.3% and 7.4% respectively for a consecutive 10 years. In addition, secondary industry underwent the most notable slowdown among them with a decline from 15% in the second quarter of 2007 to 5.3% in the first quarter of 2009, a fall of 65%. Therefore, the financial crisis brought about the most severe impact to China's secondary industry as export trade values, the most vulnerable area during the crisis, make up a significant proportion of secondary industry. In contrast, China's service trade, which accounts for a large portion of tertiary industry, suffered only limited impact due to its domestic orientation and limited external exposure.

Impact of the financial crisis on China's industries

China's industries were impacted in different degrees by the financial crisis after its outbreak, as Chart 5-10 shows.

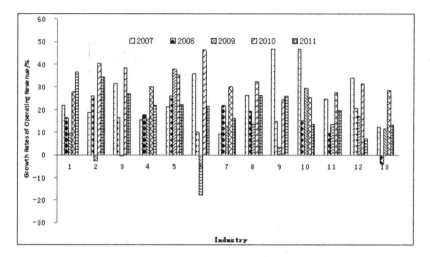

Chart 5-10 Revenue Growth Rates of China's Industries from 2007 to 2011

Note: from 1 to 13 are industries in agriculture, forestry, husbandry and fishery; extractive industry; manufacturing; building industry; transportation; IT; wholesale and retail; finance and insurance; real estate industry; social services industry; communication and culture and other integrated industries.

(Data Source: CEIC Data Base, data of 2011 only refers to that of the first six months in 2011)

From chart 5-10, it can be seen that the manufacturing, extractive and transportation and storage industries were the most crisis-stricken industries as growth rates of their operating revenue declined drastically into negative figures in 2009. The building industry, however, thanks to the large inflow of capital from China's economic stimulus plan, remains the only one with growing operating revenue among the above 13 industries during the crisis period (2007-2009).

Impact of the financial crisis on China's different regions

As an important aspect of China's economy, provincial economies were, more or less, affected by the crisis between 2008 and 2009 according to their differences in provincial conditions and industrial structures. In 2008, with the exception of Qinghai, Jiangxi, Shaanxi and Tianjin, growth rates of GDP in China's other 27 provinces or municipalities directly under the Central Government decreased more or less compared with that of 2007. Specifically, the growth rates of GDP in Shanxi, Shanghai, Hainan, Beijing, Fujian, Zhejiang and Guangdong dropped by 7.4%, 5.5%, 5.5%, 5.4%, 4.6% and 4.5% respectively compared with those in 2007. Although China's economy, on the whole, began to rise steadily in 2009, including gains in Hainan, Beijing, Tibet, Sichuan, Guangxi, Yunnan, Anhui, Chongqing and Tianjin, the growth rate of GDP for the remaining 22 provinces or municipalities, particularly in Fujian, Qinghai, Shanxi, Xinjiang, Shaanxi and Jilin, witnessed a slight slowdown compared with their performance in 2008. However, growth rate of GDP in all regions of China started to recover between 2010 and 2011 as a result of the decreasing impact from the crisis. Changes in the growth rate of GDP in some heavily affected provinces or municipalities in China were depicted in the following chart 5-10.

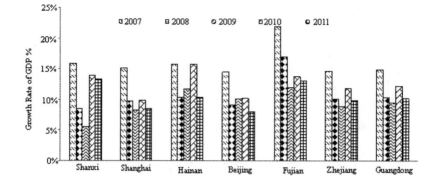

Chart 5-11 Relatively Heavy Declines in Growth Rate of GDP for Some Provinces or Municipalities in China between 2007-2011 (%)

Note: from left to right are Shanxi, Shanghai, Hainan, Beijing, Fujian, Zhejiang, Guangdong.

(Data Source: CEIC Data Base, data of 2011 only refers to that of the first six months in 2011)

In the 7 provinces or municipalities depicted in chart 5-11, decline of economic growth in Shanghai, Fujian, Zhejiang and Guangdong, due to their relatively high dependence upon foreign trade, had a close relation with the deterioration of global trade during the financial crisis. In respect of the other three provinces or municipalities in the above chart, Shanxi relies heavily on its coal production, and Hainan's pillar industries are tourism and agriculture, both heavily impacted by the crisis while Beijing's industrial growth amplitude also dropped drastically in 2008 in an obvious response to the crisis.

Quantitative analysis of the impact of the American financial crisis on China's export trade

By means of applying the VAR measure, we analyzed the impact of the American financial crisis upon China's economy in terms of foreign trade, investment and finance. Results show that foreign trade was the most effective channel through which the crisis affected the growth rate of China's economy, which indicates that their economic structure had a relatively heavy dependence on foreign trade. Clearly, the rapid development of export trade has been an important factor in driving China's economy forward. After the outbreak of the American financial crisis, major global economies, also being China's major trade partners, underwent a notable decline in their economic growth rate with a limited consumer motivation, which curbed China's export to these countries, thus directly affecting our economic growth. This being the case, we conducted a quantitative analysis, in particular, on the impacts of the crisis upon China's foreign trade in terms of various trade types, trade partners, destinations and products of their export.

Impacts of the financial crisis on China's trade types

China's processing trade and general trade accounts for 90% or more of its gross export value. In addition, volumes of processing trade are higher than those of general trade as the following chart 5-12 shows through their year-on-year changes.

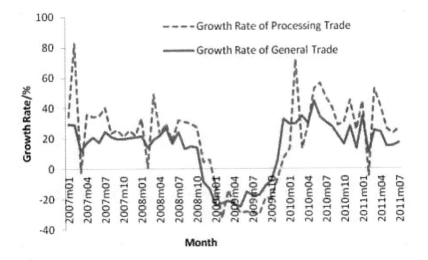

Chart 5-12 Year-on-Year Changes between Processing Trade and General Trade of China's Exports
(Source: CEIC Data Base)

Chart 5-12 indicates that there were matching fluctuations between processing trade and general trade of China's export as both of them experienced sharp declines after the outbreak of the crisis. However, processing trade dropped less than general trade and the former recovered faster than the latter during the subsequent process of recovery. Clearly, processing trade is more sensitive and vulnerable to the external economic environment.

Impacts of the financial crisis on the destinations for China's export

Asia, Europe and North America are the three most important destinations for China's export as volumes of average annual export to these three regions accounted for approximately 90% of China's total over the last 10 years. Changes of year-on-year growth rate for these three regions, irrespective of factors of periodicity, show, as in chart 5-13, that fluctuations of China's export to Europe were more severe than those of the other two regions.

Chart 5-13 Changes of Year-on-Year Growth Rate for China's Export to Asia, Europe and North America
(Source: Wind Database)

As the largest destination of China's export, Asia, on average, took 50% of China's total export in the last 5 years with a fluctuation range of only ±10%. We further analyzed changes in Asia without Hong Kong, in consideration that a certain volume of transit trade to Hong Kong was also covered by China's total export. Results of our analysis show that with Hong Kong removed from China's total export to Asia, data differences between Asia on the whole and Asia without Hong Kong have gradually declined since 2000 in line with the declining proportion of transit trade to Hong Kong in China's total export, caused by China's WTO entry and the benefits of opening up trade with the rest of the world.

Analysis on impacts from the financial crisis on export of China's major trade partners

EU, America and Japan are three major trade partners of China. Chart 5-14 depicts their year-on-year growth rate of export.

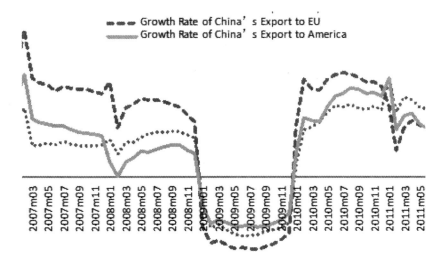

Chart 5-14 Year-on-Year Growth Rate of China's Export to EU, Japan and America (Source: Wind Database)

Chart 5-14 shows that the year-on-year growth rate of China's export to EU maintained its historical rise before the crisis, yet with the greatest volatility from the maximum of 50% in 2007 to the lowest rate of -25% in 2009. Growth in China's export to Japan was relatively low with limited fluctuations. The year-on-year growth rate of China's export to America declined by the largest proportion at the exact time of the outbreak of the 2007 subprime crisis, being lower than the EU by 10 percentage points. However, this growth rate, along with the expansion of the crisis to the real economy, declined by the lowest proportion among the three trade partners between the second half of 2008 and 2009.

Analysis of the impacts from the financial crisis on different goods of China's export

According to Standard International Trade Classification (SITC), goods of China's export are classified into 10 major categories. Machinery and Transport Equipment in the 7th category, Miscellaneous Products in the 8th category and Manufactured Products classified by raw material in the 6th category are the three largest categories as they account for 49%, 25% and 15% of the total of 10 categories respectively. Chemical Products and Relevant Products in the 5th category, Food and Live Animals in the zero category, Fossil Fuel, Lubricant Oil and Relevant Raw Materials in the 3rd category and Non-food Materials (fuels not included) of the 2nd category account for 5%, 3%, 2% and 1% of the total respectively. The remaining categories make up a proportion of less than 1% of the total.

In order to better understand the impacts, development and performance of different goods among China's exports during the crisis, disregarding those accounting for 5% or less, we took the major proportions only, namely, the 5th, 6th, 7th and 8th categories into our consideration as they account for 94% of China's total export. In addition, we also included High-Tech Products as counted by China Customs into our comparison for analysis. Chart 5-15 shows the accumulative year-on-year export value of the products mentioned in the above 5 categories.

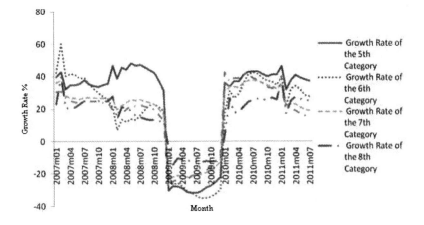

Chart 5-15 Accumulative Year-on-Year Export Value of the Major Categories

Note: the 5th category is chemicals and related products, the 6th category is manufactured goods according to the raw material classification, the 8th category is machinery and transport equipment (Source: Wind Database).

Chart 5-15 shows that the miscellaneous products of the 8th category remained relatively unaffected by the crisis. This is because products of the 8th category are mainly labor-intensive daily use necessities with a relatively low elasticity of demand, such as clothes and footwear, which have a price advantage in their export as a result of China's cheap and plentiful labor force. Therefore, products of the 8th category, though declining to a certain extent in their export after the outbreak of the crisis, remained relatively strong compared with the total, yet recovered more slowly than the others during the crisis recovery. The impact of the financial crisis on the 7th category, namely, Machinery and Transport Equipment as well as High Tech products counted by China Customs, stands between the 8th category and the 5th and 6th. Export for these two categories declined in large numbers as a result of the financial crisis, yet began to rebound rapidly as soon as it hit the bottom line because high-tech products, which are poor in substitutability due to their technical exclusiveness, recovered quickly as a result of demand increases during the late period of the crisis. Categories of the 5th (Chemical Products and the Related) and the 6th (Manufactured Goods Classified by Raw Materials such as iron and steel, aluminum materials and other resource-based products) were affected most by the financial crisis in combination with severe competitiveness in global markets, specifically declining both in quantity and price.

Analysis of the above shows that the financial crisis exerted a relatively small impact upon labor-intensive products in China's export industry. However, primary processing industries with high resource consumption were the most heavily hit by the crisis. Moreover, high-tech industries recovered at a faster speed than others after the crisis.

Causality analysis and regression analysis of export volume influenced by the financial crisis

In order to analyze the relationship between our export and the world economy, we built up the regression model and VAR model to further analyze the degree of international economic influence on our exports after the analysis of the causal relationship between our export performance and the token variable of the world economy.

In the regression model and the causal relationship analysis of our exports and the world economy, the dependent variable we selected was the value of exports, and the independent variables included token variables of global economy fluctuation impulse (global oil price index, global stocks index and global trade amount), monthly average nominal exchange rate (RMB to euro, RMB to USD, RMB to Japanese yen, euro to USD, and Japanese yen to USD), all the sample variables being based on monthly data ranging from Jan. 2000 to Sep. 2009.

In the causal relationship examination, the report applied the Granger causality test on the variable selected, and made a judgment about whether a causal relationship existed between our value of exports and the different independent variables. The lag values 1-5 are selected out to be analyzed by the Granger test, so as to analyze short and longer period causal relationships among variables. The results are shown in table 5-1:

lag	Export				
	1	2	3	4	5
lnoil_g	l(2.E-05)	l(9.E-05)	l(1.E-06)	l(8.E-06)	l(5.E-06)
lnstock_g	n	n	n	l(0.0623)	l(0.0372)
lntrade	l(0.0001)	d(0.0003,0.0282)	l(0.0013)	d(2.E-06,0.0166)	d(4.E-07,0.0249)
lnex_cnyeur	n	n	n	N	n
lnex_cnyjpy	n	n	d(0.07,0.02)	d(0.0407,0.0591)	d(0.068,0.063)
lnex_cnyusd	r(8.E-08)	r(0.0016)	r(0.03)	r(0.0753)	n
lnex_eurusd	l(0.0365)	n	n	N	n
lnex_jpyusd	r(0.0044)	r(0.0229)	r(0.0058)	r(0.012)	r(0.0307)
lnner	l0.0903	l(9.E-05)	l(1.E-06)	l(8.E-06)	l(5.E-06)

Table 5-1 Results of Granger Causality Analysis

Note: 1: **is the cause for export; r: export is the cause for granger of **; d: mutually causes of granger; n: no causality relationship.

The values in () are refusal probabilities to suppose false.

213

It is clear that the lag values 1-5 of global trade amount and global oil price are the Granger causes for China export, lag values 3-5 of RMB converting to Japanese Yen and lag values 4-5 of Japanese Yen converting to USD for China export. In accordance with the results, the further regression analysis of our exports and token variables of the world economy is to test the influence of the world economy on our exports around the time of the crisis. Taking the probable co-linearity issue among the variables of different lag values into consideration, we select the smallest value of p in the values with a causal relationship in lag value 1-5 and exports, then put it into the regression model. Furthermore, we choose China's value of exports as the dependent variable, the variable of world economy as the independent variable, the data of 2000-2006 collected before the crisis as the model of relations between China's export and world economy under the crisis as well as the data of 2000-2010 collected during the crisis as the model of relations between China's export and world economy. The results of the above application shows clearly in chart 5-2, as model 1 is a regression model only covering the result before the crisis, and model 2 is the one covering that of both before and after the crisis.

Variable	Model 1 2000m1-2010m12	Model 2 2000m1-2006m12
C	4.973488***	4.798437***
LNTRADE	2.012776***	1.951773***
LNSTOCK_G(-4)	-0.433969***	-0.368998***
LNOIL_G	-0.161476	-0.002598
LNOIL_G(-4)	0.147502	0.064751
R-squared	0.974370	0.970999
Adjusted R-squared	0.973516	0.969618
S.E. of regression	0.104506	0.095148
Sum squared resid	1.310574	0.760459
Log likelihood	107.4982	85.64435
Durbin-Watson stat	1.259877	1.320347

Table 5-2 Results of Our Export and Token Variable of World Economy Regression Model

(Note: ***1%confidence level, **1%confidence level, *10%confidence level)

Coefficients of two models in the regression results charts show that the coefficients of oil price, global stock indexes and global trade volumes grew larger after the crisis, meaning that our exports became more sensitive to these factors. Model results show that the world economic situation exerts a marked influence over our exports, especially in the regression model including the crisis and the oil price index, whose 4-month-lag coefficient grew larger, indicating that the development of our national economy became more synchronous with the world economy.

What the Granger causality analysis and regression model can illustrate are only what kind of factors from the crisis influenced our exports and their changes. To analyze the different influence by different factors, the VAR model established for exports, world trade volumes, global oil price, global stock indexes and our nominal effective exchange rate index was used to analyze impulse response and variance decomposition.

The results of impulse response and variance decomposition with two time units show that we ourselves can explain most of our export fluctuation. Among the influential factors, the changes in world trade volumes have the biggest effect on our exports, meaning that our exports are mainly influenced by the world economy and individual entity economies. In the model including the crisis, it is clear that the variance containing the crisis period gives a more direct explanation of our exports than that excluding the crisis period, with particular relevance from the world trade volumes. In addition, in the impulse response model including the crisis period, the influence on our country of the world stock indexes appeared to be reverse, from minus to plus and plus all the way.

The above results show that our exports were substantially influenced during the crisis, and models including the crisis period prove the linkage between our exports and the world economy, with an even closer connection to world trade volumes. The influence exerted in general by the crisis on our exports cannot be neglected, and the different impacts from the crisis make that influence extremely complex. In impulse response, the world trade volumes, compared to other variables, always stay on the plus side and give the most direct explanation for our exports in the variance decomposition including the crisis period, meaning that our exports are still mainly influenced by world trade volumes more than other indicators, and therefore that the main influence on our exports was from the fluctuations of the real economy. There were no large changes happening to the nominal effective exchange rate and the global oil price index, regardless of the crisis period, and in fact this was influenced by our fixed exchange rate and to some degree, by the separation of our oil market from the world oil market.

Quantitative analysis on the different exported products influenced by the financial crisis

The statistics show the differences in the exported products affected by the financial crisis while the quantitative analysis results manifest the influence on our country's total export volume of the world economic situation. For this reason, the report chooses the growth rates from the 3 major trade partners and the year-on-year acceleration of other investments (the acting variable of trade credit) as the acting variable to our exports influenced by the external economy. Taking the export volume of four major products as the dependent variable, the report analyzes the effect on those products of the economies of 3 major trade partners. The data samples spanned from the 1st quarter of 2000 to the 4th quarter of 2010. For the stability of the model, the root of unity test was applied to the dependent variable in advance and the ADF test showcases all the variables are the single-order integrations.

We also build up 4 VAR models separately for the products of the 5th, the 6th, the 7th and the 8th, taking those 4 kind of products as the response variables and the year-on-year growth acceleration of the GDP of the EU, Japan and the U.S. and the other investments as impact variables. Each VAR model will be estimated individually according to 2000q1-2006q4 and 2000q1-2010q4.

If we consider the export model of the 5th kind of chemical and related products, a comparison between the two time units lead us to conclude that the change in Japan and the U.S. was relatively smaller whereas EU was the largest in impulse response models. Moreover, reversed impulse response appeared in crisis-included models to crisis-excluded models; yet, the variance decomposition at a certain degree meet the result of impulse response; Other investments of EU, which lies into crisis-included models, have a much higher explanation on fluctuation of the export of China's 5th chemical categories and its related products, while in the crisis-excluded models, Japanese other investments are more plausible in this regard.

The comparison between export models of products classified according to the raw materials used in two time units concludes that in impulse response models the products in the crisis-included models appeared reverse to those in the crisis-excluded models; furthermore, variance decomposition shows explanation of each variable of EU's GDP and Japanese other investments in pre-crisis models to export of manufactured products classified by raw materials is relatively weak; however the explanation of EU's GDP improved significantly from 3% up to 17% in the crisis-included models.

As for the machines and transportation equipment export model, the comparison between the time units concludes that EU changed most in the impulse response model. In the period of crisis-included models, the export of machines and transportation equipment was apparently influenced by fluctuations in the EU's GDP and vice versa. The variance analysis supports this result in some sense in that it explains how growth in the EU's GDP improved exports by 100% to200%.

In the miscellaneous products export model, the comparison between two time units concludes that in the impulse response model the EU still registered the greatest change so that the EU's GDP and other investments all reversed in the crisis-included models period. However, in the variance analysis, the explanation of both EU and U.S. GDP on miscellaneous products substantially improved in this regard.

Based on the results models, the conclusion can be reached that in the balance of international payments other investments have been the substitute variable for trade credit status. After the financial crisis, the other investments of the EU showed a remarkable relationship with the chemical products of the 5th and the finished products classified by their raw materials of the 6th. The other investments of Japan showed a notable relationship with machines and transportation equipment of the 7th. The most dramatic relationship, however, was between the GDP of the U.S. and the miscellaneous products of the 8th. From this it is clear that our exported chemical finished products and primary finished products classified by raw materials are closely affected by the EU economic situation, the machines and transportation equipment most affected by the economic situation of Japan and the EU, and the miscellaneous products by the EU and the U.S. Meanwhile, the results show the EU economic situation casts a strong influence upon our country's major exported products in that its economic situation is closely paralleled by the fluctuation of our exported products. In the model comparisons including and excluding the crisis, it is clear that the EU's influence on China's exported products showed marked changes after the financial crisis, especially in that the impact direction against those products has reversed in impulse response. It is reasonable to conclude that since the EU is China's largest trade partner, there will be full linkage with China's trade; Japan's strong influence on China's exports of machines and transportation equipment is owing to the fact that it has a strong manufacturing industry that needs to import those commodities; the prevailing influence of the U.S. on the export of China's labor-intensive products is mainly attributable to it being the largest consumer economy where China's cheap, labor-intensive products can find a correspondingly large market.

Summary

Results of the above statistical and quantitative analyses show that the financial crisis had a significant impact upon China's macro economy by influencing China's export trade.

1. China's economic fluctuation was affected greatly by major economies such as America, Europe and Japan. Moreover, changes in China's economic growth rate were largely consistent with those of the major economies in the world.

2. This financial crisis spread into China mainly through foreign trade rather than through channels of the fictitious economy such as FDI and finance as they had only a very limited impact on the economy of China.

3. Export of high-tech products w fell to its lowest point in the early period during the crisis, yet it recovered at a faster speed than others products. The crisis had only a limited impact on the export of labor-intensive products, and this recovered more slowly than other exports. Furthermore, the export of resources-consuming products was the most vulnerable to the crisis.

4. The EU had a strong influence on China's export of products in the major categories. Japan and America had strong impacts upon China's export of machinery and transportation equipment and labor-intensive products respectively.

6.

China's Countermeasures against the Financial Crisis and their Effects

Under the influence of the global financial crisis, China, an economy that kept double-digit growth from 2004 to 2007, also experienced a slowdown. It grew at 10.0% in 2003, 10.1% in 2004, 10.4% in 2005, 11.6% in 2006, and 13% in 2007, reaching the peak of this economic climb. The double action from the global financial crisis and China's own economic cycle dragged the country's growth rate back by 3.4 percentage points to 9.6% in 2008, and 9.2% in 2009. If we judge from the quarterly data, the growth rate was 11% in the fourth quarter of 2007, 11.3% in the first quarter of 2008, 10.1% in the second, 9% in the third and 6.8% in the fourth. It can be seen that China's economic decline accelerated in the third quarter of 2008, leaving China facing a very difficult situation. To ensure sustained and sound growth, the country took a series of effective measures. By 2010, the impact of the financial crisis started to fade away and China's economic growth for this year rebounded to 10.3%.

China's economic stimulus package

In November 2008, at an executive meeting, the State Council decided on a proactive fiscal policy and a moderately easy monetary policy, unveiling forceful measures to boost domestic demand, improve programs concerning people's welfare, infrastructure, environment and post-disaster reconstruction, and raise the income of the working population especially of the low-income earners to mitigate the impact of the financial crisis and ensure fast yet steady growth. The meeting also specified 10 measures to be adopted currently to expand domestic demand and promote economic growth.

First, accelerating the construction of low-income housing. Low-rent housing and shanty-town reconstruction will be given more support. The government aims to build permanent housing for nomads and increase pilot projects for the renovation of dilapidated rural buildings.

Second, speeding up rural infrastructure construction. Methane gas usage, drinking water safety projects, and road construction will be strengthened. Rural power grid, key water conservancy projects such as the South-to-North Water Diversion, reinforcement of deteriorating reservoirs and large irrigated area reformation all need to be enhanced. Efforts will be intensified to fight poverty.

Third, the development of key infrastructure including railway lines, expressways and airports. Priority will be given to a series of passenger transport lines, coal transport systems and the Western Line. The expressway network, the trunk line airports and branch line airports of the central and western region as well as urban distribution networks all need to be enhanced.

Fourth, the promotion of medical and health care as well as cultural and education programs. The primary-level medical and health care service system will be intensified, the renovation of middle school buildings in China's central and western rural areas will be accelerated, and the development of special education schools as well as township culture centers will be advanced .

Fifth, improvement of the ecological environment. The construction of sewage and garbage disposal facilities and the prevention of water pollution in key river basins will be strengthened. The key shelter forests and natural forest resources must be protected, and the key energy-saving and emission-cutting projects be supported.

Sixth, the encouragement of independent innovation and structural readjustment. High-tech industrialization and industrial progress as well as the development of service industries will be given strong support.

Seventh, continuation of the post-disaster reconstruction of the earthquake stricken area.

Eighth, raising the income of urban and rural populations. The minimum purchase prices of foodstuff should be increased, the levels of several subsidies including the direct subsidy and subsidy to high-quality seeds and agricultural implements should be adjusted, and the income of farmers raised. There will also be improvement in the level of treatment to the beneficiaries of social welfare such as low-income workers, an increase in the subsidies to urban and rural low-income people, and improvements in the pensions of retired people from enterprises as well as subsidies to the disabled or for the families of the deceased.

Ninth, the implementation of value-added tax reform in all the regions and industries in China. Enterprises will be encouraged to upgrade technologies and there will be a 120 billion RMB relief of burden for the enterprises.

Tenth, the increase of financial support to economic growth. Restrictions on the credit size of commercial banks will be cancelled and appropriate expansion permitted. Credit support will be enhanced to key projects such as agriculture, farmers and the rural area, SMEs and technical reform, as well as acquisition and consolidation. Consumer credit growth with clear objectives will be developed and consolidated.

Based on preliminary calculation, 4 trillion RMB is needed for the above projects by the end of 2010.

This stimulus package, on the one hand, gives support to infrastructure construction such as railways, roads and airports as well as rural infrastructure, housing projects for low-income families, energy conservation and emission reduction, culture and education, independent innovation, and post-disaster reconstruction. On the other hand, the package plan aims to promote the key industries of China. In 2009 the State Council executive meetings successively deliberated on, approved and implemented the top ten industrial revitalization plan covering automobiles, steel, textiles, equipment manufacturing, shipping, electronic communication, petrochemicals, light industry, non-ferrous metal and logistics.

The countermeasures against the financial crisis, featuring a proactive fiscal policy and a moderately easy monetary policy, mainly cover the following aspects:

First is financial expenditure. The government has formulated relevant policies for expanding investment and transfer payment to highlight the leverage role of "achieving the great by doing the little", attracting social investment and stimulating consumption. The central finance is providing an additional RMB 1.18 trillion of investment to spur the investment plan of RMB 4 trillion. In 2009 the central finance accomplished RMB 924.3 billion of public investment, 503.8 billion more than the previous year. Of this, 44% was invested in low-income housing, projects to improve the wellbeing of rural residents, and social programs, 16% in independent innovation, restructuring, energy conservation, emissions reductions, and ecological improvement, 23% in major infrastructure projects, and 14% in post-Wenchuan earthquake recovery and reconstruction. Fixed asset investment nationwide increased by 30.1%, reaching RMB 22.5 trillion, 5.2 trillion more than the previous year.

Second is expanding consumer spending. The central government has provided RMB 45 billion in subsidies for rural residents to purchase home appliances and motor vehicles including motorbikes. Part of the subsidies also supported trading-in old motor vehicles and home appliances for new ones and purchasing agricultural machinery and tools. The scope and variety of subsidized "home appliances going to the countryside" has been expanded. The government adjusted the rate of vehicle consumption tax and halved the purchase tax on small-displacement automobiles. It also reduced or exempted taxes on buying and selling homes to support the purchase of homes to be used as their owners' residences. Subsidies have been allocated to support small and medium-sized enterprises (SMEs) for the credit guarantee. Special funds were also utilized to support the technical innovation and progress of SMEs.

Third is fiscal revenue. This mainly refers to reform on individual income tax and corporation tax. The individual income tax on savings deposit interest income (otherwise called interest tax) was temporarily exempted from October 9, 2008. In December of the same year, the value-added tax deduction policies were promulgated.

Fourth is credit policy. The government took measures to expand loan size and ease credit constraints. By the end of 2009 the loan balance in RMB was 9.6 trillion more than the year-end balances of 2008. With the addition of foreign currency loans, the total newly-added loans in 2009 exceeded RMB10 trillion.

Fifth is interest rate policy. Measures on deposit reserve requirement ratio and benchmark interest for deposit and loan were taken. Since September 2008, the People's Bank of China (PBOC) has lowered the benchmark interest rate5 times consecutively in less than 3 months, ending at 2.16%. It also reduced the deposit reserve ratio three times consecutively on September 15, October 8, and November 26. Since October 27, 2008, the PBOC has expanded the floating range of personal commercial housing loan interest rate, adjusted the minimum down payment ratio and lowered the loan interest rate for the personal housing accumulation fund.

Sixth is foreign trade policy. The export rebate rate and export tariff on some labor-intensive products and mechanical and electrical products have been raised. Since August 2008, China has, 7 times in a row, raised the export rebate rate, and reduced or canceled the export tariff or special export tariff on some of the steel, aluminum, chemical and food products.

With regard to employment, the government has adopted three solutions:

First is to create employment through investment. The RMB4 trillion of investment plan would attract 24.16 million jobs within two years.

Second is to help enterprises stabilize their job positions. The *"five-*

four-three-two" employment support policies allow qualified enterprises to postpone their payments of *five* types of social security contributions including endowment insurance, medical insurance, workers' compensation, unemployment insurance and maternity insurance; reduce the contributions to *four* types of insurance funds (namely the above-mentioned five except endowment insurance); utilize unemployment insurance funds to provide qualified enterprises with *three* types of subsidy including social insurance subsidy, job subsidy and staff training subsidy; sign installment payment agreement or other types of payment contracts when the enterprise must conduct downsizing but can truly not afford lump-sum compensation, based on equal *consultation* with the trade union or employees themselves, and shorten working hours or adjust salaries to combat difficulties and stabilize labor relations, based on collective *consultation*. The government planned to alleviate tax burdens of RMB200 billion on enterprises and stabilize 20 million jobs in 2009.

Third is to strengthen policy support. The policies encourage entrepreneurship and promote employment, help college graduates and rural migrant workers find jobs and help urban laid-off personnel get reemployed. Vocational training is to be strengthened to improve the employability of people.

The RMB4 trillion Yuan investment is expected to play six roles:

First is to create more jobs. Employment has all along been a key economic and social problem for China. For the past several years of rapid economic growth, the employment figures have continued to increase. In 2007, 12 million jobs were provided, but employment pressure still existed. 9-10 million graduates of all types each year need jobs; current laid-off employees amount to 6 million and are increasing each year; 9 million rural workers are will move to cities. According to the research from the Chinese Academy of Social Sciences (CASS), China's registered urban unemployment rate by the end of 2007 was 4.0%, but the actual unemployment rate reached 9.6% [1].Preliminary estimates show that about one million jobs would be lost each time the GDP dropped one percentage point. Affected by the financial crisis, the number of new jobs in urban areas continued a substantial decline, totaling only 380,000 in December 2008, down by 54.2% compared with January. Before the Spring Festival of 2009, among the 130 million rural migrant workers, 20 million lost their jobs or returned home through not finding jobs due to the recession. Many of them could no longer adapt back to rural life, and the rural labor surplus also made them decide to stay in large and medium-sized cities, creating social problems. Investment in infrastructure and housing construction may create more jobs to mitigate employment pressure.

Second is to encourage the demand for means of production such as steel and cement. China's production of steel and cement has been growing fast in recent years, ranking the first in the world. Hit by the financial crisis, their production dropped dramatically, as did the price. Expanding infrastructure investment could push up demand for them.

Third is to better conserve energy and protect the environment. The rapid growth of China's economy for the past several years was achieved to some extent at the cost of energy and the environment. Estimates show that the cost of energy consumption, ecological degradation and environmental pollution of China in 2005 reached RMB275 million, accounting for 13.9% of the GDP [2]. Part of the 4-trillion investment would be used for energy conservation and consumption reduction to ensure the sustainable development of China's economy.

Fourth is to improve the housing system. Approximately RMB 900 billion of the 4 trillion would be utilized in building low-rent housing and affordable housing to ensure accommodation for low-income and homeless people, which is also conducive to increase their consumer spending.

Fifth is to strengthen the impetus for consumption. 20% of the RMB4-trillion investment would be translated into purchasing power through staff salaries and thereby boost consumption.

Sixth is to prevent deflation. Under the impact of the financial crisis, China's Consumer Price Index (CPI) and Producer Price Index (PPI) dropped substantially from the third quarter of 2008. By the end of January 2009, the CPI growth rate had been decreasing for nine consecutive months and PPI had sustained two months of negative growth, indicating a deflation risk. The RMB4-trillion investment could help the CPI and PPI go up to a reasonable level to guard against deflation.

Research method and scenario planning

This section highlights the positive and negative effects of the financial expenditure and credit policies among the countermeasures against the financial crisis.

The research integrates statistics-based empirical analysis and macro-economy-based simulation methods. The simulation, which is mainly based on the CGE (Computable General Equilibrium) and input-output modeling, analyzes how the economy reacts to circumstances of no financial crisis, taking measures against the crisis and not adopting measures against it.

The CGE model is based on the Input-Output Table 2007 and SAM Table 2007 compiled according to relevant customs, revenue, balance of payments and money flow. The model involves 39 sectors (See Table 6-1), 2 groups of residents (urban and rural), and 3 factors of production (labor, capital and resources). The 39 sectors comprise 1 agricultural sector, 36 industrial sectors and 2 service sectors. The 9 energy sectors involve coal, petroleum, natural gas, petroleum-processed goods, coke, fuel gas, thermal power, other electric power and heating power.

The elasticity of substitution among energy factors, between energy and capital, between energy-capital mix and labor referenced the research made by Wu Yajun and Xuan Xiaowei [3], as well as the parameter setting of SGM, MIT-EPPA, G-Cubed, AIM and AMIGA models. The elasticity of substitution between import and domestic commodities referenced the empirical value of GTAP (6th Edition) model. Labor data of various sectors comes from *The Fifth National Population Census of China* and *China economic census yearbook 2004*. Data of fixed asset investment and population comes from the *China Statistical Yearbook*. National and industrial energy consumption data is from the *Energy Statistics Yearbook*.

Modeling dynamism is realized through capital accumulation, la-

Table 6-1 Sector Classification of SAM

No.	Sector	No.	Sector	No.	Sector
1	Agriculture	14	Printing, reproduction of recording media, manufacture of articles for culture, education and sports	27	Standard machinery, manufacture of special purpose machinery
2	Coal mining & washing	15	Petroleum and processing of nuclear fuel	28	Manufacture of Transport Equipment
3	Extraction of Petroleum	16	Coking	29	Electrical machinery and equipment, electronics and communications equipment manufacturing
4	Extraction of Natural Gas	17	Manufacture of raw chemical materials and chemical products	30	Manufacture of measuring instrument and machinery for cultural activity & office work
5	Mining of ferrous metal ores	18	Manufacture of medicines	31	Other industries
6	Mining of non-ferrous metal ores	19	Manufacture of chemical fiber	32	Thermal power production supply
7	Mining of other ores	20	Rubber product industry, plastic product industry	33	Other power production supply
8	Food and beverage processing	21	Manufacturing of cement, lime and gypsum	34	Heating power production supply
9	Tobacco manufacturing	22	Manufacture of glass and glass product	35	Production and supply of gas
10	Textile	23	Manufacture of other nonmetallic minerals	36	Production and supply of water
11	Manufacture of clothing, leather and other fiber products	24	Manufacture and processing of ferrous metals	37	Construction
12	Processing of timbers, manufacture of bamboo products and furniture	25	Manufacture and processing of non-ferrous metals	38	Transport, storage, post and telecommunications
13	Paper and paper products	26	Metal products	39	Other service industries

Figure 6-1 Production Module of CGE

bor growth and technical progress. Please see specifications of the simulation design for the setting of the three parameters. The time interval for the simulation is from 2007 to 2015.

We apply the simulation method to analyze the policy effect of investment. First is the normal circumstance: the financial crisis did not happen and China's economy develops as usual. Second is the laissez-faire circumstance: after the financial crisis broke out, no countermeasures were taken against it. Third is the response circumstance: countermeasures were taken after the crisis (mainly for increasing investment and expanding domestic demand). Time interval for the simulation is 2007-2015.

Normal circumstance: In terms of model parameters, the elasticity of substitution is exogenous and some parameters are corrected according to the base year. TFP and labor growth rates are exogenous; gross fixed capital formation is endogenous. Research has shown that the TFP growth rate for the last 30 years moved between 2% and 4%. Sun Linlin and Ren Ruo'en [4] estimated a 3.14% growth rate of TFP 1981-2002. Wang Xiaolu and others [5] estimated 3.63% growth of TFP 1999-2007. If restructuring is promoted, policy administration cost is curbed, education, social security and public services are improved, and the income disparities are restrained, then the TFP 2008-2020 is expected to grow at 3.95%. Based on such research findings and in view of the fact that the future economy may not be able to return to the original level completely, we set the TFP growth rate 2008-2010 at 3.2% under normal circumstance, and suppose it will drop slightly after 2011 to 2.8% in the 2011-2015 period. Within the simulation period, the proportion of effective labor force to total population is fixed, that is, the labor force increases with the total population. Furthermore, under normal circumstance, the price index of commodities consumed by the population and government is exogenous. The mean of CPI 1990-2009 was 104.8. The CPI from 1993 to 1995 all exceeded 114 and even reached 124.1 in 1994. Taking out these particular values, we set the mean at 102.4. In the model we assume the yearly average of price index consumed by residents and the government under normal circumstance to be 103.

Laissez-faire circumstance: This circumstance considers the two impacts exerted by the financial crisis including the decline of import and export as well as of productivity. The crisis had a serious impact on import and export trade, which on one hand led to reduction of foreign demand, and resulted in declining prices of import and export on the other. From the fourth quarter of 2008, import and export prices were seriously hurt. Suppose the prices of 2008 decreased by 5%, and the export price of 2009 dropped by 15%, import price dropped by 5%, but after 2010 it returned to the level of 2007. Suppose the gross fixed asset formation grows as much as that of the normal circumstance, then the gross fixed asset formation of 2007, 2009 and 2015 is 10.54 trillion, 12.82 trillion and 19.40 trillion respectively. Since investment influences the CPI, the CPI under crisis circumstance is endogenous in relation to the exogenous investment. Furthermore, the financial crisis led to idle capital and labor, and thereby a declining TFP growth rate. According to Wang Xiaolu and other researchers, against the background of financial crisis, China's annual TFP growth rate 2008-2020 may have dropped to 1.79%. Consequently, this circumstance sets the TFP growth rate 2009 at 1.8%, and it is expected to reach 2.5% after 2010, till in 2011 it returns to the level of normal circumstance, an annual TFP growth rate of 2.8%.

Response circumstance: This circumstance mainly considers the effect of expanding investment to mitigate the impact of the crisis. If we set the gross fixed asset formation of 2009 at what it actually was, then according to the contribution rate of gross capital formation to GDP in 2009, we get 14.13 trillion of gross fixed asset formation. The growth rate afterwards approaches the level of normal circumstance, being 20.22 trillion in 2015. Under such a circumstance the TFP growth rate 2008-2009 is corrected based on actual GDP, standing at 3.1% in 2008 and 2.5% in 2009. Since investment may bring about utilization of idle capital and labor, the TFP growth rate 2009 recovered to some extent compared with the crisis circumstance, till after 2010 it returned to the level of normal circumstance, with an average 2.8%.

Simulated result

Economic growth

The simulated result of China's economic growth under the three circumstances is as shown in Figure 6-2, 6-3 and Table 6-2.

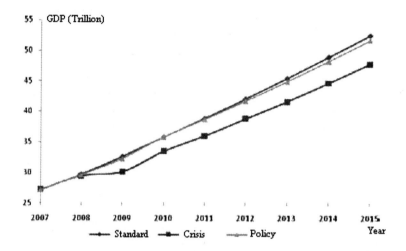

Figure 6-2 GDP(trillion)under Different Circumstances

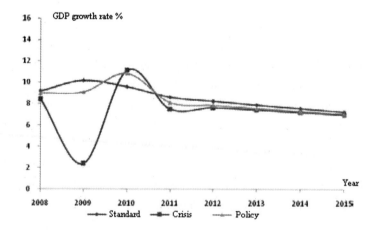

Figure 6-3 GDP Growth Rate(%) under Different Circumstances

Table 6-2 GDP Growth Rate(%)under Different Circumstances

	2008	2009	2010	2011	2012	2013	2014	2015
Normal	9.17	10.17	9.59	8.63	8.26	7.92	7.59	7.30
Laissez-faire	8.39	2.36	11.12	7.52	7.65	7.45	7.23	7.02
Response	9.00	9.10	10.82	8.12	7.87	7.61	7.34	7.09

We can see from the Table that calculated by the prices in 2007, China's GDP, under normal, laissez-faire and response circumstance, increases from RMB 27.16166 trillion in 2007 to RMB 52.46161 trillion, RMB 47.79544 trillion and RMB 51.64125 trillion respectively in 2015. Under laissez-faire circumstance, the GDP growth rate of 2009, with no countermeasures taken against the financial crisis, drops to 2.36%, and rebounds dramatically in 2010, but stays slightly lower than that of normal circumstance. Under response circumstances, after investment policies are adopted against the crisis, the macro economy recovers to a large extent. The GDP growth rate of 2009 rises from 2.36% of the crisis circumstance to 9.1%. The substantial increase of investment helps the GDP growth rate of 2010 score higher than normal circumstance. Afterwards the GDP growth rate is slightly lower than normal circumstance, but as time goes by, the gap gets gradually smaller, indicating that it can be concluded that the measures of increasing investment and expanding domestic demand to a large extent mitigate the impact of declining foreign demand and reduce the fluctuations of economic performance.

Import and export

The simulated result of China's import and export under the three circumstances is as shown in Figure 6-2, 6-4, 6-5, 6-6, 6-7 and Table 6-3, 6-4.

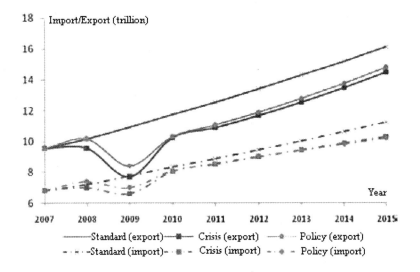

Figure 6-4 Import and Export (trillion) under Different Circumstances

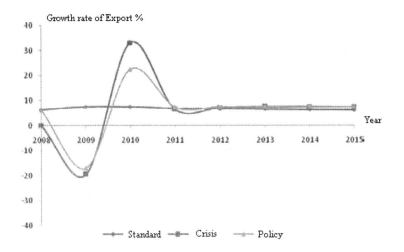

Figure 6-5 Growth Rate (%) of Export under Different Circumstances

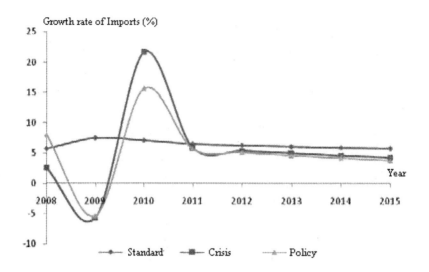

Figure 6-6 Growth Rate (%) of Import under Different Circumstances

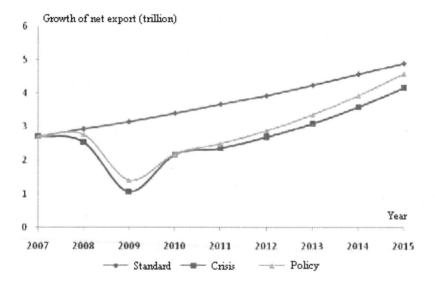

Figure 6-7 Net Export (trillion) under Different Circumstances
(Note: The export share of the above-mentioned 15 industries in 2007 amounted to 91.5%, size down by export share.)

Table 6-3 Change Rate of Export (%) for Key Export-Oriented Enterprises in 2009 (Laissez-faire VS Normal)

Key export-oriented enterprises	Change rate (%) of export
Electrical machinery and equipment, electronics and communications equipment manufacturing communications equipment manufacturing	-20.73
Other Service industries	-12.76
Textile	-18.68
Standard machinery, manufacture of special purpose machinery	-14.97
Manufacture of clothing, leather and other fiber products	-17.74
Transport, storage, post and telecommunications	-13.25
Manufacture and processing of ferrous metals	-14.75
Manufacture of metals	-16.14
Manufacture of raw chemical materials chemical products	-15.68
Manufacture of Transport Equipment	-15.16
Manufacture of measuring instruments machinery for cultural activity & office work	-26.98
Rubber product industry, plastic product industry	-16.38
Processing of timbers, manufacture of bamboo products and furniture	-15.43
Printing, reproduction of recording media, manufacture of articles for culture, education and sports	-15.27
Food and beverage processing, manufacturing	-13.07

Table 6-4 Change Rate of Import (%) for Key Import-Oriented Enterprises in 2009 (Laissez-faire VS Normal)

Key import-oriented enterprises	Change rate (%) of import
Electrical machinery and equipment, electronics and communications equipment manufacturing	-9.17
Manufacture of raw chemical materials and chemical products	-11.07
Standard machinery, manufacture of special purpose machinery	-8.26
Other service industries	-9.99
Extraction of Petroleum	-13.90
Manufacture of measuring instruments machinery for cultural activity & office work for	-5.55
Manufacture of Transport Equipment	-6.97
Mining and dressing of ferrous metals	-8.41
Mining and dressing of non-ferrous metals	-11.63
Agriculture	-14.51
Manufacture and processing of ferrous metals	-10.98
Other industries	-13.87
Food and beverage processing, manufacturing	-12.10
Extraction of natural gas	-16.01
Petroleum and processing of nuclear fuel	-11.22

(Note: The import share of the above-mentioned 15 industries in 2007 amounted to 88.8%%, size down by import share.)

The Table shows that under normal circumstance, China's annual export growth rate 2007-2015 in real terms is about 6.2-7.5%, and the annual import growth rate is 5.8-7.5%. Under laissez-faire circumstance, the financial crisis exerts a serious impact on import and export. In 2008 they start to be affected, and the total export begins to fall. The imports and exports of 2009 demonstrate a substantially negative growth, with total export decreasing by 19.6% and total imports declining by 6%. The post-crisis import and export dramatically rebound and even increase rapidly in 2010, with total import and export growing 32% and 21% respectively. Their growth rates become gentler afterwards. The total import and export under response circumstance are slightly higher than that of the laissez-faire circumstance, but their growth rates stay negative, with exports decreasing by about 17% and imports declining by about 5% compared with 2008. The decline rate of import and export resulting from the financial crisis is mitigated only to a small extent. Similar to the laissez-faire circumstance, imports and exports of 2010 started to rebound dramatically, and their growth rates became gentler afterwards. Since exports are worse hurt by the crisis, the post-crisis total export is far below the level of normal circumstance, but the annual growth rate compared with the previous is slightly higher than that of the normal circumstance.

As is shown in Figure 6-7, under normal circumstance, China's net export gradually increases as time goes, but the increase rate gets lower and lower, from 8.2% in 2008 to 7.1% in 2015. Under laissez-faire and response circumstances, the growth rate of net export in 2009 is negative, being -58% and -48% respectively. After the financial crisis, net export starts to rebound and move toward the level of normal circumstance, growing faster under policy circumstance than under crisis circumstance.

Table 6-3 and 6-4 represent the changing rates of import and export in 2009 for the key sectors under laissez-faire circumstance versus normal circumstance. Impacted by the financial crisis, the decline rate of export for most of the key export-oriented sectors is above 15% compared with the normal circumstance, especially for the two sectors:

manufacture of measuring instruments and machinery for cultural activity and office work, as well as electrical machinery and equipment, electronics and communications equipment manufacturing, both exceeding 20%. The decline rate of imports for most of the key import-oriented sectors also exceeds 10%, with the energy exploitation sector being hurt most.

Consumption and income

The simulated result of China's consumption and income under the three circumstances is as shown in Figure 6- 8, 6-9 and 6-10.

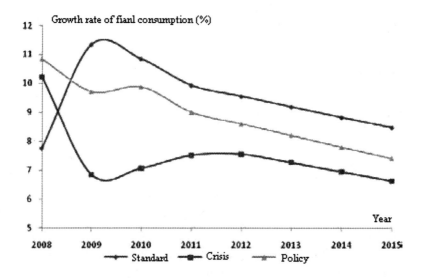

Figure 6-8 Growth Rate (%) of Final Consumption under Different Circumstances

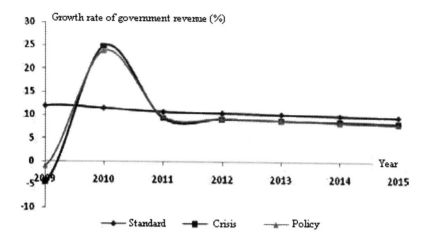

Figure 6-9 Income for Urban and Rural Residents under Different Circumstances(trillion)

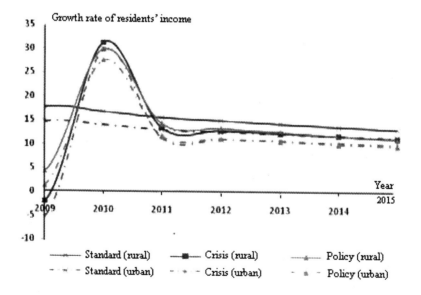

Figure 6-10 Growth Rate (%) of Income for Urban and Rural Residents under Different Circumstances

From Figure 6-8 we can see the variation of final consumption is gentler compared with net export and GDP. Under normal circumstance, the final consumption grows fastest in 2009, and then decreases from 11% to 8.5% in 2015. Based on laissez-faire conditions, the decline rate of final consumption in 2009 is high, and then picks up, but drops after 2012. The growth rate of final consumption from 2009 to 2015 remains between 6.8% and 7.5%. Under the response circumstance, investment helps the decline rate of final consumption in 2009 score lower than that under the crisis circumstance. The growth rate after 2010 gradually reduces, moving between 1.5-2% higher than that of the laissez-faire conditions and 1% lower than that of the normal circumstance.

Figures 6-9 and 6-10 show that government revenue and personal income under different circumstances represent basically the same trend of variation. Under normal circumstance these two indicators both rise dramatically but their growth rates gradually slow down. The growth rate of government revenue declines from 12% in 2009 to 9.7% in 2015. The growth rates of income for rural and urban residents drop from 17.7% and 14.7% in 2009 to 13.3% and 11.5% in 2015 respectively. Under laissez-faire conditions, government revenue and personal income both experience negative growth in 2009. The former grows at -4.4%, and the latter grows at -5.3% (urban) and -2.0% (rural), indicating a bigger impact of the financial crisis on urban residents than on rural residents. After a dramatic rebound in 2010, the growth rate of government revenue and private income becomes more stable, though slightly less than under normal circumstances. Under the response circumstance, investment helps government revenue, and personal income of 2009 achieves substantial growth rates compared with that under crisis circumstance. Afterwards their variation trend resembles that under normal and laissez-faire circumstance.

GDP composition

The simulated result of China's GDP composition under the three circumstances is as shown in Table 6-5, 6-6.

Table 6-5 GDP Composition under Different Circumstances

		2007	2009	2015
Normal	Net export	9.97	9.64	9.31
	Final consumption	48.50	48.39	51.86
	Capital formation	41.52	41.97	38.83
Laissez-faire	Net export	9.97	3.54	8.70
	Final consumption	48.50	51.48	49.17
	Capital formation	41.52	44.98	42.13
Response	Net export	9.97	4.37	8.87
	Final consumption	48.50	49.60	50.56
	Capital formation	41.52	46.03	40.57

Table 6-6 Contribution Rate to GDP of Consumption, Investment and Net Export under Different Circumstances

		2009	2010	2012	2015
Normal	Net export	7.22	8.13	8.71	9.14
	Final consumption	53.39	54.67	57.28	59.64
	Capital formation	39.39	37.20	34.01	31.22
Laissez-faire	Net export	-211.92	32.87	11.85	18.26
	Final consumption	143.10	32.75	48.97	46.63
	Capital formation	168.82	34.38	39.18	35.10
Response	Net export	-44.93	22.44	12.75	19.11
	Final consumption	52.66	45.28	54.24	52.66
	Capital formation	92.27	32.28	33.02	28.23

We can see from Table 6-5 and 6-6 that under normal circumstances, the proportion of consumption to GDP gets higher and higher through time, while the proportion of net export and gross capital formation to GDP get smaller. The contribution of final consumption and net export to GDP rises gradually, whereas the contribution of gross capital formation to GDP growth rate gets smaller and smaller. Based on the laissez-faire situation, however, the proportion of net export to GDP in 2009 decreases rapidly, 6 percentage points lower than under normal circumstances. At this moment the GDP grows only at 2.36% and the rate of decline for net export is twice as much as the GDP growth rate. The post-crisis contribution of net export to GDP experiences a quick rebound till gradual recovery, and its contribution to GDP rises, too. Under the response circumstance, investment policies serve as a key driver of GDP, and the proportion of investment to GDP is 4 percentage points higher than under normal circumstances. In 2009 the increment of gross capital formation occupied 92.3% of the GDP increment, and net export substantially decreased, with a decline rate reaching -44.9% of the GDP growth rate.

The simulated result indicates that adopting investment policies against the financial crisis, compared with not adopting them, can drive the 2009 GDP growth rate of 6.7 percentage points higher, and may narrow the gap between post-2010 GDP growth rate and the GDP under normal circumstances. It can be concluded that the measures of increasing investment and expanding domestic demand to a large extent mitigate the impact of declining foreign demand and even out the fluctuations of economic performance.

Employment

Investment itself is a key factor in promoting employment, and the expansion of investment can increase the demand for investment goods, thereby leading to stronger demand for labor and more employment. Since different industrial sectors have varied absorptive capabilities of employment, different investment allocation structures will bring about diverse effects in promoting employment. Cai Fang applied the Input-Output Method to reach a conclusion that the 4-trillion-yuan investment plan would create approximately 51.35 million jobs [6]. A report on the effect of employment policies, issued by the Ministry of Human Resources and Social Security of China, showed that the 4-trillion-yuan investment plan would promote 24.16 million jobs within two years [7]. The Social Development Institute of National Development and Reform Commission speculated that the investment package would promote 5.6 million jobs in long-term employment and 50 million jobs in short-term employment [8]. It is evident that different scholars utilize different methods to conclude different effects on employment. We adopted the input-out analysis method to estimate the effects of increasing investment to expand employment.

As has been noted, the natural growth rate of fixed asset investment in 2009 may be set at 18%. Without stimulus policies, the total investment in fixed assets 2009 would have been RMB20.3937 trillion; the stimulus package brought an increment of RMB2.090896 trillion of fixed asset investment. According to our model, such an increment might create a full employment effect of 8.5297 million people. To be specific, increasing investment in construction would create a full employment effect of 4.8126 million people; expanding investment in water conservancy, environment and public utilities management would create a full employment effect of 3.5482 million people. The sum of the two number accounts for 98% of total employment increment. In fact, the data released by the National Bureau of Statistics [9] showed that by the end of 2009, China's total employment reached 779,950,000, 5.15 million more than the previous year. Among them, urban employment totaled 311,200,000, 9.1 million more than the previous year, and there were 11.02 million newly employed urban residents in that total.

Negative effect of the stimulus package

To cope with the financial crisis, the Chinese government launched a RMB4 trillion- stimulus package in November 2008. Of the RMB4 trillion, 1.18 trillion was funded by the central government. Newly increased financial investment reached RMB104 billion in the fourth quarter of 2008, and RMB 503.8 billion in 2009. Bank credit increased RMB9.6 trillion in 2009, and total investment in fixed assets totaled RMB22.4846 trillion, up by 30.1% compared with the previous year.

Loan increment grew rapidly in 2009. The newly increased loan of RMB and foreign currencies reached RMB10.55 trillion, 2.5 times as much as 2008. Of the 10.55 trillion, newly increased household loan stood at RMB 2.47 trillion, 3.86 times as much as 2008; newly added loans to non-financial corporations and other sectors amounted to RMB8.08 trillion, 2.25 times as much as 2008 (See Table 6-7).

Table 6-7 Comparison of Credit Funds Composition 2008-2009

Item	1st half of 2009		2nd half of 2009		2009		2008	
	Amount	Composition	Amount	Composition	Amount	Composition	Amount	Composition
I. All loans	77578.9		27969.0		105547.9		42302.2	
1.Household loan	10748.2	13.9	13988.6	50.0	24736.8	23.4	6407.8	15.2
(1)Consumer loan	6656.8	8.6	11474.4	41.0	18131.2	17.2	4483.4	10.6
Short-term	955.4	1.2	1292.7	4.6	2248.2	2.1	1035.8	2.5
Medium and long-term	5701.3	7.3	10181.7	36.4	15883.0	15.0	3447.7	8.2
(2)Business loan	4091.5	5.3	2514.2	9.0	6605.7	6.3	1924.4	4.6
Short-term	3366.9	4.3	1628.5	5.8	4995.4	4.7	1762.7	4.2
Farmer credit	2336.5	3.0	314.7	1.1	2651.3	2.5	1294.3	3.1
Medium and long-term	724.5	0.9	885.7	3.2	1610.2	1.5	161.7	0.4
2.Non-financial corporate loan and loan of other sectors	66830.6	86.1	13980.5	50.0	80811.1	76.6	35894.4	84.9
(1)Short-term and bill financing	30556.8	39.4	-10605.2	-37.9	19951.6	18.9	13251.9	31.3
Short-term	13485.6	17.4	1901.4	6.8	15387.0	14.6	6822.1	16.1
Bill financing	17071.1	22.0	-12506.6	-44.7	4564.5	4.3	6429.0	15.2
(2)Medium and long-term	32230.7	41.5	18868.9	67.5	51099.6	48.4	19159.0	45.3
(3)Other loans	4043.2	5.2	5716.8	20.4	9760.0	9.2	3482.0	8.2

(Note: a. Source data: official website of the People's Bank of China: http://www.pbc.gov.cn/; b. Unit of the amount: hundred million; composition: the proportion of the said loan to total loans of the same period. Unit: %)

247

The above-mentioned measures helped China achieve a 9.1% economic growth and maintain social and economic stability, testifying the necessity of adopting stimulus measures under special circumstances. The negative effect, however, of relying on huge investment to stimulate the economy, started to reveal itself from 2010, as Premier Wen Jiabao said in this year's Report on the Work of the Government, "Although this year's development environment may be better than last year's, we still face a very complex situation. Some positive changes and negative influences are growing while others are diminishing. Short-term and long-term problems are interwoven, domestic and international factors mutually affect each other, and the dilemmas facing economic and social development are increasing". Such adverse impacts must be considered seriously and removed in a timely fashion.

Overcapacity

Since China has long been relying on huge investment to boost economic growth, quite a few industries have approached saturation in their production, and the overcapacity problem was exacerbated under the impact of the U.S. financial crisis. Reports say 21 among the 24 industrial sectors of China have an overcapacity problem. Some cities, however, for the sake of economic growth rate and relying excessively on increasing investment to boost GDP, not only substantially added new projects, but also revitalized some outdated capacity and developed their industries with excessive production capacity, which exacerbated the general overcapacity problem.

For instance, China's steel production has become the highest in the world, reaching 568 million tons in 2009, and 730 million tons in early 2010, which was already excessive in capacity. It is reported [11] that in the first half of 2009, investment in the steel industry exceeded RMB140 billion. By the end of December, the crude steel production for projects in progress totaled 58 million tons, most of which were not approved by the government. If not controlled in time, overcapacity could reach 200 million tons. If calculated at RMB5000 investment per ton of crude steel production, then approximately RMB1 trillion would be added to the economic growth rate in terms of investment, but this would no longer be conducive to real economic growth.

Overcapacity inevitably causes stockpiling of goods. Though some products have already been produced and their added value calculated into the GDP, they have never actually been sold on the market and the value they created only stayed on paper rather than forming social wealth. Such waste of resources would reduce the cost effectiveness of enterprises. Moreover, the investment-stimulated economic growth could lead to a decline of investment returns when rash decision-making increases the occurrence of mistakes.

There are also some places failing to conduct environmental impact assessment due to anxious start-up of new projects. Compounded by the resumption of outdated capacity, environmental pollution has reappeared or deteriorated.

The overcapacity problem has already attracted the attention of the Chinese government and got restrained in the fourth quarter of 2009. *Several Opinions of the General Office of the State Council on Strengthening Energy Conservation and Emission Reduction and Accelerating Restructuring of the Steel Industry*, issued in June 2010, specified that, excluding the state approved projects already carrying out preliminary work, no steel projects for capacity expansion could be approved or filed before the end of 2011; the concentration ratio of China's steel industry needs to be enhanced to form 3-5 super-size steel conglomerates with relatively strong international competitiveness and 6-7 conglomerates with relatively strong performances. It is expected that by 2015, the proportion of steel production for the top 10 domestic steel conglomerates could be raised to above 60% from the 44% in 2009. In addition, the National Development and Reform Commission, the Ministry of Land and Resources, and the Ministry of Environmental Protection will take the lead in the investigations of construction projects, illegal land use cases and environment impact assessment or excessive pollution since 2005 [11].

Increasing inflation risks

Chief measures of price inflation normally include the Consumer Price Index (CPI) and Producer Price Index (PPI). CPI measures the average change over time in the prices paid by consumers for a market basket of consumer goods and services; PPI measures the average change in the selling prices received by manufacturers and farmers for their output, mainly reflecting the price changes of means of production and is usually used to measure the cost price changes of various commodities in different production phases.

Figure 6-11 shows the CPI and PPI year-on-year growth before and after the financial crisis.

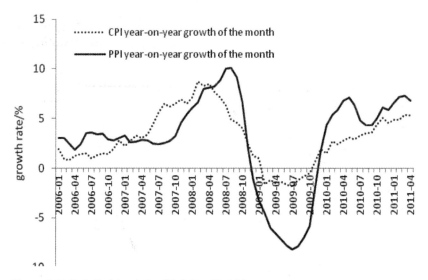

Figure 6-11 Statistical Analysis of Inflation Variable

We can see from Figure 6-11 that the change of inflation representation variable has two rise phases and one decline stage. Taking CPI as an example, from January 2007 to April 2008, CPI year-on-year growth rate of a month rose slowly, with an average of 5.61%. During this period, the highest CPI year-on-year growth rate reached 8.7% in February 2008, and started to decrease rapidly from May 2008, with an average growth rate of 2%. It touched bottom in July 2009, standing at -1.8%, and started to pick up in August, till turning positive in November 2009. The data of June 2011 shows that the CPI year-on-year growth rose up to 6.4%. The variation of PPI is similar to CPI, only with bigger fluctuations.

Inflation risks exist in the environment of expansive fiscal policy and easy monetary policy. In July 2009, Professor Cheng Siwei pointed out the need to guard against inflation, saying "inflation occurs when a greater money supply than is needed by the real economy causes erosion in the purchasing power of that money. When the price of financial assets rises, the inflation may not be obvious since they have absorbed some of the currency. But once the bubble bursts, inflation will follow promptly. Currently an expectation of inflation has appeared amongst the general public, and we must guard against any positive feedback. We must know where the limit is in implementing a moderately easy monetary policy, ensure the consistency and stability of policies, prevent the increase of non-performing loans and avoid substantial fluctuations of money supply."[12]

Besides the year-on-year growth (compared with the same period of the previous year), the sequential growth rate (compared with the same period of the previous month) is also needed when observing inflation. All data should be seasonally adjusted. Figure 6-12 lists the monthly data of CPI year-on-year growth and sequential growth based on seasonal adjustment.

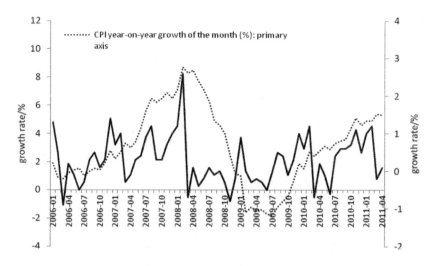

Figure 6-12 Monthly Data of CPI Year-on-Year Growth and Sequential Growth

We can see from Figure 6-12 that in July 2009, though the CPI year-on-year growth was negative, its sequential growth in January started to turn positive, indicating that the general level of prices had started to rise. However, most people looked only at the year-on-year growth data and neglected the risk of inflation till November when CPI year-on-year growth data turned positive. Some still did not take it seriously and believed the CPI growth in 2010 could possibly be controlled below 3%. Considering the impossibility of hasty tightening an easy monetary policy and taking into account the inertia of inflation, such a goal was hard to achieve. In fact the CPI year-on-year growth in the first three quarters of 2010 had reached 2.9%, and 3.6% in September, and 3.3% for the whole year. The CPI year-on-year growth in the first quarter of 2011 was as high as 5%.

It must also be observed that the variation of inflation index fell obviously behind the currency policies, which started declining in September 2007 and rebounded in November 2008. However, the inflation indicator did not slide until May 2008, and started to recover in August 2009. The analysis in Table 6-8 and the time difference analysis show that the average lag of CPI variation against money supply was 8 months. However, since the time for the money supply indicator to change was later than the promulgation time of monetary policies, the actual lag might be longer than 8 months. The pre-crisis lag was about 10 months.

Table 6-8 Peak and Valley Analysis of Money Supply and CPI Before and After the Financial Crisis

Money Supply (year-on-year growth of the month)	CPI (year-on-year growth of the month)
2007-08 (peak)	2008-04 (peak)
2008-11 (valley)	2009-07 (valley)
2009-11 (peak)	
Analysis result: The peak is 8 months ahead, and the valley is 8 months ahead.	

6.4.3 Expansion of Local Government Debt

Local government financing vehicles (LGFVs) are the financing corporations set up by local governments through the appropriation of land, stock, fees or government debt. The corporations must meet standard assets and cash flow requirements, and may receive fiscal subsidies when necessary to achieve the goal of taking over funds from all sides, which will be used in municipal construction, public utilities, real estate development and so on.

Since the reform and opening up to the outside world, the acceleration of industrialization and urbanization has been calling for more construction-oriented local financing. From the 1990s on, some local governments started to organize financing corporations and gradually formed their debt on a certain scale. Before the financial crisis broke out, the size of local government financing platform loans was relatively limited and the existing institutional problems did not attract attention.

In early 2009, to cope with the financial crisis, the People's Bank of China and the China Banking Regulatory Commission (CBRC) jointly released *Guiding Opinions on Further Adjusting the Credit Structure to Promote the Rapid yet Steady Development of the National Economy*, saying "it is also necessary to encourage the local governments with conditions to set up investment and financing vehicles and issue such financing instruments as corporate bonds and mid-term bills so as to diversify the channels for raising funds in support of centrally-funded projects". Since the central government allows and encourages local governments to borrow a lot from banks to fund their infrastructure spending, the provincial, city and county level governments, using their credit and finance as loan collateral, actively set up a huge number of local financing vehicles. It is estimated that the total sum of vehicles reached 8000. With the support of an easy monetary policy and the trust of bank regulators, local governments obtained huge amounts of funding from the banks. Such local government financing vehicles have played an important role in mitigating the impact of the international financial crisis and ensuring the sound development of local economies.

According to the estimates by China International Capital Corporation Limited (CICC) [13] the LGFV loan balance (excluding negotiable instruments) of financial institutions by the end of 2009 totaled RMB7.2 trillion , making up 18% of total loans. Of the newly-increased credit in 2009, as much as RMB3.7 trillion of loans flowed into various LGFVs, accounting for nearly 40% of total loans for the whole year and 51% of LGFV's total loan balance. Figure 6-13 shows the administrative level and geographical distribution of LGFV loan balance 2009.

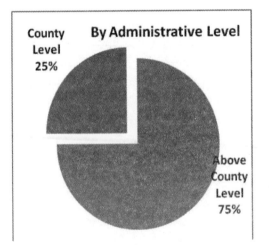

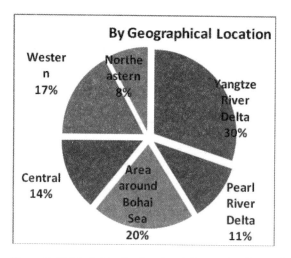

Figure 6-13 Administrative Level and Geographical Distribution of LGFV Loan Balance 2009

We can see from Figure 6-13 that nearly a quarter of the loans to LGFVs by financial institutions flowed into the county-level units. In terms of regional distribution, the Yangtze River Delta and the Area around the Bohai Sea occupied half of the total loans. However, data from the People's Bank of China showed that of the RMB8 trillion credit by the end of August 2009, the financing obtained by the 4 municipalities directly under the Central Government through LGFVs had already reached RMB1 trillion.

Figure 6-14 shows the proportion of loan balance for bank financing to total loans 2009. Since the major provider of county-level local government financing vehicle is the China Development Bank, the proportion of its loan balance reached 68.7%, the highest among all banks providing funds to LGFV. Meanwhile, the loans to government financing vehicles by 14 domestic listed banks occupied 50% of total loans in 2009.

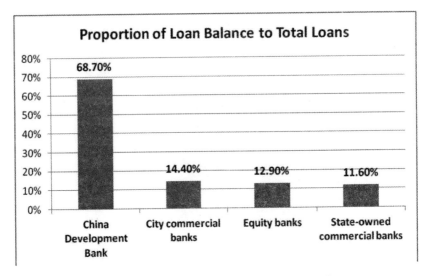

Figure 6-14 Proportion of Loan Balance for Bank Financing to Total Loans 2009

(Note: The loans from China Development Bank, city commercial banks and equity banks are Capital Construction Loans. Data source: report from China International Capital Corporation Limited)

According to the *Auditing Work Report on the Execution of the Central Budgets for 2009 and Other State Revenues and Expenditures* issued by the National Audit Office on June 23, 2010, 18 provincial, 16 city and 36 county-level governments that were audited had accumulated debts of RMB 2.79 trillion by the end of 2009. The indebted local governments had repayment obligations of approximately RMB1.8 trillion, 64.5% of the total debt. Obligations under bond accounted for 11.8% of the total, reaching RMB0.33 trillion and obligations to render assistance made up the last 23.7% , standing at RMB0.66 trillion. The percentage of debt balances over fiscal income last year was more than 100 percent in 7 provinces, 10 cities and 14 counties, with the highest reaching 364.8%. These indebted regions repaid capital and interest worth RMB274.546 billion via new lending in 2009, accounting for 48% of the total amount of capital and interest repayment, indicating these regions' inability to repay debt through fiscal income. This reflects the fact that excessive debt of local governments, most of which were medium and long-term debt, had exceeded their abilities of repayment through fiscal income. According to CBRC statistics, as of June 2010, debt incurred by the local government financing vehicles amounted to RMB7.66 trillion; in addition, the bond market data shows that as of June 2010, the city construction investment bond (including medium-term notes and short-term financing securities) amounted to RMB488.25 billion , together with the RMB267 billion local government bonds issued by the Ministry of Finance, the calculable total debt released by local governments exceeded RMB8.42 trillion. [14] To prevent debt default, the CBRC plans to liquidate RMB3 trillion of local government debt within the third quarter of 2011, and the losses incurred will be assumed by the Central Government and state-owned banks.

I pointed out, early in November 2009, that the swelling local government debt must be taken seriously. The U.S. "subprime" was to issue loans to individuals having difficulties in paying back, and "China's subprime" might be the lending to local governments unable to repay debt, which would also increase financial risks and bring considerable risks and potential danger to the overall economy and its long-term development [15]. Some scholars played down the local government debt problem with a firm belief that the Central Government's fiscal strength could render adequate support. However, if the central budget bails out local governments by repaying debt for them, the other spending on social security and people's welfare will definitely be impaired. In addition, it is highly probable that a part of the debt unable to be paid back by local governments might turn into non-performing loans for the banks, which increases financial risk. Some local governments, under repayment pressure, would certainly sell state-owned assets such as land at a high price or raise taxes, which would handicap the sound development of China's economy.

Quite a number of local government financing vehicles have played an admittedly important role in fighting against the financial crisis in 2009, but the excessive debt problem must not be ignored. Fortunately the local government debt bubble has aroused the close concern of the Central Government. Currently the regulators are sorting out the debts by local government financing vehicles, which is conducive to regulating existing debt and allaying debt crisis pressure. Moreover, such measures of tightening regulation play the role of curbing excessive borrowing by local governments. First, the local government financing vehicles only undertaking public welfare project financing and mainly relying on fiscal funds to repay debt are no longer allowed to engage in financing, so the financing entity for local governments will be limited; second, the public-welfare assets are not allowed to be injected as a sort of capital into local financing vehicles, so the asset size for local government financing vehicles will be restrained to a large extent, with lower financing capabilities; third, local finance is not allowed to be used as collateral for financing, which will also erode the financing abilities of local government. In general, these regulation requirements are conducive to both existing-debt regulation and future-debt expansion, exerting tighter control over local government debt risk. In this process, the regulation must be reasonably exerted to prevent the occurrence of uncompleted projects resulting from the "broken link" of follow-up investment when the over-hasty restriction in the short term fails to provide an alternative channel for funds.

Bigger risks in the fictitious economy

Guided by an easy monetary policy, a huge number of credit funds flew into the fields of the fictitious economy such as the real estate and stock markets. *The Statistical Report 2009 on Investment Direction of the Loans from Financial Institutions*, issued by the People's Bank of China in early 2010, shows that in 2009, the increment of real estate development loan from major financial institutions, rural cooperative financial institutions and urban credit cooperatives totaled RMB576.4 billion; increment in individual consumer housing loans reached RMB1.4 trillion. However, according to the China Economic Information Network, among real estate investment funds in 2009, domestic loans reached RMB 1.13 trillion. Adding the RMB1.4 trillion housing loans, we could work out a figure as big as RMB2.53 trillion flowing into the real estate market, accounting for 25% of the total loan increment in 2009.

The stock market in 2009 was even more vibrant than 2007, the widely-recognized "golden time" when the stock market approached madness and the accumulated stock transaction volume reached RMB46.06 trillion. In 2009, however, against the background of the international financial crisis, the stock transaction volume totaled 53.60 trillion, 7.54 trillion more than that in the "golden time". The stock market touched bottom by the end of 2008, and the Central Government rolled out an economic stimulus package, facilitating the economic recovery of 2009. The interaction of such factors might have triggered expectation of stock index rise and attracted more funds into the stock market. This, however, does not fully explain the stock market prosperity of 2009. We believe that against the background of an easy monetary policy, excessive liquidity might have been one of the most important causes.

The procedures of analyzing the impact of excessive liquidity on the stock market are as follows. First, calculate the amount of net capital inflow to the stock market ; second, set up an econometric model for the pre-October 2010 data (featuring a tightening monetary policy) to analyze the relationship between the stock index and the net inflow to the stock market without credit fund influence; third, apply the econometric model mentioned in the second step to calculate the amount of net inflow to the stock market without credit fund influence after November 2008; finally, calculate the net inflow to the stock market with credit fund influence (see first step) minus the figure without credit fund influence (see third step) to get the amount of credit funds flowing into the stock market.

Net inflow to the stock market:

$$\text{NCI}_t = \sum_{i=1}^{n} K_i(P_{it} - P_{it-1})$$

NCI_t symbolizes the net inflow at the t period; there are altogether n kinds of stock; K_i symbolizes the trading volume of the i stock at the t period; P_{it} symbolizes the price of the i stock at the t period; P_{it-1} symbolizes the price of the i stock at the t-1 period.

If we assume the stock deal structure of each month is the same, namely, the trading volume of the stocks can be calculated by using a potentially standard measurement unit (It must be specified that such an assumption of the same monthly deal structure is a little too rigorous since the actual conditions are far more complicated), the net inflow to the stock market of this month will be:

Trading volume of this month *(Trading amount of this month/ Trading volume of this month - Trading amount of last month / Trading volume of last month)

By adopting the above-mentioned method, this report calculated the monthly net inflow to the stock market from February 2001 to May 2010. The net inflow was RMB3.83 trillion in 2007 and RMB2.61 trillion in 2009. The new outflow in 2008 was RMB1.32 trillion. It can be seen that despite the financial crisis, the fund reserve of the stock market by the end of 2009 was still RMB1.29 trillion more than at the end of 2007.

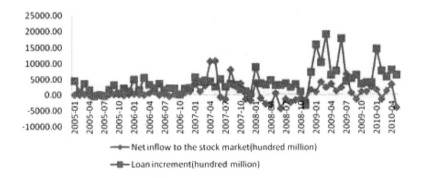

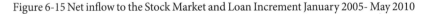

Figure 6-15 Net inflow to the Stock Market and Loan Increment January 2005- May 2010

In 2009 the monthly net inflow to the stock market had a similar trend in relation to the monthly loan increment, though with a lag of a month as shown in Figure 6-15. Then net inflow was concentrated in the first half of the year, amounting to RMB2.08 trillion from February to July 2009 and RMB0.4 trillion from August to December. It was the same with the loan increment in 2009, totaling RMB7.76 trillion in the first half of 2009 and only RMB2.80 trillion in the second half. It can be seen that the monthly net inflow to the stock market bears some relationship with monthly loan increment, but there does exist a one-month lag in the growth of the two figures because loans could not flow directly into the stock market, but had to undergo some sort of turnover and packaging after the enterprises obtained them.

In the first half of 2009 the huge amount of credit fund into the stock market aroused enormous worries from all social circles as well as the regulators. In the second half of 2009, China Banking Regulatory Commission (CBRC) successively formulated *The Interim Measures for the Administration of Fixed Asset Loans, Guidelines on Project Financing, Interim Measures for the Administration of Working Capital Loans* and *Interim Measures for the Administration of the Basic Data of Individual Credit Information* (called *"three sets of measures and one set of guidelines" on the new loan regulations*) to enhance the management of where the credit went. With tightening regulation on credit funds, the amount of loan increment dropped substantially, and part of the credit funds were squeezed out of the stock market.

For most of the time before October 2008, against the background of a tightening monetary policy, the credit funds into the stock market were so limited that they could even be ignored. But during the bull market period from January to September 2007, loans increase dramatically, and part of them may have flowed into the stock market. To use an econometric model to estimate the impact of the stock index on the net inflow to the stock market without the influence of the credit funds, we must take out the data from January to September 2007.

Considering the data availability, we chose the monthly data of August 2005 to December 2006 and from October 2007 to October 2008 to organize the econometric model on the relationship between the stock index and the net inflow to the stock market without credit fund influence. The explained variable is net capital in the stock market (symbolized by NĆ), and the explanatory variables include the lag phase of net capital inflow to the stock market and the Hushen 300 Index (symbolized by HS300). NC and HS300 are both stationary sequences (Table 6-9), which are co-integrated and may be regressed by using OLS. Based on Akaike and Schwarz Criteria, the optimum lag was set at 2.

In November 2008, the Central Government formulated economic stimulus policies, and resorted to an easy monetary policy. The loan increment in December of the same year was RMB732.355 billion, and the impact of credit funds on the stock market might have appeared in that month. Therefore, the starting time could be December 2008 if we analyze the impact of credit funds on the stock market.

Based on the NC and HS300 econometric model (Table 6-10), we can get the estimated net inflow to the stock market December 2008-May 2010 without credit fund influence, as shown in Figure 6-16. The net inflow with or without credit fund influence basically share the same trend in variations, with the latter reaching RMB1.352264 trillion from December 2008 to September 2009, and RMB0.655247 trillion from September to December 2009.

Table 6-9 NC and HS300 Unit Root Test

Variable	ADF Statistic	PRO	Test Format (c, t, k)	Conclusion
NC	-6.6894	0.0000	(c,t,1)	Stationary
HS300	-3.3877	0.0715	(c,t,5)	Stationary

Table 6-10 NC and HS300 Regression Result

Variable	Regression Coefficient	Standard Deviation	T Statistic	Prob.
SH300	2.8804	0.5789	4.9757	0.0000
SH300(-1)	1.6447	0.6277	2.6202	0.0147
SH300(-2)	-4.3250	0.5622	-7.6931	0.0000
R²	0.720191	AdjR²	0.697806	
DW Statistic	2.036387	Akaike Criteria	16.70041	
Sample Size	28	Schwarz Criteria	16.84314	

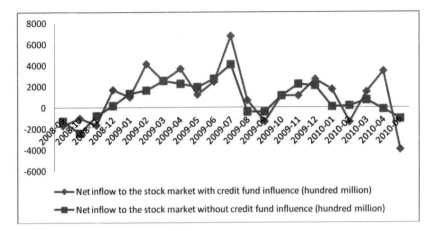

Figure 6-16 Estimated Net Inflow to the Stock Market, October 2008- May 2010 (hundred million).

The estimated net inflow to the stock market with credit fund influence was RMB2.284110 trillion from December 2008 to September 2009, and RMB0.496604 trillion from October to December 2009. By deducting the net inflow without credit fund influence (of the same period), we arrive at the amount of credit funds entering the stock market.

From December 2008 to September 2009, the net inflow of credit funds into the stock market totaled RMB0.931846 trillion, and the net outflow was RMB0.158643 trillion from September to December 2009, which might be the funds extruded from the stock market as a result of tightening control by the regulators. To neutralize each other, an estimated RMB0.773203 trillion credit fund remained in the stock market by the end of 2009.

A huge number of credit funds flowing into the stock market would spur the stock index and attract more individual investors and hot money. If without large scale credit issuance, the fund inventory of the 2009 stock market affected by the financial crisis was at most the equivalent of the 2007 level, the "golden time" for the Chinese stock market. Therefore, based on the fact that there were RMB1.29 trillion more funds in 2009 than 2007, and deducting the RMB0.773203 trillion credit funds remaining by the end of 2009, we can infer that there was RMB0.5168 trillion's worth of hot money in the stock market.

To summarize, a maximum of RMB930 billion credit funds flowed into the stock market, forcing up the stock index and attracting approximately RMB520 billion of hot money, creating a vibrant stock market in the first half of 2009 against the background of the financial crisis.

Based on above analysis we can see the credit funds flowing into the real estate market in 2009 reached RMB2.5 trillion, accounting for 25% of the total credit fund; the credit funds flowing into the stock market in disguised forms reached RMB0.78 trillion at the highest, but about RMB0.15 trillion's worth of funds were withdrawn from the market in the second half of 2009.

The injection of credit funds into the real estate and stock markets helped part of the huge liquidity created by an easy monetary policy to be absorbed by the fictitious economy, which might have postponed a CPI rise to some extent, but this part of liquidity was destined to be released into the real economy eventually, bringing about tremendous inflationary pressure. Analysis indicates that the soaring prices of some agricultural products in 2010 were precisely due to the retreat of funds from the fictitious economy to the agricultural market. Consequently, the inflow of credit funds into the fictitious economy may produce inflation risks and increasing the difficulties in economic regulation.

The injection of credit funds into the real estate and stock markets will directly cause an asset price bubble and push up market expectation of inflation, increasing economic operation risks and regulation difficulties. A huge number of credit funds flowed into the real estate market, forcing up the real estate prices of 2009 and even evolving into entire insanity by breaking away from the economic fundamentals. Meanwhile, the credit funds flowing into the real estate and stock markets brought enormous risks to banks by increasing the pressure on the control of non-performing loans. According to the *Annual Report of China Banking Regulatory Association 2009,* by the end of 2009, the real estate loan balance for banking institutions reached RMB7.33 trillion, growing 38.1% on a year-to-year basis and accounting for 17.2% of the credit balance. It can be said that the real estate industry and banking have become bound together due to very close connections.

A large quantity of credit funds flowing into the real estate market exacerbated the complexity and arduousness of real estate market regulation. The crazy market sales of 2009 and the huge credit fund flowing into the market led to over-abundant capital in the real estate market which underwent regulation in April 2010. Although the trend of excessive price hikes for some cities was curbed, the housing price for the real estate market as a whole remained strong. On the other hand, once the price drops substantially, non-prudential behavior in individual housing mortgage loans might be exacerbated and the risk chain effect for real estate development might reappear, increasing potential credit risks. As one of the pillar industries, the real estate industry undoubtedly facilitates economic growth, and a persistent regulation of the market will lead to declining investment, which might affect the economic growth rate. All of these factors provided the real estate market regulation policy-makers with a dilemma by making the process much more difficult.

More difficulties in promoting energy consumption and emission reduction

Applying the CGE-based energy-environment-economy model, we made a simulation analysis on the impact of the financial crisis countermeasures on China's promotion of energy conservation and emission reduction.

The simulated result shows that the total energy consumption in 2015 under normal, laissez-faire and response circumstances is 4.25 billion, 4.02 billion and 4.26 billion Mtce respectively. The figure for CO_2 emission is 8.37 billion, 8.02 billion and 8.42 billion tons respectively, as shown in Figure 6-17 and 6-18. Among others, the CO_2 emission by the high-energy-consuming sectors such as Thermal power production supply, Manufacture and processing of ferrous metals, Transport, storage, post and telecommunications, Manufacture of raw chemical materials and chemical products, Manufacturing of cement, lime and gypsum, Heating power production supply, Construction, Petroleum and processing of nuclear fuel, as well as Manufacture of other nonmetallic minerals accounted for about 83% (Table 6-11).

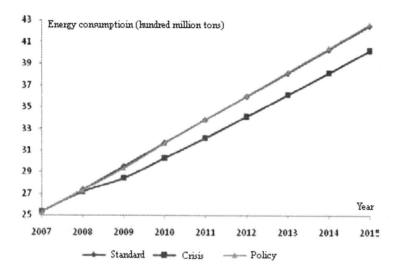

Figure 6-17 Energy Consumption under Different Circumstances

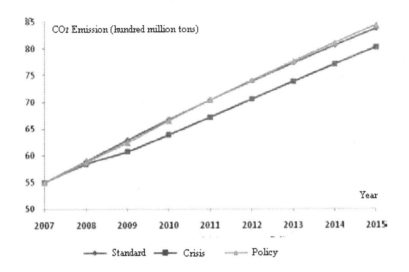

Figure 6-18 CO$_2$ Emission under Different Circumstances

Table 6-11 CO$_2$ Emission of High-Energy-Consuming Industries

(Unit: hundred million tons)

	Normal	Laissez-faire	Response
Thermal power production supply	34.21	32.90	34.50
Manufacture and processing of ferrous metals	13.19	12.97	13.43
Transport, storage, post and telecommunications	7.24	6.82	7.26
Manufacture of raw chemical materials and chemical products	4.14	4.03	4.19
Manufacturing of cement, lime and gypsum	3.39	3.48	3.50
Heating power production supply	3.04	2.87	3.04
Construction	1.12	1.09	1.14

Petroleum and processing of nuclear fuel	1.09	1.02	1.10
Manufacture of other nonmetallic minerals	1.03	1.02	1.06
Manufacture of glass and glass product	0.84	0.81	0.85
Total	69.29	67.01	70.06
Proportion to total emission (%)	82.83	83.59	83.20

With the increase of total factor productivity, the intensity of energy consumption and CO_2 emission fell gradually but the extent varies under different circumstances. Under normal circumstance, calculated by the prices in 2007 (the same below), the energy consumption per RMB10,000 GDP drops from 0.93 Mtce in 2007 to 0.81 Mtce in 2015, and the CO_2 emission per RMB10,000 GDP falls from 2.02 tons in 2007 to 1.59 tons in 2015, down by 13.2% and 21.2% respectively, as shown in Figure 6-19 and 6-20. Under laissez-faire circumstance, the decline of productivity leads to rising energy consumption and CO_2 emission. The energy consumption and CO_2 emission per RMB10,000 GDP in 2015 are 0.84 Mtce and 1.68 Mtce (Table 6-12), 9.8% and 17.1% lower than 2007 respectively. Under response circumstance, though the total energy consumption and total CO_2 emission are less than that under normal circumstance, the decline rate of energy consumption and CO_2 emission slows down. The energy consumption and CO_2 emission per RMB10,000 GDP in 2015 are 0.83 Mtce and 1.63 Mtce, 11.6% and 19.4% lower than 2007 respectively.

The simulated result shows that the energy consumption in 2010 under normal, laissez-faire and response circumstances declined by 11.1%, 9.1% and 11.2% compared with 2005. The figure for CO_2 emission was 15.1%, 13.1% and 15.4%. According to the GDP and energy consumption data issued by the National Bureau of Statistics, which was calculated based on unified caliber (due to changes in energy statistical caliber in 2008) the energy consumption of 2005-2008 decreased by

10.64%, and by 3% in 2008-2009, far from reaching the goal of 20% for the Eleventh Five-Year Plan period. The situation for energy consumption and emission reduction in 2010 was difficult, and without effective measures, it was not possible to attain the goal for the Eleventh Five-Year Plan period.

During the Twelfth Five-Year plan period, the decline rate of energy consumption in 2010 under normal, laissez-faire and response circumstances was 8.5%, 7.0% and 6.64% respectively. The figure for CO_2 emission was 14.4%, 12.0% and 12.1% respectively. Thanks to the substitution among energies, the decline rate of energy consumption was lower than that of CO_2 emission. Since energy consumption and CO_2 emission had a substantial rise in 2009, leading to bigger base numbers for 2010 and the highest decline rate of energy consumption and CO_2 emission.

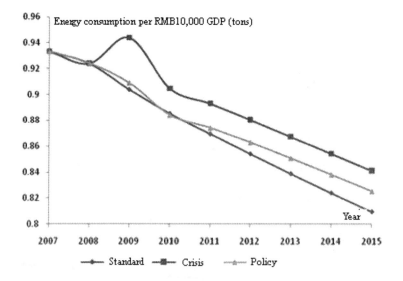

Figure 6-19 Energy Consumption per RMB10,000 GDP under Different Circumstances

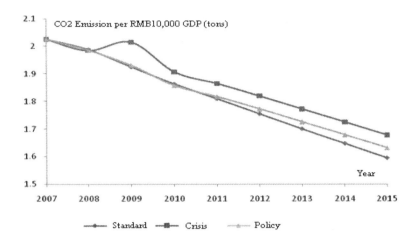

Figure 6-20 CO_2 Emission per RMB10,000 GDP under Different Circumstances

To sum up, the investment-led countermeasures against the crisis brought about rises in energy consumption and CO_2 emission, complicating China's energy conservation and emission reduction task by missing the government's goal during both the "Eleventh Five-Year Plan" period and the "Twelfth Five-Year Plan" period.

Table 6-12 Annual Decline Rate of Energy Consumption and CO_2 Emission per RMB10,000 GDP under Different Circumstances (%)

		2008	2009	2010	2011	2012	2013	2014	2015
Energy Consumption per 10, 000 Yuan GDP	Normal	1.02	2.15	2.05	1.76	1.77	1.78	1.77	1.74
	Laissez-faire	1.00	-2.17	4.16	1.29	1.39	1.47	1.52	1.54
	Response	0.98	1.64	2.72	1.11	1.29	1.41	1.48	1.52
CO_2 Emission per 10, 000 Yuan GDP	Normal	1.83	3.18	3.19	2.90	3.01	3.09	3.14	3.16
	Laissez-faire	2.00	-1.54	5.34	2.25	2.43	2.57	2.67	2.73
	Response	1.98	2.73	3.83	2.17	2.43	2.62	2.74	2.82

Summary

1. The simulation analysis of the normal circumstance (no occurrence of financial crisis), laissez-faire circumstance (no countermeasures against the crisis) and response circumstance (positive countermeasures against the financial crisis) indicates that China's countermeasures against the financial crisis effectively mitigated the impact of declining external demand, raising 6.7 percentage points of GDP growth rate in 2009, increasing 8.53 million jobs to ensure sustained yet steady economic growth and achieved the expected result of ensuring growth, promoting employment and improving people's livelihood. There were, however, negative effects of bigger risks in economic performance, slower transformation of economic growth pattern and more difficulties in energy conservation and emission reduction.

2. Inflation expectation and bigger risks for financial assets made the macroeconomic regulation more difficult; the economic stimulus package is faced with a dilemma in choosing the exit time. It is estimated that RMB2.5 trillion and RMB0.93 trillion in credit funds flowed into the real estate market and the stock market. The fictitious economy absorbed huge liquidity, creating transient borrowed prosperity in the real estate market and the stock market, postponing inflation but increasing the risk for financial assets. Too much liquidity in the real estate market also placed the real estate market regulation starting in April 2010 into a difficult situation. Part of the credit funds went into local government financing vehicles, and their excessive debt brought new risks and hidden dangers to the macro economy.

3. In 2010 real estate market regulation resulted in decreasing investment in the market, which may create new difficulties for related industries and the macro economy as a whole. Potential risks of overcapacity were far from removed. The energy conservation and emission reduction goals during the Eleventh and Twelfth Five-Year Plan period became even more difficult to achieve.

7.

Lessons from the U.S. Financial Crisis

After the outbreak of the subprime loan crisis, domestic and foreign experts and insiders in the economic arena put forward different ideas, trying to summarize the experience and lessons to be learnt. Many of the ideas are marvelous, but there are also misunderstandings. Based on a careful study of the reasons and development of the American financial crisis and combining that with the Chinese situation, we have analyzed and pondered over it, drawing the following conclusions.

The fictitious economy should not develop without the real economy

The main part of the fictitious economy is established with the economic activities based on credit system. It was born from real economy and relies on it. However, the fictitious economy has an important effect on the real economy in that it can facilitate or constrain its development. Therefore, we need to understand the relation between the two and take full notice on the double-edged effect of fictitious economy. As a result, the two of them will have a coordinated development.

The earliest development of the fictitious economy can be traced back to the business lending practice between individuals. For example, A is in urgent need of capital to purchase raw materials or commodities, but he does not have sufficient money. B happens to have some idle money. A then borrows a certain amount of money from B and promises to return the money and interest within a fixed period of time. Through such practice, A gets the right to use the money and will make a profit from real economic activity which is paid for with the borrowed capital. At the same time, B maintains the ownership of the money by IOU and the right to claim the money and interest when the loan is due. The IOU of B is the rudiment of the fictitious economy. It appreciates in the cycle of borrowing and repaying. In this process, B doesn't engage in any real economic activity, but he earns money through fictitious economic practice. Therefore, the first stage of fictitious economy development is the capitalization of idle money. In other words, idle money becomes capital which can bring interest. After that, the development of the fictitious economy goes through the following stages: the socialization of interest-bearing capital, the marketization of securities, the internationalization of financial markets, and the current financial integration [1].

Since the 1980s, firstly, the interdependence among nations and financial liberalization have been greatly increased along with economic globalization. Secondly, when the U.S. dollar was separated from the gold standard, a floating exchange rate system was formed, financial innovation was enhanced and the size of the fictitious economy began expanding. Thirdly, due to the development of information technology, fictitious capital increased its speed of flotation and volume in the financial market. These three factors have facilitated the communication among different financial markets and have strengthened the tie between domestic and international financial market. The mutual influence on both sides is increasing as well. In a word, a slight change of one part may lead to the change of the whole body [2].

Because of the strong connection between the fictitious and the real economy, the risks in the real economic system will be transferred to the fictitious economy and cause instability. The risks may include product backlog, bankruptcy etc. On the other hand, the risk in the fictitious economic system will also impact the real economy, and these risks include a fall in the stock index, a sharp decrease in housing prices, an increase in bad debts of banks, and a large depreciation of currency.

Even though fictitious economic activity doesn't create social value directly, it will accelerate the flow of capital, optimize resource allocation, improve investment efficiency, lower cost of deals, and influence public expectation. Ultimately, it will facilitate the development of the real economy. Finance has become the core of today's economic activities. The real economy cannot function without the fictitious economy. Therefore, if we consider the real economy as the hardware in terms of the economic system, then the fictitious economy is the software.

As the world entered the 21st century, the fictitious economy was expanding rapidly in developed nations like the U.S.. From 2000 to 2007, the nominal size of the fictitious economy in the world (including stock market value, outstanding amount of bonds, outstanding amount of derivatives contract value, counted at the price in that year) grew 4.5 times larger (from $163 trillion to $728 trillion), with an annual increase rate of 24%. World nominal GDP only grew 1.8 times larger (from $32 trillion to $56 trillion), with an annual growth rate of 9%.

From 2000 to 2007, the value of the world stock market grew twice as large(from $32.2 trillion to $64.6 trillion), with a yearly increase rate of 10.4%. The outstanding amount of bonds got 2.2 times larger (from $35.5 trillion to $77.9 billion), with an annual growth rate of 11.9%. The outstanding derivatives contract value grew 6.2 times larger (from $95.2 trillion to $585.9 trillion), with an annual growth rate of 29.8%. In conclusion, the swift expansion of the fictitious economy in the first seven years of this century was mainly due to the development of financial derivatives.

As stated in the first chapter of this book, from 2001 to 2007, American institutions and individuals invested large amount of capital (even borrowed money to invest) in the fictitious economy, especially in MBS, CDO and CDS which were closely connected with housing mortgage loans. Such investment brought a much higher rate of return than practice in real economy. Many American financial institutions were keen about issuing all kinds of financial derivatives to make a huge profit. At the same time, they didn't even think about investment in the real economy. Some financial institutions in developed nations followed the American example. The consequence of isolation from the real economy was finally exposed in 2008 and caused the American crisis and even the world financial crisis. We should learn a serious lesson from that and develop the fictitious and real economies in coordination.

Government should adopt cautious and proper interference in the housing market

A house is an expensive daily necessity and an investment tool which can maintain its value. The property industry is a pillar of the national economy. It affects the quality of people's life and generates demand for production materials, commodities and service. The development of the property industry has close ties with the financial system. Both the house buyer and developer have to rely on bank loans. Therefore, the price of houses and the interest rate of mortgage loans have become major factors influencing the housing market. According to economic theory, when house prices increase, the supply of houses will increase and then the demand from buyers will decrease and vice versa. When interest rate drops, both the supply and demand will increase. With a certain housing price and interest rate of loan, a balance will be reached. This is the basic function of resource allocation that the "invisible hand" plays in the housing market.

Dialectics points out that everything in the world is in constant change and there is no absolute balance, but a relative one. The emerging science of complexity says: even though every house buyer independently decides when, how large, where and what quality to buy, his decision will be affected by others and the larger environment. Buyers, developers, banks and government interact with each other and will organize themselves to promote the market in a certain direction. The market may seem to be disordered from a micro and short-term perspective, but from the macro point of view and in the long run, it has a

278

certain direction, such that the market can advance in waves and rise in spirals. This is the reason for the cyclical fluctuation of housing market.

Housing is in closely connected with the interests of individuals. In order to fulfill the responsibility of protecting social equality, government has to adopt macro-control. However, the interference must be cautious and appropriate, otherwise, there will be serious consequences. In order to gain the support of lower-income groups (especially African Americans and Latin Americans) and develop the economy, both the Clinton and Bush Administrations took a high rate of house ownership as an important target. Therefore, the American government favored housing mortgage loans (including support for Fannie Mae and Freddie Mac) and lowered the qualification requirement for loans [3]. And this is the reason for the subprime crisis. Some American Senators boasted that, "we should help all blue collar workers to have their own house." Consequently, the Department of Housing and Urban Development (HUD) stipulated a policy of housing mortgage loans which encouraged subprime loans. HUD instructed Fannie Mae and Freddie Mac to issue more loans to lower-income families and "affordable" mortgage loans to minority groups. It also suggested that the two companies should take the investment of billions of dollars in subprime loans as a public product [4]. In 1996, HUD instructed the two that 42% of the mortgage loans should go to families whose income was lower than the regional median, a target that was raised to 50% in 2000 and 52% in 2005 [5].

With the prosperity of the American housing market and the promotion of Fannie Mae and Freddie Mac, banks started to lend money to more and more high-risk borrowers, even including illegal immigrants, tempted by the prospect of high profits from high-risk loans. These loans could be divided into three types. The first was subprime loans of the type "No Income, No Job and (no) Assets" or NINJA. The second was adjustable rate mortgages, or ARM. Borrowers of this type needed to pay only the interest in the first few years, but if the interest rate rose after those years, they would face a high pressure of repayment. The third type is an optional loan which allows the borrowers to choose the amount of monthly payment. However, any unpaid interests will be counted as principal. Of the above mentioned three types, ARM loans accounted for about 80%. At the same time, the average difference between subprime loans and normal loans was reduced to 280 basis points in 2001 and 130 in 2007. Furthermore, mortgage underwriting was loosened. Among all the subprime loans in 2007, 40% were issued automatically, so there was insufficient assessment and record [6], all of which brought about the prosperity of the subprime loan market. Between 1994 and 2003, the issuance rate of subprime loans grew almost ten times larger, with an annual growth rate as high as 25% [7]. The total amount increased from $35 billion in 1994 (5% of all loans) to $160 billion in 1999 (13% of all loans) and then even to $600 billion in 2006 (20% of all loans).

Usually when the price of houses rise, demand should go down, which will contain the increasing price. However, the American government had adopted policies to support subprime loans and the Fed was carrying out a low interest rate policy, with the consequence that the American housing market was booming from 2002 on. Many low-income families received loans to purchase houses that they could not afford and they became trapped. Such policies also encouraged investment and speculation in the housing sector. In 2005, 28% of houses were purchased for investment. Another 12% were purchased for vacation use. Speculators leveraged transactions on existing homes and future housing, thus adding more risks to the market.

After the subprime crisis broke out in 2007, many low-income families couldn't fulfill the high-interest monthly payment through refinancing and were forced to default and lost their houses to foreclosure. In September 2008, the price of houses in America dropped by more than 20%, compared with the 2007 mid-term peak. Many borrowers now had zero or even negative net assets. By March 2008, it is estimated that the houses of 8.8 million borrowers (10.8% of the total) had become negative assets, statistics that grew to 12 million in 2008, leading to mass defaults by borrowers and many frauds. In 2007, the sales of new houses dropped by 28.4% which was the largest fall since 1980 (23.1%) [8]. By the end of 2007, about 4 million existing homes were waiting to be bought, 2.9 million of which were vacant [9].

The rising rate of mortgage loan default reduced the value of MBS, CDO and other securities, and as a result, weakened the net assets and financial situation of banks. Fannie Mae and Freddie Mac could not afford to service their debt (by June 30, 2008, their net assets were only $114 billion, while their loans for houses were $5.1 trillion, half of which were unpaid) and was taken over by the American government.

The subprime crisis triggered a global financial crisis and caused serious damage to other countries who thereby suffered great losses. We should learn the following lessons.

Firstly, government should not leave the problem of housing for low-income families to the market. Housing guarantee for low-income families is part of social equality. Market mechanisms cannot solve the problem. Government has the responsibility of building affordable houses and offering accommodation for families who are too poor to buy houses, and should also provide housing subsidy for households in difficulty. The main responsibility of government is to protect and do its best for low-income groups. Mechanisms should be constructed to stop disqualified people from taking advantage of subsidized houses which are public assets.

Secondly, government should not persuade and support middle-and-low-income families to buy houses. Middle-and-low-income families have unstable incomes and a poor capacity to withstand risk. Even though they buy houses with the encouragement and support of government, they have to save every penny to pay the loan. Once they fail to pay, the house will be taken away and put on auction. The beautiful dream of owning a house will become nightmare. Moreover, when the house price drops, their accumulated wealth will be diminished by the reduced value of their house.

Thirdly, government should not instruct commercial institutions to offer favorable loans to low-income families. It should be these commercial institutions that decide whether or not to issue the loan based on their own risk and trade cost.

In conclusion, when government is carrying out macro-control policy, it should respect the basic economic rules and carefully analyze the attitude and features of house buyers, developers, intermediaries, banks and other players. A balance of interests needs to be struck. In this way, policies will be launched at the right time and with appropriate effect [9-10].

Excessive debt is the culprit in undermining the stability of financial systems

The fictitious economy is a meta-stable system which has a dissipative structure. It has to exchange capital with the outer environment to maintain relative stability. Such a system can reach stability through self-organization. However, its stability is easily affected by a slight disturbance in the outer environment. When the stability of the system is damaged, it will move into a floating state and then, it will alternate between the stable and the floating state. From a macro perspective, such a system can be considered as stable in a certain area, in other words, regional stability. However, the instability of the system sometimes leads to dramatic change, even the collapse of the whole system. When the system collapses, it will either restore the meta-stable state through profound restructuring or come to an end. Usually, the stronger the inertia of the system is, the more unlikely it is to collapse [11].

There are many reasons which will lead to the meta-stable state of a fictitious economy. The fundamental cause is the inner instability of fictitious capital. When fictitious capital constantly expands with the support of a credit system, dangers of harming the credit system are formed. The instability of fictitious capital brings positive feedback in the fictitious economic system. For example, when certain financial assets are sold off, many more people will sell the same assets. This mutual influence between people is called positive feedback. It will have an amplification effect which will cause dramatic changes in the price of fictitious capital.

After WWII, America abandoned its traditional virtues and became a country that went after consumption. The consumption culture emphasizes satisfying the current demand. "Buy first and pay later" became a widely accepted principle [12]. Driven by this culture, the ratio of debt to disposable income in American families increased from 60% in 1974 to 77% in 1990, then on to 127% by the end of 2007 and even 134% in 2008. Wealth generated by the price rise of housing encouraged people to consume boldly and reduce saving. According to the Bureau of Economic Analysis, from 2005, more than 99.5% of American families' disposable income was spent or used to pay off interest. If we exclude most programs relating to self-ownership of houses, American household savings deposit has become negative since 1999. The spending has surpassed individual disposable income. In 2008, an ordinary American family had 13 credit cards, and 40% of American families had unpaid credit card debt. In 1970, it was only 6% [13].

In the first few years of the crisis, low interest rates and large amounts of capital inflow created a loose environment of credit loan which promoted sharp growth in the housing market and debt financing consumption. The basic reason for borrowers of excessive debt to maintain a meta-stable state is their capacity for repayment. The appreciation rate of borrowers' assets is required to be higher than the interest rate of the loan. This appreciation may come from pay rise, the value increase of the house or other fixed assets or profits from other investments. When all the sources of appreciation fail, the metastable state will be disrupted and borrowers may suffer default or even bankruptcy.

Financial institutions are the creditor and debtor at the same time. They are also the debtor to their investors. When borrowers go into default or bankruptcy, financial institutions have less inflow of capital and cannot make the agreed payment to their creditors. The meta-stable state is therefore destroyed and again bankruptcy may even occur. It is clear, therefore, that excessive debt will damage the stability of a financial system and cause financial crisis.

Consumption accounted for more than 70% of the American economy, so American families' excessive debt definitely led to large amounts of national debt. Between 1990 and 2004, the deficit in American current account increased by $650 billion, accounting for 5.8%

of GDP, up from 1.5%. In order to make up the deficit, the American government on the one hand issued national bonds to attract foreign capital and create a surplus in capital account; on the other hand, it took advantage of the international status of the American dollar to increase the amount of those dollars. When the financial crisis broke out, the American government had to use national wealth to inject capital into the financial system, in the hope of protecting the stability of the whole system. However, this would leave a hidden danger for the American financial system.

When a nation, bank or sovereign wealth fund is in excessive debt, it will have a sovereign debt crisis. To avoid default, government either has to borrow new debt to repay the old one (the cost of borrowing will then increase, for example, national bond will have a soaring yield), or it must sell national assets, or even restructure the debts (which is actually default in disguise). At the same time, it also has to cut government expenditure and public welfare. This is a difficult and painful process, during which the nation will suffer greatly. Therefore, an indebted government must strictly control fiscal deficit and the size of national bond. Additionally, it will need to monitor the debt of financial institutions and the sovereign wealth fund. Too much expectation of social welfare should be avoided.

Over-speculation in the financial derivatives market should be prevented

Financial innovation means all the creative changes in the financial sector which are driven by demand and interests. Financial innovation and financial supervision contain each other and promote each other. Financial institutions continuously pursue financial innovation for the purpose of getting rid of external and internal constraint, avoiding financial control, lowering trade cost, satisfying the preference of investors etc. Through innovation, efficiency can be improved and risk can be reduced by hedging. However, financial innovation will increase systematic risks, the possibility of market fluctuation and the business risk of financial institutions. Supervision is the lawful regulation and constraint carried out by financial authority on financial institutions and activities, and it should facilitate a legal and healthy development. Therefore, financial supervisors should pay close attention to financial innovation and adjust their measures in time to reduce the negative influence created by any risk from innovation. In the evolution of the subprime crisis into a global financial crisis, innovation played a crucial role. Based on the innovation, there developed a complicated relationship between institutions and individuals and a long chain was constructed by them. However, financial supervision was left to lag behind innovation.

A financial derivative is one kind of financial innovation. It aims at improving financial efficiency and hedging or spreading risk. However, it began to be used as a tool for speculation. Subprime loans led to the global financial crisis. One of the main reasons is that the American government did not prevent the excessive speculation of the derivative market through supervision.

In early 1990, large financial institutions on Wall Street securitized loans in the name of innovation. Their aim was not spreading risk, but pursuing profits. They designed and promoted derivatives which focused on the preferences of investors and ultimately formed a large market. Although, such measure will efficiently shift the risk of commercial banks and other loan institutions and provide high returns to investors, the existence and development of subprime loans lowered the quality of mortgage loans for MBSs and the quality of capital pool for CDOs. Both of them became toxic assets and were sold all over the world. The reasons include the misleading nature of government policy (encouragement of subprime loans), regulatory negligence (relaxation of scrutiny and acquiescence in the existence of unlisted entities), and misinformation by rating institutions (rating $3.2 trillion of subprime loan related MBS and CDO as AAA). In 2004, the ruling of the American Securities and Exchange Commission reduced the limit on the 10~15 investment bank leverage rate to enable them to issue more bonds. The income from selling bonds was spent on purchasing MBSs and CDOs. From

2004 to 2007, the top five American investment banks had a sharp increase in their leverage rate. In the accounting year of 2007, the debt exceeded $4.1 trillion, about 30% of American GDP in that year. It meant that the institutions would be more vulnerable when MBSs depreciated. Some financial institutions took advantage of the high leverage to issue and buy CDOs to gain high profits. Excessive speculation changed CDS from an insurance measure into a gambling speculation tool.

Excessive speculation created large bubbles in the financial market which maintained the meta-stable state with a high growth by relying on inflow of capital. If the credit system is damaged, investors will lose their confidence and bubbles will burst. Serious financial crisis will occur. The ignorance and bigger fool theory for financial derivatives (someone is a bigger fool than I am, so I can always withdraw at the highest point) prevented investors from withdrawing until the actual outbreak of the financial crisis which caused huge losses. From January 1, 2008 to October 11, the total value of the American stock market shrank from $20 trillion to $12 trillion. Markets in other countries had an average decline of about 40% [14].

We have established a dynamic game model of financial innovation and financial supervision in an environment of incomplete information. According to the model, when a nation is making financial supervision policy, it should take the following points into consideration: the risk preference of innovative institutions, the bearing capacity of the national economy, and the environment of the national economy. Based on this understanding, supervision policy should be devised with a balance between innovation and supervision. The combination of these two aspects is actually the Nash equilibrium solution obtained through the game between innovative institutions and supervisory institutions. It is a process of aggregation. By learning and interaction, the equilibrium solution can be reached, allowing the government to release policy signals based on certain economic targets to create a favorable situation which will be conducive to economic development through financial innovation and supervision.

Controlling inflation is not the only goal for the monetary policy of a central bank

Inflation is a monetary phenomenon. Currency is commonly considered as the media of exchange. In modern society, it includes notes and coins. Therefore, inflation means that the increase in the amount of currency surpasses the total growth of commodities and services, thus causing a sustained rise in prices. In other words, this is the process of currency depreciation.

A central bank, authorized by government, administrates currencies. It adjusts the supply of currency through its reserve rate, its discount rate, its open market operation and other monetary policy. As a result, inflation can be controlled within certain areas. Under the leadership of Greenspan and following economic theory, the Fed mainly paid attention to the inflation rate, rather than avoiding a property bubble, an Internet bubble or price bubbles of other assets. It usually took action when the bubbles had burst, trying to reduce the side effects to the economy without stopping the formation and expansion of other bubbles.

It should be understood that from the increase of money supply to CPI rise, there is a conduction period, usually 2~3 quarters. In addition, while the fictitious economy is expanding, if the increase of money supply is absorbed by the housing market and stock market, then there will be no inflation. Conversely, when the housing market and stock market drop, the released currency will flow into the real economy and inflation will occur. For example, from 2002, American house prices increased rapidly and the inflation rate was not high. Therefore, the Fed had the wrong impression that the interest rate could be lowered safely. Federal fund interest rate was lower than 2% between 2002 and 2004 which was the lowest recorded in the U.S. in the past 40 years. Between July 2003 and July 2004, the rate was even lower than 1%. It accelerated the formation of bubbles in the housing market. The obvious conclusion is that when the central bank uses monetary policy to cope with inflation, it should foresee the lag effect and pay attention to changes in asset price.

Similar problems have occurred in the adjustment of our monetary policy in recent years. In 2007, the American subprime crisis developed into a loan crisis and then a liquidity crisis. Its influence started to spread to other countries. Without adequate consideration of the international financial and economic crisis, in the first half of 2008, we adopted a tight monetary policy to prevent deterioration into inflation. Only after the outbreak of the Wall Street Financial Storm did China change its monetary policy to a moderately loose one in October 2008.

In conclusion, in the world of accelerating globalization, prices in any country will be affected by world commodity prices, such as oil and grain. In other words, imported inflation cannot be controlled by local government monetary policy. A tight monetary policy cannot stop imported inflation and may even have a negative effect.

Moral hazards in financial institutions and their staffs should be prevented

Financial institutions are the "factory" in the fictitious economic system. Through innovation, they produce all kinds of financial products which are sold to investors inside or outside the market. In many institutions, especially investment banks, the salaries and bonuses of staff are closely related to short-term performance. Therefore, they do not consider the healthy development of the company, but only the year-end bonus. In this financial system, from the brokers of mortgage loans to risk managers on Wall Street, people all tend to pursue short-term interest and neglect long-term responsibility. Most senior staff in banks are only concerned about a high rate of return on investment. They do not understand how a CDS and its financial tools work [15]. In order to obtain high profits, some institutions and their staff violate professional ethnics. They exaggerate benefits, hide risks and use other ways of cheating to lure investors to buy various kinds of financial derivatives.

The bonuses of investment banks staff is from the charges of the financial derivative that they have designed, not based on the performance of the product or the profits it made. Their bonus is paid by cash, not by stocks. Even if the derivatives do not perform well or even suffer loss, the bonus will not be withdrawn [16]. They benefit hugely from the adventure of a high leverage rate. In 2006, the executives on Wall Street had total bonuses of $23.9 billion. Richard Fuld Jr., CEO of Lehman Brothers, had an annual income as high as $344 million in 2007.

The fearless attitude of Wall Street executives also came from the confidence in government aid. The government wouldn't let these large financial institutions go bankrupt because of bad debts. One good example was that the Federal Reserve Bank of New York aided Long-Term Capital Management in 1998. The current financial crisis shows that executives have gained huge personal profits and left the loss from high risk to government and ultimately to the whole of society.

During the subprime crisis, some rating institutions played a sinister role. 90% of the income of rating companies is from the charges to issuers, and they have no legal responsibility for their ratings. Thus, staff in rating companies and security institutions may act in collusion. By giving a high rating to subprime derivatives, they exchanged judgment for illegal benefits. The fact that rating institutions lost their objectivity is another reason for financial crisis.

Reform of our financial system should be promoted

In the last three decades, along with reform and opening up, our financial reform has scored remarkable achievements. The reason for the relatively smaller effect of the current financial crisis on China is the government's supporting role for financial institutions and the confidence of the Chinese people in their government. Nevertheless, the financial system in China needs to be further developed. We basically do not have investment banks, rating institutions or financial derivatives. Our banks do not lack liquidity and the supervision is cautious, but we should also admit that there is a long way to go for financial reform in our country. Our overall international competitiveness is not strong enough. Despite being the No.1 trading country in the world, a big buyer and seller in the global market, we do not have enough say in the international financial market. It is imperative that financial innovation and supervision in our country be further enhanced.

Following the Wall Street financial storm, there are various opinions. Some are questioning the direction and pace of our financial reform. President Hu Jintao pointed out, "reform and opening up is a great new revolution. ... ... Its direction and path are correct. Its function and achievement should not be denied. Pause and retreat are not options. [17]" With the premise of economic and financial stability, we should follow Premier Wen Jiabao's requirement of balancing the relation between financial innovation and supervision, between the fictitious economy and the real economy and between saving and consumption [18]. We need to adhere to active and cautious financial reform, constantly promote financial services and improve financial efficiency and international competence.

Our financial reforms have the following three main directions [19].

Internationalization

Economic globalization is an irresistible historical trend. With its development, financial globalization is also under way. Regarding the trend, the features of financial globalization can be concluded as the following:

First, currency has become more fictitious and the exchange rate has become a game tool between governments. Since currency has shaken off the gold standard and gold exchange standard, its value does not have an objective measurement. In other words, it has been fictionalized to a large extent. Therefore, currency is issued based on the credit of countries, known as fiat money. Its value can be measured by its purchasing power in two markets, the domestic one and the international one. Domestic purchasing power can be measured by PPP while international purchasing power is mainly measured by exchange rate. The difference between these two purchasing powers has a close relation with the price of labor. If a country has no import trade, exchange rate has no influence on its domestic purchasing power. In contrast, if a country relies totally on imports, its domestic purchasing power will be decided by the exchange rate. Actually, any country in the world is somewhere between these two states. Thus, exchange rate cannot be decided solely by PPP. If all countries take global interests into consideration when deciding the exchange rate of their currencies, then Pareto Optimality can be obtained and everybody will benefit. Unfortunately, no country will take global interest as a priority, but only its own benefit. Therefore, exchange rate has become a policy game tool between countries.

It is generally agreed that the Plaza Accord and the Louvre Accord caused more than ten years of economic recession in Japan. When the Asian financial crisis broke out, the pressure on depreciating the RMB was quite intense. Today, the demand for appreciation of the RMB is equally strong. It means that exchange rate has become a game tool between governments. In this regard, our country has always adhered to the self-centered position and the principle of sovereignty. Even though we need to consider various other factors, exchange rate is a sovereign issue and we cannot simply follow the ideas of others.

The second feature is the increased size and pace of capital flow. Because of scientific and technological development, pushing one button can transfer trillions of dollars to thousands of miles away in no time.

The third feature is the integration of world financial markets, which means that the connection between financial markets is becoming closer and closer. One single part will affect the whole body. The Asian financial crisis started from the liquidity crisis in Thailand and its influence was felt worldwide. The American subprime crisis is affecting Europe and other regions and has even led to a world financial crisis.

The last feature is the development of financial innovation. After WWII, the European dollar was the starting point of financial innovation. In the following decades, financial innovations emerged in an endless stream and many financial derivatives were put forward. As a result, the outstanding amount of financial derivatives is more than ten times world GDP. So many derivatives dazzle people's eyes. It is important to prevent financial risk and avoid excessive investment in financial derivatives.

In the context of the integration of international finance, we have to improve our international financial competitiveness and adapt to the above features of financial globalization through reform. In the area of financial innovation, we do not have enough knowledge and have little experience, so we may be at a disadvantage in international competition. For example, we had the problems of the Zhuzhou Zinc Smelter, CAO, the central reserve of cotton and the central reserve of copper which caused great loss. Therefore, we need to carefully study and understand international financial products and their rules. At the same time, we should train talents with international vision and international financial management skills. Moreover, training and introduction of talents should be combined.

Marketization

To promote marketization, we need to first have a market-decided interest rate. Interest is the cost of capital. It depends on risks and trade cost. Therefore, we should have a market-decided interest rate, including the loan interest rate and deposit interest rate. There should be a floating scale based on risk and trade cost.

Secondly, we need a market exchange rate which reflects the ever changing international purchasing power. Our exchange rate system should be improved according to market demand, purchasing power and demand and supply relations.

Since July 2005, we have adopted a set of managed floating exchange rates. Up to now, the RMB has appreciated by 20%. However, this change did not fully follow the market rule. I think we need to allow the exchange rate to float in an administrated area. When exchange rate exceeds the target limit, central bank will carry out measures. Of course, the RMB will definitely go to free exchange. In 1996, we deregulated the current account, but a capital account has not been opened. Among the 43 accounts required by the IMF, 20 have been opened, but still need to be improved. It is firstly decided by our capacity of administration. Only when we can administrate properly, can we open it. Secondly, we need to choose an appropriate time when U.S. dollar, euro and Japanese yen are relatively weaker. To realize the free exchange of the RMB is a matter of time. Even if we don't have a timetable, it won't be long. When the RMB becomes one of the world currencies, we can say that our exchange rate system has fully merged into the market.

The third point about marketization is the need to constantly increase market participants. Currently, the state has majority shares in banks, security companies and insurance companies. Foreign investment and individual investors have very few shares. "36 Articles on Non-Public Economy" has clearly required that private capital should flow into medium and small financial institutions. More market participants will help complete our financial market. Of course, there are rules for participation from concern for national security. For example, currently we require that the percentage of foreign shares should be no more than 20% for a single bank and no more than 25% in total.

Systemization

First, finance and economy cannot be separated. We cannot talk about finance without mentioning economy. Finance belongs to the fictitious economy. However, its production, distribution, exchange and other activities are in the area of real economy. Problems in the fictitious economy can spread to the real economy and vice versa. The American government made great efforts to save the financial market, its purpose being to prevent the financial crisis from becoming an economic crisis. It was for this reason that the report of the 16th CPC Central Committee pointed out that we should correctly handle the relationship between the fictitious and the real economy.

Second, finance is a complete system. It is not an isolated entity. The securities market, stock market, loan market, insurance and futures intertwine with each other. Therefore, we should think systematically. We cannot only address the symptoms. In the long term, we should steadily promote mixed operation and comprehensive supervision, because only through comprehensive supervision, can we avoid comprehensive risk. Otherwise, supervisors will work separately. If the Chinese Securities Regulatory Commission (CSRC) only guarantees that the securities market has no problem, then risks will be transferred to the insurance market or the foreign exchange market. If the other two have any problem, they will affect the securities market.

Thirdly, we should build a multi-layered financial market with various types. The current securities market has a large size, but our loan market is not developed. It has its own features. The benefits of loan are smaller than that of stocks, but they are safer. An important reason for the American government to save Fannie Mae and Freddie Mac was to avoid their problem of repaying bonds. If there was problem, it would not only be a social problem, but also an international problem. The international credit of America would be affected, because the government has guaranteed the MBS issued by the two companies. We should develop our stock market, while developing a bond market, a foreign exchange market and a futures market. Financial futures could start with stock index futures. During their development, excessive speculation should be prevented to avoid risks. Institutional economics has a famous saying, "trade before system." No trade is done only after the system is complete. Through trade, problems are identified and the system can be gradually improved.

Fourthly, supervision should be systemized. The current supervision system of one bank and three commissions should have a coordinating institution. Systemized supervision should focus on the following points: first, that the purpose of supervision is to protect people's interests and to be people-centered. Unfortunately, when problems occur, supervisors usually think about protecting the interests of institutions, because banks, insurance companies and securities companies are state-owned. Their loss is the loss of the country. On the other hand, national wealth and people's wealth are related to each other. As the saying goes, when large river has water, the small river will also be full. It seems that only when the nation is wealthy, can the people be rich. Conversely, if there is no water in the small river, the large river will dry too. So rich people and strong country are related. We must protect the interests of the people because it is also protection for the national interest.

Supervision should start with information disclosure. Supervision should first be transparent. Information disclosure means the financial consumers' (investors, account holders, policy holders etc.) right to be informed. When information is disclosed, analysis can be carried out and problems identified, publicized and dealt with. Supervisors are not responsible for the fluctuations of the market, but need to provide true, complete and timely information.

Lastly, service should be systemized. Insurance companies, security companies, banks and other financial institutions should establish the sense of service. The financial sector is part of the service industry, so it should have high standards and constantly improve the quality of its service.

Reflecting on this financial crisis, we should see the double-edged effects of fictitious capital and the fictitious economy on the real economy. On one hand, the fictitious economy can drive real economic development. On the other hand, over-expansion of the fictitious economy and fictitious capital can harm the real economy. The risks in the fictitious economy can spread to the real economy. So we should carefully think about, analyze and conclude the lessons of this crisis, improve our confidence and push forward our financial reform under the leadership of central government.

8.

"Six Balances" and Scientific Development

In 2001, the issue of "Global Imbalance" was raised by Maurice Obstfeld and Kenneth Rogoff in their research report [1]. Rodrigo de Rato, the IMF Managing Director, enumerated at the G20 Finance Ministers and Central Bank Governors Meeting held on October 15-16, 2005, the major manifestations of global economic imbalance: the huge U.S. current account deficit and soaring growth of debt, the trade surpluses of Japan, China and other emerging Asian economies against the U.S., as well as the rising trade surplus of oil-producing nations including Russia and Middle East countries. He warned that such imbalances might handicap the sustainable development of the global economy and threaten world prosperity. De Rato saw mounting risks facing the global economy, with trade protectionism leading them [2]. "Global Imbalance" has become an issue of great concern ever since, especially after the outbreak of the U.S. financial crisis. Some even see it, the China-U.S. trade imbalance in particular, as one of the major causes of the financial crisis in the U.S. [3].

If we merely interpret economic imbalance as disequilibrium in trade, namely, one party suffering a massive trade deficit while the other enjoys a substantial surplus, then it already existed in the trade between the West and the Middle East countries during the oil crisis period of the late 1960s and early 1970s, as well as the trade between the U.S. and Japan and West Germany at the beginning of the 1980s.

However, this time the imbalance occurs in an environment of economic globalization, and is therefore more significant in both depth and breadth.

The world economy, for the first several years of the 21st century, maintained a good momentum for development, featuring steady growth, low inflation, prosperous international trade and accelerated international capital flows, so that some economists took global economic imbalance as an inevitable result of the backward finance of the emerging economies, and even as a "win-win" phenomenon. On one hand, the imbalance enabled the savings of developing countries to be secure and fluid; on the other, it allowed developed countries to borrow on more relaxed conditions [4,5]. The biggest defect of such a stance was to assume the capital markets of developed countries to be fully equipped to sustain a rising leverage ratio. The fact was, however, that soaring housing prices, regular account deficits and decreasing leverage ratios already foretold a financial and economic crisis, just like a turbulent wind preceding a mountain storm.

In the final analysis, economic imbalance is nothing but a superficial indicator, and the root cause lies within certain countries themselves. As Lorenzo Bini Smaghi points out, "The external imbalance often indicates and even heralds internal imbalance" [6]. It should be seen that balance is only temporary and relative, whereas imbalance can be perpetual and absolute. The world is in constant change, and interaction among countries could break down the old balance and bring about all sorts of changes.

"The Golden Mean", as one of the core values of ancient Chinese philosophy, emphasizes "the eclectic approach", and the concept of balance and limit. A higher and broader perspective is needed to reflect on global imbalance especially after the global financial crisis. That is why I put forward the idea of "Six Balances" at the annual conference of the 18th Pacific Economic Cooperation Council (PECC) held in Washington in May 2009 [7]. This Chapter aims to study the post-crisis situation and probe further into ways of keeping the "Six Balances".

Balance between savings and consumption

On March 10 and again on April 14, 2005, Ben Bernanke, then a member of the United States Federal Reserve made remarks on "The Global Saving Glut and the United States Current Account Deficit" [8,9], blaming the excessive savings of developing countries such as China for the U.S. regular account deficit. This view has often been quoted by researchers on global imbalance and the U.S. financial crisis, and has also been refuted by some scholars [10], arousing concerns about the savings rate and discussions on elements influencing it [11].

Barry Eichengreen has summarized the explanations of global imbalance into four categories. The first is the shortage of U.S. savings, recognizing the reduction of the U.S. national savings rate as an important factor in global and U.S. economic imbalance. The second is the New Economics perspective, namely that the high productivity of the U.S. attracts savings and investment from other countries. The third is excessive global savings, which prompt capital flow into and investment in the United States. The fourth category is Sino-U.S. interdependence, and this explanation blames China's export-oriented growth and under-valued RMB for the dramatic increase of U.S. imports. Eichengreen regards all four perspectives as one-sided explanations, similar to those of "the blind men and the elephant" (A Chinese idiom saying four blind men touch an elephant to figure out what it is like. Each one only touches a part of the elephant and claims that that describes the whole of the animal)[12].

Savings rate in a broad sense means the national savings rate, that is, the proportion of total savings, including residents, enterprises and the government, to the GDP of the same year. Savings rate in a narrower sense refers to residents' savings rate, namely, the percentage of savings to the residents' total disposable income.

Table 8-1 lists the national savings rate of China and other countries and regions in 1996 and 2007.

Table 8-1 National Savings Rate of China and other Countries and Regions

1996	The United States	France	Germany	Japan	South Korea	Chinese Taiwan	India	Chinese Mainland
Residents	5	10	11	11	14	13	16	19
Enterprises (Financial and Non-financial)	11	8	9	16	12	12	5	13
Government	1	0	-1	3	10	0	2	4
Total	17	17	20	30	35	26	23	36
2007	The United States	France	Germany	Japan	South Korea	Chinese Taiwan	India	Chinese Mainland
Residents	3	10	11	5	3	10	24	22
Enterprises (Financial and Non-financial)	11	7	10	21	14	19	9	18
Government	1	1	2	0	11	1	4	11
Total	14	19	24	26	29	30	38	51

(Quoted from a second source, "*China's Savings Rate and Its Long-term Trend*", Gao Hua Global Economic Research Report: 191st Issue, Gao Hua Global Economic Research Website, October 16, 2009).

It can be seen from the Table that China's national savings rate ranks the first, and is much higher than Western countries such as the U.S., France and Germany.

The "Rostovian take-off model" [13] identifies all societies, in their economic dimensions, as lying within one of five categories: the traditional society, the preconditions for take-off, the take-off, the drive to maturity, and the age of high mass-consumption. Entering the stage of take-off, a society requires a high savings rate to support the huge investment required for growth.

Figure 8-1 shows the proportion of final consumption, investment and net export to GDP (as calculated in the constant price of 1990).

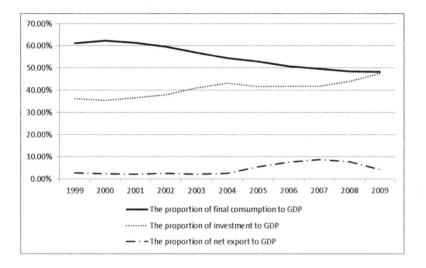

Figure 8-1 Proportion of Financial Consumption, Investment and Net Export to GDP (as calculated in the constant price of 1990)

(Data from *China Statistical Yearbook*)

It can be seen that since 2000 the proportion of China's investment to GDP has been rising whereas the final consumption dropped dramatically. Meanwhile, the capital formation rate (contribution rate of investment to economic growth, or so-called investment rate) went up to nearly 50%. It is evident that China's high savings rate lends support to the high investment rate, and has managed to sustain the rapid growth of its economy.

The structure of China's national savings rate is shown in Figure 8-2.

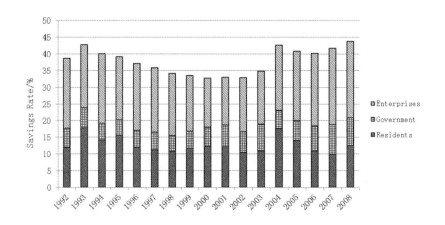

Figure 8-2 The Structure of China's National Savings Rate
(Data from *China Statistical Yearbook*)

We can see that the savings rates of the government sector and enterprises (including financial and non-financial sectors) grow at such a fast rate that the sum of the two equals the residential savings rate.

Some economists believe that the decrease in the U.S. national savings rate is due to the growing deficit of the federal government as well as the improved social security system which discourages residents from saving for risk prevention [14]. Some American scholars attribute the low savings rate to the financial deficit [15] or twin deficits (financial deficit and trade deficit) [16]. In fact, the major cause is American consumption of debt under the influence of consumerism after WWII. Furthermore, the capital inflow from developing countries including China enhances the liquidity of the U.S. financial market and facilitates Americans' consumption of debt. However, China's high savings rate is not the major cause of the imbalanced U.S. current account. What should have been considered was the ability to repay when a loan was raised, for this is a basic principle of financing.

In addition, U.S. fiscal and monetary policies also encourage people to raise a loan for their expenditures. Under such expansionary fiscal policy, the deficit of the U.S. government has been growing rapidly. Under a loose monetary policy, the interest rate dropped 13 times in three and a half years after 2001, and the federal funds rate decreased from 6.5% to 1% and kept going down for one year (July 2003 to July 2004). During that time, negative interest rate occurred and lasted for almost three years, which further stimulated Americans' consumption of debt. Consequently, China's high interest rate is not an excuse for U.S. monetary and fiscal authorities to evade their responsibility.

Our focus should be placed not only on the national savings rate, but also on the household savings rate. According to Keynes' economic theory, income is the major and basic determinant of savings, and the functions of consumption and saving are complementary. That is to say, one part of household income is for consumption, and the other for savings, but it is one-sided to consider only the influence of current income on consumption. According to the Life Cycle Hypothesis [17,18], income for life has more influence on savings than current income does. However, these two theories cannot fully explain the differences in people's saving behaviors.

Figure 8-3 shows the changes in household savings rates in China and the U.S. in the past 30 years.

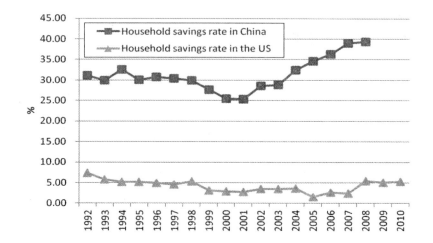

Figure 8-3 Household savings rates in China and the U.S.

(Note: U.S. household savings rate data comes from U.S. Department of Commerce. Bureau of Economic Analysis.

China's household savings rate is calculated.

Formula:

Household savings rate=aggregate savings (household sector)/disposable income (household sector)*100%

Note: Aggregate savings and disposable income data of household sector all come from the fund flow statement (barter) of each year's *China Statistical Yearbook*

This figure shows that China's household savings rate has remained continuously above 25% and in recent years has been up to almost 40%. Although the income of Americans is much higher than that of Chinese, the savings rate in the U.S. is lower, only about 5%, and was even below 5% from 1999 to 2007.

From the perspective of the fictitious economy, household income is an economic flow, one part for consumption and the rest becoming the increment of household wealth. To maintain or increase the value of their wealth, people tend to change it into tangible assets (house property, gold, etc.) or intangible assets (deposit receipts, stocks, bonds, etc.). In the future, the assets will be for consumption, left to family members or donated to social communities. Therefore, savings rate is determined by the people's choice between consumption and wealth accumulation. Factors influencing people's saving behaviors include traditional and cultural factors existing for a long time, as well as social economic factors in the present situation.

Influenced by traditional culture, Chinese people value "rearing sons for help in old age and storing up grains against famine"; they save present income for future use. In contrast, Americans are influenced by consumerism and advocate "buy now, repay later"; they borrow tomorrow's money to spend today. This is the root cause of the gap between the savings rates in China and the U.S. In addition, Chinese family members are more dependent on each other. When their children grow up and begin to work, Chinese parents will still give them financial aid for their wedding and house purchase. In the U.S., however, parents have finished their obligations when their children grow up and start to work. Therefore, Chinese people have a stronger intention to leave their wealth to their descendants. Some researchers even believe that China's rising national savings rate has been partly due to its gender imbalance. With fewer females, males are in a much more difficult situation to find a spouse, thus putting more pressure on parents to save money. In this regard, the savings rate in China will probably keep rising[19].

Furthermore, there are other reasons for China's high savings rate. First, the national income has increased rapidly with the development of China's economy. Second, China's social security system remains to be improved. People have to save money for self-protection. Third, Chinese people worry about the risks of investment, especially direct investment. Though saving money is not very profitable, it is safer because banks are state-owned and will not fail to pay the interest. Thus Chinese consumption behaviors are less influenced by interest rate reduction. Fourth, China has a low overall consumption level: its people are frugal and do not spend too much [20].

It thus seems clear that Americans' excessive consumption is a major cause of the financial crisis in the U.S. However, Chinese oversaving also has negative impacts on China's economy[21]. Because of the high savings rate, a large amount of money is deposited in the banks, and banks want to lend the money, thus making easy credit terms. As a result, people are enjoying low cost and easy loans from the banks and tend to use the loans for investment (personal consumption credit only accounts for 15% of the total), leading to high demand for investment in China. Due to the low domestic consumption capacity, the goods produced with the investment will be exported. China's low labor cost and the fierce competition among exporters make Chinese export products very competitive in the foreign market, resulting in the increasing Sino-U.S. trade surplus and growth in China's foreign reserves. A large part of China's foreign reserves is used to buy U.S. national debt, thus increasing the liquidity of the U.S. financial market.

Entering the 21st century, U.S. trade deficit and foreign loans have been increasing. As early as 2003, the G7 summit and Dubai Conference all urged the United States to take measures to increase national savings. But due to the fact that the U.S. could raise loans at a very low interest rate, the government continued borrowing money on a large scale. The increase rate of foreign debt exceeded that of the trade deficit. By the end of 2006, the foreign debt of the United States had reached 6% of its GDP, but the savings rate had been kept at a very low level. Since 2008 in the aftermath of the financial crisis, the foreign debt of the U.S. has been growing rapidly, now accounting for 30% of its GDP. Since the U.S. dollar is the major reserve currency in the world, the United States can print paper money to repay its debt and transfer its inflation to other countries, but this will result in serious problems. Therefore, it is fundamental that U.S. take measures to increase revenues and reduce expenditures, increase export, and put restrictions on residents' excessive consumption of debt, in order to bring the savings rate back to the level of the 1980s (about 10%).

China should make efforts to increase its imports and reduce the trade surplus to 4% of its GDP or even less. At the same time, it should consume its high foreign reserves through investment abroad or other means to keep the foreign reserves down to 20% of GDP. Moreover, the government should encourage people to spend more and lower the savings rate to an appropriate level, about 30%, in the following ten years.

Balance between domestic and foreign demands

Foreign trade is another pillar of China's rapid economic development in recent years, especially after China entered the WTO in 2001. Figure 8-4 shows the changes in China's total import and export volume and its trade surplus.

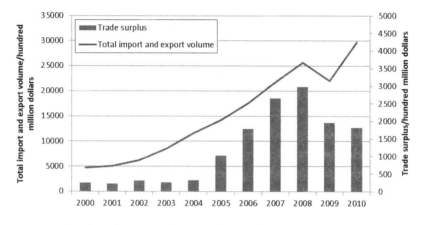

Figure 8-4 China's total import and export volume and trade surplus
(Source: *China Statistical Yearbook*)

The figure shows that when China's economy kept a double-digit growth from 2003 to 2007, China's foreign trade volume and trade surplus also increased rapidly. During that time, net exports contributed as much as 20% to China's economic development. China has many export-oriented enterprises, and processing trade in which orders and markets are both abroad takes half of its foreign trade.

After the U.S. financial crisis, the economy went into recession and demands declined in the U.S., Europe, and Japan, the three largest trading partners of China, which damaged China's foreign trade in 2009 and hindered its economic development. In 2009, the contribution rate of net export to China's economic growth was 39.1% negative. In 2010, the number was 7.9% positive, but this was still far below the level before the financial crisis.

Since this global financial crisis, the developed economies still have a long way to go to their recovery. This is also a "de-leveraging" process, in which governments, financial institutions, enterprises, and families should gradually lower their debt ratio and change the present operation and consumption patterns, which are so reliant on high liabilities. The leverage ratio in the U.S. financial sector has now dropped from 26% at the beginning of 2008 to the present 20.6%. The de-leveraging in developed countries will lead to contraction in government expenditure, bank loans, enterprise investment, and family consumption, reducing China's foreign demand. Under such circumstances, some export-oriented enterprises are facing production capacity surplus or even bankruptcy. Moreover, some developed countries have increased protectionism and thus have more trade conflicts with China, which further reduces China's net export. Only the expansion of domestic demand can offset the negative impacts of the de-leveraging in developed countries on China's economy. A balance should therefore be established between domestic and foreign demands.

Domestic demand can be expanded through investment, and more importantly, consumption. Investment can stimulate demand for means of production, creating more job opportunities, and a part of investment will be transferred into consumption through salaries. Nevertheless, too much reliance on investment to stimulate domestic demand will result in production capacity surplus, overstocked products, low productivity, and recurring pollution. Sustainable development cannot be achieved in this way. In the long run, we should focus on consumption to expand domestic demand. Only when people pay for more goods and services can we effectively stimulate the economy. In the 12th "Five-Year Plan" period, the Chinese government prioritized the transformation of the economic development pattern and further expansion of domestic demand, especially household consumption demand.

To stimulate household consumption demand, we first need to

improve people's consumption capacity, including both salary income and property income. In this regard, some important institutional arrangements should be made. First, people's income should grow in step with economic growth. I pointed out that this is the primary standard for economic development as early as the beginning of 2007 [21]. Wealth is made by the people, but for a long time in China has been allocated in the order of the country, the enterprises, and only then the individuals. Thus the people's income grows more slowly than the economy. Figure 8-5 compares the rural and urban disposable income (at constant prices) with GDP and CPI from 2000.

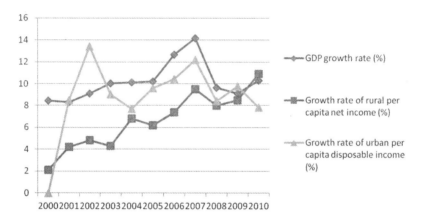

Figure 8-5 Comparison between the rural and urban disposable income (at constant prices), GDP and CPI
(Source: *China Statistical Yearbook*)

The 12th "Five-Year Plan" clearly set the goal that people's income should grow in step with economic development, and that per capita urban disposable income and rural net income should surpass the average annual economic growth goal (7%).

To increase people's purchasing power, personal income tax threshold should be raised appropriately (the threshold has been adjusted from RMB 2000 to 3500 Yuan recently) and the minimum living standard should be improved. Besides, we should promote credit consumption. Now, individual consumption loan only accounts for 15% of the total loan in China, while the figure can be 60% to 70% for developed countries. Thus, there is still a long way to go to promote credit consumption and to change the traditional idea that prefers saving to consumption.

Second, people's wage should be adjusted with the inflation rate. China's inflation rate has been growing since the end of 2009 and reached 6.5% in July, 2011. Inflation can reduce people's actual income, bringing troubles to people with low income. Therefore, a system adjusting people's wage with the inflation rate should be established. At present in provinces, cities, and autonomous regions in China, the minimum wage is generally linked with CPI, but a system encompassing wage and inflation rate is yet to be set up. In addition, a high inflation rate can cause a negative interest rate, causing savings to decrease in value. Therefore, we should increase the interest rate or adopt inflation-proof bank savings.

Third, remuneration should grow in pace with labor productivity. With the development of our economy, we should gradually increase the proportion of labor in primary distribution, and the essential measure to achieve this is to make remuneration grow in pace with labor productivity. It is reported that China is the largest manufacturing country in the world, but the manufacturing sector's labor productivity in China is less than one third of that in the United States (180,000 USD per capita a year). Consequently, many medium and large-scale manufacturing enterprises have introduced foreign technology and equipment. To improve labor productivity, we should stimulate innovation in systems, management, and technology, encourage staff and workers to actively participate, and optimize utilization of the technology and equipment introduced.

The next step is to improve the social security system to stimulate consumption. With improved social security, people will no longer hesitate to spend money on other things because of the high cost of medical care, selecting a school, renting or purchasing a house.

Last, enterprises should produce products people desire, making them willing to spend their money. On one hand, enterprises should develop new cost-effective products through innovation to attract consumers, like Apple. On the other hand, they should improve the quality of products as well as after-sale service to establish business reputation and create famous brands in China and even throughout the world.

Besides expanding domestic demand, we should also make efforts to develop and improve our foreign trade to adjust to the new situation after the financial crisis. This will also help cope with the imbalance of the global economy. Figure 8-6 shows the basic conditions of foreign trade in China and the U.S. since 2000.

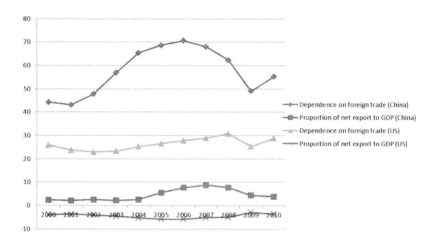

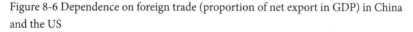

Figure 8-6 Dependence on foreign trade (proportion of net export in GDP) in China and the US

From the above figure, China should make some changes in the development of foreign trade.

First, the key point of China's foreign trade should be changed from quantity to quality. As a developing country, China should not have high dependence on foreign trade (proportion of net export to GDP) and should gradually lower it to less than 40%.

Next is to increase import to an appropriate level and try to maintain an overall balance with little surplus. An overlarge trade surplus will rapidly increase China's foreign reserves as well as related risks and will also cause trade frictions. Therefore, net export should be reduced to less than 4% of GDP.

The final need is to improve China's foreign trade structure. First, processing trade should be reduced to avoid the risks associated with changes in market demand. Second, export goods should be changed from low-end products to high-end ones. With the increasing labor cost in China, labor intensive products have lost their competitive advantages. Third, export destinations should be transferred from the traditional ones like the United States and Europe, to South-East Asia, Latin America, and Africa.

Balance between financial innovation and regulation

Financial innovation includes designing financial derivatives under the principles of financial engineering, and also refers to the narrow sense of financial innovation in foreign countries. When developing financial derivatives, China should also take into consideration the innovation of financial regulation and financial management. On the one hand, transaction of financial derivatives can enhance financial efficiency, stimulate the fictitious economy, and promote the development of the real economy. On the other hand, financial innovation can also lead to excessive speculation, which, without strict regulation, will have a deadly impact on the economy. Following the outbreak of the financial crisis, some in China strongly oppose the development of financial derivatives. According to them, China can survive this crisis only because it does not develop financial derivatives. This seems one-sided to me. It is true that China's financial derivatives are not developed, and thus China does not have subordinated debt or poisonous financial products and does not buy many poisonous financial products from foreign countries. However, it is also because of the lack of financial innovation that China has a very low financial efficiency. For example, China has foreign reserves of over 3 trillion USD but mainly uses them to buy foreign bonds, which means lending money to foreign investors and helping them make more returns. The return rate is about 8%, and we can receive the interest of 4% but at the same time have to take the risk of foreign currency depreciation. From this perspective, without the development of financial derivatives, China can neither improve its international financial competitiveness nor have a say in the international financial market, which does not match its financial capacity. In my view, we should draw a lesson from this global financial crisis, keep up with the times and steadily promote the development of financial derivatives.

Financial innovation, which continually develops throughout the game with regulators, brings opportunities to investors and poses challenges to currency regulators. Financial innovation began with the euro-dollar. After the Second World War, a large quantity of dollars should have been introduced into Europe according to the Marshall Plan. However, U.S. financial regulations put restrictions on deposit reserve, and foreign loans of U.S. banks and transnational corporations. The eurodollar, however, was neither limited by the U.S. bank interest rate nor financial regulations in the host countries. Under such circumstances, U.S. banks had to find a way out through innovation. Thus the Negotiable Order of Withdrawal (NOW) was developed to avoid the regulation that the checking account should not have any interest. The Negotiable Certificate of Deposit (CD) was designed to avoid the restriction on the highest interest rate, and the Repurchase Agreement (REPO) to avoid deposit reserve and insurance premium. Regulators will make new regulations to restrict and supervise new financial products, while at the same time, financial institutions will find new ways to avoid those regulations. This is the game between the two sides.

Consequently, financial innovation comes along and develops with new products and improvement of regulation. In recent years, financial innovation has been developing fast. According to the data from BIC, outstanding financial derivatives totaled 95 trillion USD at the end of 2000, and increased to 600 trillion USD at the end of 2010. The United States was the country with the largest volume of transaction, which, in the absence of appropriate regulation, finally led to the financial crisis.

The main responsibility of financial regulators is to create an open, equal, and fair market and ensure the legitimate rights and interests of investors. Market trend is determined by market forces, the game between bulls and bears. Too much intervention may not function well, but it is important to make the market open, equal, and fair, and to avoid false information, internal transaction, and malicious manipulation of the market, so as to ensure the legitimate investors' rights and interests. This is easier said than done. In fact, China's regulators are in a dilemma. Most listed companies in China are state-owned, so if problems arise, special help will be extended to them. Furthermore, the securities companies are also state-owned, and therefore, regulators tend to have a bias towards those securities companies and listed companies rather than investors. Finally, even the fines for listed companies are levied by the national government, and thus the rights and interests of investors cannot be ensured. In addition to ensuring legitimate rights, financial regulation should itself be legitimate, reasonable, appropriate, and effective. First, there should be related laws. The Securities Law has been revised, which in my view has been very successful. It has laid the foundation and left some space for the development of financing bonds, financial derivatives, and Privately Offered Funds. But laws are not easy to make. I have been working in the NPC for ten years and find that making laws is a long process of compromise and coordination of the interests of different parties. In this case, we can make some regulations first. Economic laws are there to adjust the behavior of market entities, the basic relations between the entities, and the competition order of the market, but there is a well-known saying in institutional economics, "transaction ahead of regulation", which means that transactions should not be conducted only after regulations are perfectly made. Generally, transactions come first, and then the regulations are gradually improved. We should not develop financial derivatives only after the regulations are improved; instead, we should accumulate experience through development, and improve and standardize the market step by step.

To be reasonable regulation must satisfy four requirements. First, regulation should be carried out in a scientific manner. Some believe that financial derivatives are profiteering, and that any industry with a profit margin higher than the average is a profiteering industry. This seems to be reasonable but in fact is wrong. Average profit margin is calculated from the profit margin of all industries. Therefore, if we assume that any industry with a profit margin higher than the average is a profiteering industry, then half of those industries belong to that group. In addition, risk is directly proportional to return; higher risks come with higher returns. Financial derivatives may bring huge profits, but can also lead to great losses. Thus the mathematical expectation value of the return rate is not so high. Secondly, to be reasonable also means to abide by rules which cannot be easily changed. Regulators should comply with their obligations and not easily break their original promises just because of a change in their leaders.

Thirdly, financial regulation should be appropriate, which is also very important. Since the financial crisis, the whole world has put greater emphasis on the role of the government in regulation. However, China's market economy is not yet sufficiently developed, and the government often plays a big role in the market, while in other countries, governments seldom intervene, a situation which needs to be improved. Nevertheless, inappropriate intensification of regulation in China will result in further restriction. Moreover, regulation has its cost. In the pose-Enron era, the United States passed the Sarbanes-Oxley Act in 2002 to strengthen the internal control of listed companies, including accounting, auditing, corporate governance, etc. With stricter regulation, accountants have to produce more financial statements, which will raise the total cost. It is said that the cost for a listed company was increased by 700 to 800 USD per hour. For a period, the United States even faced a shortage of accountants. China's Ministry of Finance, Securities Regulatory Commission, National Audit Office, Banking Regulatory Commission, and Insurance Regulatory Commission issued Basic Internal Control Norms for Enterprises on June 23, 2008, and Implementation Guidelines for Enterprise Internal Control on April 26, 2010. According to preliminary estimation, if the nearly 2000 listed companies in the stock markets of Shanghai and Shenzhen and their branches are all equipped with internal control offices, and we assume that each headquarter needs 3 to 5 professional internal control staff members, and each branch needs about 10, then we will produce more than 50,000 job opportunities, and over 1 million potential ones. This proves that regulation does have a cost, and it is therefore imperative that it be appropriate. Stricter regulation is not necessarily good.

The final consideration is effectiveness. To give full play to the regulatory measures in the market, the key is to change people's standard of behavior and expectations; otherwise the measures may become ineffective. A market may seem disordered, but in fact, the interaction between participants and the influence of participants and the external environment on each other will organize the market and promote its development. Regulation is an external force, which cannot reach its goals without changing people's standard of behavior and expectations. For example, the bull stock market keeps going up though the stamp tax is increased, and the bear market keeps falling though the stamp tax is reduced. That's because these measures do not change people's expectations concerning the ups and downs of the stock market. According to dialectics, internal cause is the basis, and external cause is the condition for changes. Only through internal cause can the external cause exert its function. Therefore, only when we change the internal cause, the standard of behavior and expectations of market participants, can we take effective regulatory measures. Excessive and inadequate regulation will both have serious consequences.

I believe financial regulation should start with comprehensive, accurate, and timely information disclosure for analysis and handling. If information disclosure is not true or accurate, the analysis will not make any sense.

At the early stage of the market, it is necessary to have stricter regulation because of lack of experience. Thus we should make efforts to prevent risks and excessive speculation. With the development of the market, regulation can be relaxed to some extent.

Before its opening, I made a visit to the China Financial Futures Exchange and gave my advice. I argued that it was necessary to take stricter measures, like higher margin rate and higher demands for investors because without experience too many participants would create chaos. However, strict regulation would have a negative impact on the active market, and thus should be relaxed with the development of that market, so that more people will take part, making the market more active. For example, with ten years of practice, Hong Kong Hang Seng Index launched the Mini Hang Seng Index of 10 HKD one point, which has attracted many investors. Therefore, regulation should be appropriately improved according to the maturity level of the market and the accumulation of regulatory experience.

Balance between fictitious economy and real economy

The fictitious economy is an economic activity model which is the opposite of the real economy in all ways, including its structure and evolution. It describes the circulation of fictitious capital on financial platforms, and the relations involved in the process.

The fictitious economy can be represented by the total value of stock markets, the balance of bonds, and the contract balance of outstanding financial derivatives. Entering the 21st century, foreign fictitious economy has been developing rapidly. Figure 8-7 shows the changes in the scale of world fictitious economy and GDP since 2000.

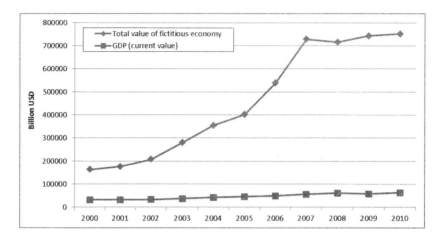

Figure 8-7 Changes of the scale of world fictitious economy and GDP since 2000
(Source: Bank for International Settlements and World Bank)

The figure shows that the scale of world fictitious economy was 160 trillion USD at the end of 2000, 5 times the GDP of that year. It increased to 752 trillion USD by the end of 2010, 12 times the GDP that year. Currently, the daily trading volume in world foreign exchange markets alone is as much as 4 trillion USD, over 50 times the real total of international trade per day. The scale is too large. It is estimated that after this financial crisis, the scale of foreign fictitious economy will contract to some extent; it should keep a balance with the real economy.

The fictitious economy comes from and relies on the real economy. The two are closely connected and have impacts on each other. The real economic system refers to the production, allocation, exchange, and consumption of material goods, which can be regarded as the circulatory movement of capital. For example, if capitalists in the production sector gain funds from the financial market, they use those funds as their capital to purchase (exchange for) equipment, raw materials, and labor for production. Then the products become commodities in the circulation process, and funds again in the process of sales (exchange). This is the cycle of entity capital. Capitalists use the funds they get back (including profits) to repay the principal and interest provided in the contract and put an end to the loan relationship, which is the cycle of fictitious capital.

Since fictitious and real economic systems are closely connected, the risks produced in the real economic system, like excessive inventory, or enterprise bankruptcy, will influence and destabilize the fictitious economic system. Risks in the fictitious economic system, like huge drops in the share index, a plunge in property prices, a sharp increase of banks' bad debts, or great depreciation of currency, will also have serious negative impacts on the real economy. Now, finance is the core of the modern economy, so the real economy cannot function well without a healthy fictitious economic system. Therefore, if we regard the real economy as the hardware of the economic system, then the fictitious economy is the software.

The fictitious economy can improve the structure and effectiveness of the real economy, but can also increase its risks and hamper its function. Thus the two should be balanced. At present, the CAS Research Center on Fictitious Economy and Data Science is conducting research to establish an accounting system for the fictitious economy and thus construct a fictitious economic index.

Figure 8-8 shows the changes of the scale of China's fictitious economy and GDP since 2000.

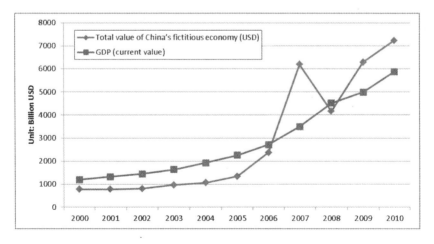

Figure 8-8 Changes of the scale of China's fictitious economy and GDP since 2000
(Source: *China Statistical Yearbook*)

The figure shows that at present, the scale of China's fictitious economy is small with relatively slow development. The fictitious economy was only 0.65 of GDP at the end of 2000, and increased to only 1.23 times GDP in 2010. In 2007, the scale of the fictitious economy was at its largest, but still less than twice GDP. Accordingly, China's leverage rate is low. Therefore, we should establish and improve China's stock markets, bond markets, foreign exchange markets, financial derivatives markets at all levels, promote the reform of commercial banks so that qualified securities companies can change into investment banks, and increase the leverage rate to steadily develop China's fictitious economy and facilitate its active influence on the real economy.

Balance between economic growth and sustainable development

As a developing country, China has taken economic construction as its central task since the reform and opening-up and has set development as the primary task in recent years. With rapid economic growth over more than 30 years, China's per capita GDP has surpassed 4000 USD, reaching the level of middle-income countries. Due to these achievements, some government officials falsely believe that economic growth equals development, thus simply pursuing fast economic growth. Their enthusiasm for GDP is simply a mistaken idea: "everything for growth; growth is everything", is the criticism by institutional economists. Some other economists also believe that China's annual economic growth rate should not be less than 8%, "China's economy is better overheated than cold." With such ideas, China' total fixed assets investment accounts for an increasingly large part of GDP, as shown in Figure 8-9.

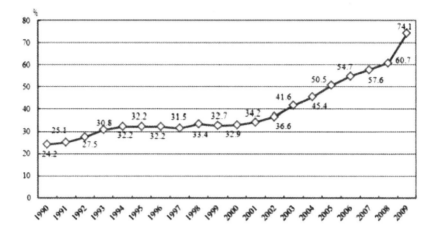

Figure 8-9 Proportion of fixed assets investment to GDP (fixed price in 1990)
   (Source: *China Statistical Yearbook*)

The figure shows that the proportion of social fixed assets investment to GDP has been increasing since 2001, from 32.9% in 2000 to 74.1% in 2010. This results in overheated investment, production capacity surplus, overstocked products, low investment efficiency, as well as social and environmental problems.

After the financial crisis, China should not seek such a fast economic growth rate and instead should attach more importance to problems other than the traditional national income account. While still taking GDP as the major indicator of economic development, we should pay more attention to non-market economic activities (for example activities in the sectors of education, scientific research, charities, etc.) and environmental costs, the costs to resources, ecology, and the environment in the process of economic growth. According to preliminary estimation, in 2005, China's environmental cost was 13.5% of GDP, but the GDP growth that year was only 10.4%. If we keep going like this, the environmental consequences will be passed down to our descendants. Therefore, we should change our system of economic development and strive for sustainable development.

Sustainable development is an active concept of environmental protection, which can satisfy people's current needs but will not impair future development capacity for our descendants. Human society is developing and will not go back to a primitive one, but we should seek development at the least possible expense. After the agricultural society lasting thousands of years and the industrial society of the last few hundred years, we are now embracing the knowledge society, which requires a new culture emphasizing resource saving, environmental protection, ecological improvement, and harmony between man and nature.

The focus now of sustainable development should be on a green economy [22]. The concept of a "green economy" was first introduced by British economist David Pearce in his book *Blueprint for a Green Economy* in 1989. In October 2008, the United Nations Environment Program launched the Green Economy Initiative, pointing out that a green economy will not be a burden of growth but an engine of growth instead. A green economy not only encompasses a low-carbon economy, but also a recycling economy, and an ecological economy. A recycling economy mainly solves problems regarding resources consumption and environmental protection, emphasizing low environmental load. A low-carbon economy focuses on energy consumption and greenhouse gas emission reduction. An ecological economy is mainly centered around recovery, utilization, and development; for example, ecological agriculture, as well as ecological systems (grasslands, forests, oceans, wetlands, etc.).

The development of China's green economy should be based on the following two national conditions:

First, China is a developing country with the largest population in the world. Along with its economic development, China's energy consumption has increased from 0.57 billion tce (ton of standard coal equivalent) in 1978 to 3.25 billion tce in 2010. The surge in consumption has been particularly steep since 2000, as shown in Figure 8-10.

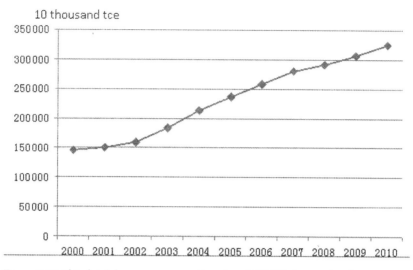

10 thousand tce

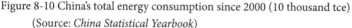

Figure 8-10 China's total energy consumption since 2000 (10 thousand tce)
(Source: *China Statistical Yearbook*)

The figure shows that China's energy consumption has been increasing rapidly since 2002, and by 2010 had doubled the amount of 2002.

China is still a developing country with its per capita energy consumption only a quarter of that in the United States. The nation is in the middle of industrialization; the heavy and chemical industries including steel and petrochemicals are developing continuously, so its energy consumption will keep increasing. It is estimated that in 2020, China's energy consumption will surpass 5 billion tce, twice the amount in 2007.

Second, coal is China's major energy source, accounting for more than 70% of both primary and secondary energy, while oil and natural gas account for 20% and non-fossil energy only for 9%. To reduce the emission of carbon dioxide, we should develop new energy industries. The Chinese government has announced that the proportion of non-fossil energy will be raised to 15% by 2020. Therefore, for a long period of time, fossil energy will still be the major source, and its consumption will keep going up.

Personally, I believe that to develop a low-carbon economy requires measures that address the following four needs. First, we must develop industries that do not emit carbon dioxide, including a new energy industry, the modern service industry, the cultural industry, and the leisure industry. Second, we must reduce carbon dioxide emission, including energy saving, other emission reduction, and clean coal technology. Third is the utilization of carbon dioxide, and fourth is the disposal of carbon dioxide, i.e. Carbon Capture and Storage (CSS).

At present, China's basis for the development of new energy is still weak, and only a small proportion of carbon dioxide is utilized, resulting in high storage cost. Therefore, the development of China's low-carbon economy should focus on "less emission", which is different from western countries. China now stresses "less energy consumption, less pollution, less emission" to reduce the intensity of carbon emission (emission of carbon dioxide of per unit GDP growth) and lower the growth rate of total carbon emission.

The Chinese government has announced that by 2020, emission of carbon dioxide of per unit GDP growth will be reduced by 40-45% on the basis of the data in 2005, an inspiring statistic that will put pressure on enterprises to reduce carbon emission and attach more attention to environmental protection. Thus enterprises should adjust their production techniques, product structure, and environmental practice to this goal. It is very important to restructure and upgrade present industries, which means moving along a new path of industrialization promoted by informatization, which can bring many benefits. First is a reduction of transaction cost. Second is an increase of added value. Third is a shorter transaction time. Fourth is an improved transaction transparency. And fifth is enhanced transaction flexibility. Thus to change traditional industries with information technology is also an important measure through which China can cope with climate change.

At the same time, China should develop new energy because new energy, renewable energy, and low-carbon energy are fundamental measures for dealing with climate change. Development of new energy can, first, cut carbon dioxide emission, and second, reduce pressure on oil demand. At present world oil demand is around 90 million barrels daily, and fluctuation is plus or minus 10%. But through the operation of the futures market, fluctuation can reach ± 200%. In 2010, China imported 239 million tons of crude oil, 17.4% higher than that in 2009, the dependence level on imported crude oil being 53.8%. It is reported that with the development of industrialization and urbanization, China's dependence level on imported oil will be 60% by 2020 and 65% by 2030. Third, development of new energy enables us to produce bio fuel with cellulose and hemicellulose instead of corn in the U.S. and sugarcane in Brazil. In this way we no longer have to consume food for bio fuel and thus can have more land to grow crops on. Fourth, China needs a new economic growth engine after the financial crisis, and new energy, including the electric motorcar, will provide precisely that.

In recent years, China has made huge efforts to develop new energy. According to data from the Bloomberg New Energy Finance Summit in Britain in March, 2010, China's input into new energy has reached an annual average increase of 44.3% in the past 3 years, and in 2009, its investment in new energy was the largest in the world. According to China's preliminary plan for new energy development, by 2020, the installation volume of hydropower will be increased to 300 million KW from the present 190 million KW; installation volume of nuclear power will be increased to 60 million KW from the present 10 million KW; installation volume of wind power will be increased to 120 million KW from the present 30 million KW; and solar electricity generation will be increased to 20 million KW from the present 5.5 million KW. The total investment is 5 trillion RMB.

Balance between globalization and regional integration

"Regional Integration" refers to a multi-national economic region composed of neighboring countries. Within this region, countries can establish multi-national economic organizations through consultation; reduce or remove trade barriers so that factors of production can circulate more freely, coordinate the currencies of different countries, and even discuss political issues like regional security.

I believe regional integration and economic globalization are not contradictory but can supplement each other [23]. Countries in the same region are closer to each other, with long historical connection and a large number of immigrants from each country. They influence each other in economy, science and technology, and culture. Thus these countries tend to form an economic alliance. A good example is the establishment of NAFTA and the EU in the process of globalization.

Practice has proved that regional integration contributes to economic cooperation and the common development of the countries under the principle of mutual benefit. It is especially beneficial to the development of less developed countries in the region (e.g. Ireland in the EU and Mexico in NAFTA) and the economic communication and development among regions.

In the late 1990s, with the trend towards economic globalization and the impact of the East Asia financial crisis, ASEAN countries decided to carry out export-oriented economic cooperation. For many years, China has been working to promote our economic cooperation with countries in East Asia. The "10+3" and "10+1" cooperative mechanisms were established as the times required.

In November 2002, at the Sixth China-ASEAN Summit in Phnom Penh, capital of Cambodia, China signed the Framework Agreement on Comprehensive Economic Cooperation between China and ASEAN with leaders from 10 ASEAN countries (10+1), determined on the establishment of a China-ASEAN Free Trade Area (CAFTA) by 2010. In addition, China and ASEAN signed an Agreement on Trade in Goods in November 2004, an Agreement on Trade in Services in January 2007, and the CAFTA Agreement on Investment on August 15, 2009. CAFTA was officially established on January 1, 2010 and is expected to be fully developed by 2015. The FTA covers 11 countries and involves 1.9 billion people. Its GDP accounts for 10% of the world total, and its trade volume 13%.

On December 15, 1997, the first summit between ASEAN, China, Japan and ROK (9+3, transformed into 10+3 after Cambodia joined ASEAN) was held in Malaysia, which was the beginning of East Asia regional cooperation. From then, the summit has been held each year, further promoting East Asia regional cooperation. The third summit in Manila, Philippines, issued a Joint Statement on East Asia Cooperation, setting the direction and key sectors for regional development. At the seventh summit in Bali in Indonesia, Premier Wen Jiabao proposed research into the feasibility of the establishment of an East Asia FTA, and at the eighth summit the next year, research was officially started. On November 20, 2007, the eleventh summit in Singapore passed the Second Joint Statement on East Asia Cooperation and the ASEAN Plus Three Cooperation Work Plan (2007-2017) and decided on the establishment of a 10+3 cooperative fund [24].

The establishment of East Asia foreign exchange reserve funds is to provide short-term funds to help those countries involved get through financial crises. The 13 members promised a total investment of 120 billion USD. The investment by China, Japan and South Korea account for 80% altogether--32%, 32%, and 16% respectively-- and the 10 ASEAN countries cover the remaining 20%. On May 3, 2011, the 10+3 Vice Finance Ministers Summit in Hanoi, capital of Vietnam, officially announced the establishment of the ASEAN+3 Macroeconomic Research Office (AMRO), whose goal is to "form an independent macroeconomic monitoring and crisis aid mechanism with Asian characteristics" [25].

The GDP of "10+3" now accounts for 22.6% of the world total, just behind that of NAFTA (27.3%) and the EU (25.8%). It has 30.7% of the world's population, much larger than that of NAFTA (6.6%) and the EU (7.3%). This region has huge potential for future development.

Figure 8-11 shows the changes in the shares of the EU, NAFTA, and the "10+3" in the world's total GDP

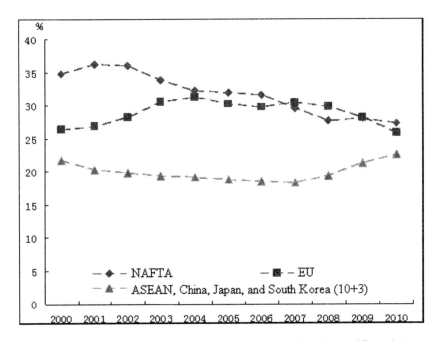

Figure 8-11 Changes in the shares of EU, NAFTA, and "10+3" in the world's total GDP

(Note: major data source is the World Bank. All data of Burma and data of Brunei in 2010 are from IMF, and the latter is estimated value)

The figure shows that the three regions' economic powers are getting closer and closer. If the "10+3"is brought into full play, then those regions will become the three largest and most influential participants in the global economy, which will contribute to world peace and development.

With the efforts of the countries involved, the"10+1" has started operating in all respects, and the "10+3" has been actively promoted, but we are still facing many difficulties and problems.

First, due to various historical and present-day factors, countries are still lacking in trust of each other. On one hand, some countries recognize the trend of peace and development in China and, as our neighbors, are determined to strengthen cooperation with us. On the other hand, some countries still have territorial disputes with China because of differences in social systems and ideologies. They still believe in the

"China threat theory" and are unwilling to establish close relations with China. Some countries even want to offset China's influence with external forces. This makes East Asia cooperation very fragile, and any progress requires huge efforts.

Second, East Asian countries have large variations in their degree of development, much larger than those in the EU and NAFTA, and this will also bring problems to the economic cooperation and trade balance between those countries.

Third, trade volume within "10+3" countries is much smaller than the trade volume between them and other countries, a situation which is very different from that of the EU and NAFTA and will set up barriers for closer economic and trade cooperation among the "10+3" countries.

Fourth, a number of countries are not willing to accept China's growing influence in Asia, and even the world, because of their own global strategy. They may even take measures to delay or impede East Asian integration.

As a prudent optimist, I believe that East Asia integration will gradually develop following the historic trend. The model of the "10+3" is definitely different from that of the EU and NAFTA, but we should borrow their experiences and learn from their lessons.

Regional integration usually starts with liberalization of trade, which means the reduction or removal of tariff barriers. As early as January, 2005, the "10+1" had already begun the process of cutting tariffs, and it is estimated that all products will enjoy conditions of zero tariff by 2018. The opening-up of trade in services began in July, 2007, and liberalization will be gradually realized. However, some "10+1" countries have signed free trade agreements with external countries and regions, so measures should be taken to prevent products in those countries and regions from entering "10+1" countries through some short-cut.

The second stage of regional integration is the facilitation of investment, which creates convenience for the flow of funds within "10+1" countries. The CAFTA Agreement on Investment signed in 2009 stipulates that both should give investors from the other side national treatment, most-favored-nation treatment, and equal and fair investment treatment so as to improve the transparency of investment-related laws and regulations, create a free, convenient, transparent, and equal investment environment and provide legal protection for investors from both sides, and further promote the facilitation of investment and gradual liberalization of both sides. It is reported [26] that the Deputy Secretary General of ASEAN, Mr. S. Pushpanathan, said, during the ASEAN Finance Ministers Summit, that ASEAN expects China to make more investment in ASEAN. To achieve this goal, ASEAN has to take measures to improve the investment environment, and simplify investment procedures to attract more investment from China. With further trade and investment relations with important dialogue and cooperation partners like China, Japan, and ROK, ASEAN can deal with external impacts like the U.S. debt.

The third stage is that of industrial transfer and free flow of the labor force, which means that labor-intensive industries will be transferred from developed countries to countries with lower labor costs, and that the labor force will flow from countries with rich supplies to countries facing shortages. Some labor-intensive industries have already started to be transferred from China to Vietnam, Laos, Cambodia, Burma, and so on, but the free flow of labor forces cannot be realized within a short period of time because it involves many complicated factors.

The fourth is monetary integration. According to the optimal currency area theory, in regions where factor flow, financial transactions, and merchandise trade are highly integrated, monetary integration can effectively coordinate internal and external balance and also bring more returns. At present, the euro area covers most European Union countries, but the recent sovereign debt crisis in some countries in the euro area shows that monetary integration still has some problems and may even lead to the collapse of the currency. It is difficult to realize monetary integration in East Asia because the development gap among "10+3" countries is so huge. The euro took ten years to be put into practice, and the projected "Asian Currency" will take an even longer time. However, with the development of the "10+3", financial cooperation among the members will be strengthened. For example, the People's Bank of China has signed Credit Swap Agreements with the central banks of Japan and South Korea, and special drawing rights in Asia are also on the way.

China has not only made huge efforts to promote regional economic integration and improve the current cooperative mechanisms of the "10+1" and "10+3", but also embraces other regional cooperation ideas. We welcome countries outside the region to play a constructive role in regional peace and development.

The human-oriented, comprehensive, coordinated, and sustainable Scientific Outlook on Development demonstrates the great progress of Marxism with Chinese characteristics as well as being an important concept which can meet the requirements for the further development of human society. Scientific development respects and follows the rules of economic, social, and natural development. Taking economic development as our central task, we should make relentless efforts to further liberate and develop social productivity. The Scientific Outlook on Development lays down the important guidelines for China's economic and social development. We firmly take development as our primary aim, insist on a human-oriented approach, and respect human rights and the value of people. In this way, we can further satisfy people's growing demands for material and cultural advancement, realize common prosperity and promote the comprehensive development of the whole population. Development is for the people, reliant on the people, and shared by the people. Furthermore, we should adhere to this principle, promoting economic, political, cultural, and social development, to produce an ecologically sensitive civilization that coordinates all links and aspects of modernization. We should make overall plans and take all factors into consideration, as we establish and properly handle the important relations in the great undertaking of socialism with Chinese characteristics. Urban and rural development inside the country will match, regional development outside, while economic and social development will be achieved alongside a harmonious development between man and nature, as China continues its domestic development and opens up to the wider world.

On September 6, 2011, the Information Office of the State Council issued the White Paper *China's Peaceful Development* [27]. Once again, China has solemnly declared to the world that peaceful development is China's strategic choice to achieve modernization, create more wealth and enhance national power, and make greater contribution to the civilization of the world. China will continue on the path of peaceful development, leading to harmony and external cooperation and peace.

We should seek new impetus and opportunities through the above six balances, analyze and reflect on specific problems facing us, and promote the fulfillment of the Scientific Outlook on Development and the building of a harmonious world.

Endnotes

Chapter 1. Notes

1. Knox, N. *43% of first-time home buyers put no money down*, USA Today. http://www.usatoday.com/money/perfi/housing/2006-01-17-real-estate-usat_x.htm. January 18, 2006

2. Timeline. *Sub-prime losses*, BBC News (Business). (http://news.bbc.co.uk/2/hi/business/7096845.stm). May 19, 2008

3. Onaran, Y. *Wall Street Firms Cut 34,000 Jobs, Most Since 2001 Dot-Com Bust*, Bloomberg. (http://www.bloomberg.com/apps/news?pid=newsarchive&sid=aTAR UhP3w5xE), March 24, 2008

4. *Bear Stearns gets emergency funds*, BBC News. (http://news.bbc.co.uk/2/hi/7296678.stm). March 14, 2008

5. Li Jun: *From US Subprime Crisis to Global Financial Crisis: Its Development and Analysis, Research on Development* (a journal published in Chinese in Gansu Province), No. 6, 2008.

6. TIMELINE: *U.S. plan for Fannie, Freddie to hit shareholders*, Reuters. http://www.reuters.com/article/2008/09/07/us-fanniefreddie-chronology-idUSN0672604420080907. September 6, 2008

7. Landers, K. *Lehman tumbles, Merrill Lynch totters on Meltdown Monday*, ABC News. http://www.abc.net.au/news/2008-09-16/lehman-tumbles-merrill-lynch-totters-on-meltdown/511426. September 16, 2008

8. Saporito, B. *Getting Suckered by Wall Street – Again*, TIME. http://www.time.com/time/business/article/0,8599,1841567,00.html. September 16, 2008.

9. *The Fed Bails Out AIG*, Business Week. http://www.businessweek.com/bwdaily/dnflash/content/sep2008/db20080916_387203.htm. September 16, 2008

10. Fox, J. *Why the Government Wouldn't Let AIG Fail*, TIME. http://www.time.com/time/business/article/0,8599,1841699,00.html. September 16, 2008

11. *Which Country Is the First One Bankrupted under Global Financial Crisis* (in Chinese), Finance 21CN. http://finance.21cn.com/stock/2008/10/10/5301982.shtml. October 10, 2008

12. Zhu Zhouliang: *Red Alert of Ice Island Indicates Continued Deterioration of European Financial Crisis* (in Chinese). www.cnstock.com, China main securities website. http://finance.sina.com.cn/world/gjjj/20081008/06005365408.shtml. October 8, 2008

13. *Pressure from IMF Leads to Ice Land 600 Basis Point Sharp Interest Reduction*, Ori-

ental Morning Post (a Chinese newspaper published in Shanghai). http://finance. qq.com/a/20081029/002979.htm. October 29, 2008

14. *Declaration Announced at G20 Financial Market and World Economy Summit.* http://paper.people.com.cn/rmrbhwb/html/2008-11/17/content_140321.htm (in Chinese).   November 16, 2008

15. *APEC Announced Its Timetable for Curing Financial Crisis* (in Chinese), Xinhua-net.comhttp://news.xinhuanet.com/fortune/2008-11/25/content_10409956.htm. [2008-11-25]

16. Fu Xueying, Chen Cai, Liu Jisheng: *Geographical Hierarchy of Global Financial Crisis Transmission and Its Inspiration to China in Preventing Financial Crisis.* Geographical Science, April, 2010.

17. *G20 Financial Summit with Hu's Attendance Achieved Significant Results, People's Daily.* April 4, 2009.http://paper.people.com.cn/rmrb/html/2009-04/01/nw.D110000renmrb_20090401_2-01.htm.

18. *Nordea Bank Believes World Economy Begins to Recover* (in Chinese published on Xinhuanet.com, September 2, 2009). http://news.xinhuanet.com/world/2009-09/02/content_11983696.htm.

19. *OECD Says World Economic Depression Will See an Earlier End than Expected* (a report in Chinese on www.xinhuanet.com, September 4, 2009). http://finance.sina.com.cn/j/20090904/13206708600.shtml.

20. *G20 Pittsburgh Summit Announced 8-Point Statement, A Significant Breakthrough* (a report in Chinese by *Guangzhou Daily* on September 27, 2009) http://finance.people.com.cn/GB/10121883.html.

21. *London Security Market Closed Sharply Down* (a report in Chinese by www.xinhua-net.com on November 27, 2009). http://news.xinhuanet.com/fortune/2009-11/27/content_12546655.htm.

22. *Dubai Debt Crisis Leads to Down Across Board in New York* (a report in Chinese by www.xinhuanet.com on November 28, 2009). http://news.xinhuanet.com/fortune/2009-11/28/content_12552723.htm.

23. *Asia-Pacific Stock Exchanges See Overall Decline* (a report in Chinese by www.xinhuanet.com on November 27, 2009). http://news.xinhuanet.com/fortune/2009-11/27/content_12551213.htm.

24. *Shanghai and Shenzhen Security Exchanges Continued Decline* (a report in Chinese published on www.xinhuanet.com on November 27, 2009) http://news.xinhuanet.com/fortune/2009-11/27/content_12550560.htm.

25. *Chronicle of International Financial Crisis* by China Banking Association, November 17, 2009. http://www.china-cba.net/bencandy.php?fid=135&id=4270.

26. *Chronicle of International Financial Crisis in 2010* by China Banking Association, July 14, 2010. http://www.china-cba.net/bencandy.php?fid=135&id=4551.

27. *Chronicle of Greek Debt Crisis: From A Sparklet to Whole Europe*, a article in Chinese by Huaxia Bank on March 4, 2010. http://fund.hxb.com.cn/WebUI/Fund-News/FinanceNewsDetails.aspx?newsid=201003041007571480.

28. *Development of European Debt Crisis*, an article published in Chinese on www. eastmoney. com. http:// topic.eastmoney.com/europedebt/.

29. *Eurozone Deficit in 2009 Soars 6.3 percent*, a report in Chinese by www.xinhuanet. com on April 22, 2010. http://finance.sina.com.cn/j/20100422/19427808722.shtml.

30. *Greek Debt Cloud over Global Stock Market*, a report in Chinese by *Shanghai Securities News* on April 23, 2010. http://finance.qq.com/a/20100423/000398.htm.

31. *Spain Surged Its Public Debt Last Year*, a report in Chinese by *China Securities News* on April 28, 2010. http://finance.591hx.com/article/2010-04-28/0000049087s.shtml.

32. *EU Releases 750 Bln Euros to Market*, a report in Chinese by *Shenzhen Special Zone Daily* on May 11, 2010. http://sztqb.sznews.com/html/2010-05/11/content_1068781.htm.

33. German Cabinet Supports Government's tighten Fiscal Plan, a report in Chinese by China News Service on June 8, 2010. http://www.chinanews.com.cn/cj/cj-gjcj/news/2010/06-08/2329507.shtml.

34. *British New Government Declared Its Budget Focusing on Cutting Deficit*, a report in Chinese by www.xinhuanet.com on June 22, 2010. http://news.xinhuanet.com/world/2010-06/22/c_12249744.htm. [2010-06-22]

35. Yu Yongding: *US, Still the Biggest Threat to World Financial Stability*, a report in Chinese on *Finance 21cn* on June 19, 2010. http://finance.qq.com/a/20100619/000547.htm.

36. *Eurozone ministers approve second installment of Greek bailout loan*, *Earth Times*, September 7, 2010

37. *IMF approves second installment of Greek bailout loan*, *M&G News*, September 11, 2010

38. *Global Foreign Exchange Market*, The Star online, November 17, 2010

39. Cheng Siwei: *Global Economic Recovery in 2011*, a report in Chinese on *Information Times*, November 25, 2008

40. APEC Determined Timetable for Curing Crisis: 18 months to settle it, a report in Chinese by www.xinhuanet.com, November 25, 2008. http://news.xinhuanet.com/fortune/2008-11/25/content_10409956.htm.

41. Cheng Siwei: Six Balance Theories for Financial Crisis, a report in Chinese on Finance 21cn on November 17, 2009. http://money.163.com/09/1117/02/5O9OJH4400253B0H.html.

42. IMF: *World Economic Outlook update*. http://www.imf.org/external/pubs/ft/weo/2010/update/01/pdf/0110.pdf.

Chapter 2. Notes

1. Cheng Siwei: *Basic Theory of Virtual Economics and Research Methodology*, Management Review, No.21, 2009.

2. *Will subprime mess ripple through economy?* msnbc.com. March 13, 2007

3. Bernanke B. S.: *The Recent Financial Turmoil and its Economic and Policy Consequences*, Speech at the Economic Club of New York. New York.http://www.federalreserve.gov/newsevents/speech/bernanke20071015a.htm. [2007-10-15]

4. Bernanke B. S.: *Financial Markets, the Economic Outlook, and Monetary Policy*, Speech at the Women in Housing and Finance and Exchequer Club Joint Luncheon, Washington, D.C. , January 10, 2008.

5. Bernanke B. S.: *Mortgage Delinquencies and Foreclosures*, Speech at the Columbia Business School's 32nd Annual Dinner, New York, May 5, 2008

6. *U.S. foreclosure activity increases 75 percent in 2007.* realtytrac.com, January 29, 2008http://www.realtytrac.com/content/press-releases/us-foreclosure-activity-increases-75-percent-in-2007-3604.

7. *Foreclosure activity increases 75 percent in 2008*, RealtyTrac Inc. January 15, 2009.http://www.realtytrac.com/content/press-releases/foreclosure-activity-increases-81-percent-in-2008-4551.

8. *The End of the Affair*, Economist, November 20, 2008. http://www.economist.com/node/14742624.

9. Katz A. , Katz I.: *Greenspan Slept as Off-Books Debt Escaped Scrutiny.* Bloomberg, October 30, 2008. http://www.bloomberg.com/apps/news?pid=newsarchive&sid=aspN..hVXJC4.

10. Bernard T.: *Money Market Funds Enter a World of Risk*, New York Times, September 17, 2008. http://www.nytimes.com/2008/09/18/business/yourmoney/18money.html.

11. Gray M.: *Almost Armageddon: Markets Were 500 Trades from a Meltdown.* New York Post, September 21, 2008. http://www.nypost.com/p/news/business/item_6Ir9jcaDd2knbCMbFFzotL.

12. Dash E., Sorkin A.: *Government Seizes Wa Mu and Sells Some Assets*, The New York Times, September 25, 2008. http://www.nytimes.com/2008/09/26/business/26wamu.html?pagewanted=all.

13. Twin A: *Stocks crushed*, CNN Money, September 29, 2008. http://money.cnn.com/2008/09/29/markets/markets_newyork/index.htm.

14. Guha K., Morris H., Politi J., and Paul J Davies: *Banking's crisis of confidence deepens.* The Financial Times, September 30, 2008. http://www.ft.com/cms/s/0/17ce4468-8f22-11dd-946c-0000779fd18c.html#axzz1iYhQvaVF.

15. *How the Happiest Country Crack Down?* A report in Chinese by Qilu Evening News, October 12, 2008. http://www.qlwb.com.cn/display.asp?id=344934.

Chapter 3. Notes

1. Wu Xizhi: *Statistics, from Data to Conclusion* (in Chinese), published by China Statistic Press in Beijing, 2004.

2. Wang Huoyan, Huang Zhijin: *Financial Crisis Hurts World Trade, World Trade Review in 2008 and Prospect in 2009 (Part One)*, published on World Trade Organization Focus (a journal run by Shanghai Institute of Foreign Trade), No. 5, 2009, in Shanghai.

3. Lu Yan: *Trade in World Economic Dilemma, Review of 2009 and Prospect of 2010*, published on No. 2 issue of Theory Front (*Li Lun Qian Yan* in Chinese) magazine in 2010, in Beijing.

4. Ren Ruo'en, Wang Huiwen: *Multivariate Statistic Analysis, Its Theory, Methodology and Examples*, published by National Defense Press in Beijing, 1999.

5. Ramsay J., Silverman B.: *Functional Data Analysis*, Second Edition, published by in Beijing by Science Press, 2006.

Chapter 4. Notes

1. *Financial Stability Report*, Bank of England, June 2010, Issue No. 27

2. *Annual Report 2010*, Bank of England, July 11, 2011. http://www.bankofengland. co.uk/publications/annualreport/index.htm.

3. *The Impact of the Financial Crisis on Supply*, Bank of England Quarterly Bulletin, 2010 Q2

4. *Inflation Report*, Bank of England, May 2010.

5. *Economic Crisis Comes to Social Problem, and Britain again Faces More Risks* (a report by *Economic Daily* in Chinese on August 11, 2011). http://www.chinanews. com/cj/2011/08-11/3251383.shtml.

6. *Introduction to Germany Economy*, East International Exhibition Co. Ltd., November 28, 2007. http://www.eieco.com/country_news.asp?cnewsid=8.

7. Zheng Keqing: *Financial Supervision in German and Its Inspiration*, August 9, 2007. http://www.zcj.com.cn/news/show.php?id=1352.

8. Jin Pei, Yuan Lei: *Influence of World Financial Crisis to Germany*, September 17, 2009. http://acs.mofcom.gov.cn/sites/aqzn/jrkd.jsp?contentId=2503948837147.

9. *Russia*, http://baike.baidu.com/view/2403.html?wtp=tt

10. *Russian Financial Crisis*. http://baike.baidu.com/view/964857.htm

11. *Russian Financial Market*, published in Chinese at Information Website of Heilongjiang Province on March 9, 2006.http://www.hljic.gov.cn/zehz/zelt/ t20060309_148346.htm.

12. *Uncertainty in Russian Economy*, a report in Chinese by Xinhua News Agency on November 6, 2009. http://chn.chinamil.com.cn/xwpdxw/2009-11/06/con-tent_4074903.htm.

13. Feng Lianyong, Wang Yue: *Influence of Financial Crisis to Russian Oil Industry*, published in Chinese on *Russian Central Asian & East European Studies*, February, 2009,

14. Ma Weiyun: *Influence of World Financial Crisis to Fast East of Russia*, published in Chinese on *Russian Central Asian & East European Studies*, February, 2009,

15. *Introduction to Australia*, website of the Ministry of Foreign Affairs, the People's Republic of China, July 13, 2011. http://www.fmprc.gov.cn/chn/pds/gjhdq/gj/dyz/1206/.

16. *Australian Economic Development and Specialties, China Economic Times,* on October 22, 2007.http://finance.sina.com.cn/roll/20071022/09081734499.shtml.

17. *Introduction to Australian Economy*, published in Chinese on China Commodity Net on July 14, 2008. http://ccn.mofcom.gov.cn/spbg/show.php?id=7791.

18. *Survey of Investment in Australia*, published in Chinese by China Investment Guide on July 19, 2007. http://www.fdi.gov.cn/pub/FDI/dwtz/ggtzzc/dyz/adly/t20070719_81148.htm.

19. *Introduction to Australian Finance Industry*, a speech at Training Program on Contemporary Financial Company System and Law hosted by Fujian Province in Australia, published in Chinese on Fujian Finance, April 2006.

20. Li Bonan: *Introduction to Australian Monetary Supervision*, published in Chinese on *Journal of Henan Institute of Monetary Carders*, February 2003.

21. Han Yingtong: *Finance Industry in Australia, China Wai Tong*, 2009

22. Li Ming, Zhang Dai, Zhang Yudong, Xie Guo, Deng Min: *Global Financial Crisis: Its Influence to Australia and Inspiration to China*, a survey by China Development Bank, 2008.

23. *Financial Stability Review*. Reserve Bank of Australia, September 2008

24. *Financial Stability Review*. Reserve Bank of Australia, March 2010

25. *Statement on Monetary Policy*. Reserve Bank of Australia, May 2010

26. *Bulletin*. Reserve Bank of Australia, June quarter 2010

27. *Saving Greek: Way to Recover Greek Economy by Greek Economy Minister,* a report published in Chinese on *China Business News*, April 23, 2010. http://finance.sina.com.cn/world/ozjj/20100423/01127809701.shtml. [2010-04-23]

28. Introduction to Greece: Economic and Commercial Counsellor's Office of the Embassy of the People's Republic of China in Hellenic Republic on March 12, 2002. http://gr.mofcom.gov.cn/aarticle/ddgk/zwjingji/200203/20020300003440.html.

29. Liargovas P., Repousis S.: *The Impact of Mergers and Acquisitions on the Performance of the Greek Banking Sector: An Event Study Approach, International Journal of Economics and Finance*, March 2011, 89-100.

30. *Greece Banking and Finance, The Library of Congress Country Studies;* CIA World Factbook, November 4, 2011. http://www.photius.com/countries/greece/economy/

greece_economy_banking_and_finance.html. [2010-11-04]

31. *Introduction to Greece*, ChinaGreece Web, September 20, 2010. http://www.cgw.gr/html/hyxt/qcyp_572_37.html

32. *Some 100 Thousands Greek to Lose Jobs*, a report in Chinese on *Beijing Evening News* on May 12, 2010. http://news.sina.com.cn/w/2010-05-12/142517500060s.shtml.

33. *Greece: Economy Withers, Unemployment Soars*, China Everbright Bank, August 12, 2010. http://www.cebbank.com/Info/41957408.

34. *Greece to Attract Tourists by Reducing Airport Cost*, a report on *China Daily* on April 22, 2010. http://www.chinadaily.com.cn/hqcj/zxqxb/2010-04-22/content_198510.html.

35. *Tourism Hurt by Debt Crisis, Hundreds of Hotels in Greek Listed for Sale*, a report in Chinese on *Global Times* on May 26, 2010. http://news.sohu.com/20100526/n272369523.shtml.

36. Investors Eyes on Greek Shipping Industry, a report in Chinese at www.sina.com on May 12, 2009. http://finance.sina.com.cn/roll/20090512/17582836369.shtml.

37. *Investor Compensation System in France and Greece and Its Inspiration to China.* The Ministry of Finance, PRC, January, 2006. http://www.mof.gov.cn/pub/jinrong-si/zhengwuxinxi/jingyanjiaoliu/200806/t20080623_47815.htm

38. Feng Yifan: *Aiding Plan to Greece, Bailout or Rescue?* a feature in Chinese published on Finance magazine on May 2010: 95-96

39. *Is Greece the Next in Global Sovereign Debt?* A report in Chinese by China Business News on December 15, 2009. http://money.163.com/09/1215/02/5QHRN6PL00253B0H.html.

40. *Fitch Downgraded Greek Sovereign Credit to "BBB+"*, a report in Chinese on www.xinhuanet.com on December 9, 2009. http://news.qq.com/a/20091209/001959.htm.

41. Li Caiyuan: *Financial Civil War*, a book in Chinese published by Jincheng Press, Beijing, 2010.

42. *Greek Parliament Passed Crisis Budget in 2010*, a report in Chinese on www.xinhuanet.com, December 24, 2009. http://www.cs.com.cn/xwzx/04/200912/t20091224_2301447.htm.

43. *Greek Debt to Lose Control and Deficit Reduction to Fail*, a Chinese on *Xin Jing Bao* on September 2, 2011. http://www.chinanews.com/fortune/2011/09-02/3301999.shtml.

44. *Greek Debt to Lose Control but Deny Withdraw from Eurozone*, a report in Chinese on Beijing Daily on September 3, 2011. http://news.sohu.com/20110903/n318210564.shtml.

45. *European and American Finance Ministers to Meet This Week for Greece to Debt Deadline*, a report in Chinese on *China Security News* on September 14, 2011.

http://www.cnr.cn/newscenter/eco/business%20c/201109/t20110914_508498202.
shtml.

46. *Eurozone Finance Minister Conference Affirms New Round Aid to Reach Greece in October*, a report in Chinese on *21cn Economic Reports*, September 17, 2011. http://
finance.eastmoney.com/news/1351,20110917163719128.html.

47. *Eurozone Finance Minister Conference Postpones Discussion on Aiding Greece*, a report in China on *Hong Kong Commercial Daily* on September 17, 2011. http://news.
hexun.com/2011-10-05/133944109.html.

Chapter 5. Notes

1. Huang Wei: *Infection mechanism in Financial Crisis and Its Role in Southeast Asia Crisis*, an essay in Chinese published on *Foreign Economy Management* magazine on 2000, 23(5): 33-36.

2. Zhou Pan: *Options of Infection Channels of American Financial Crisis*, a MA essay of Xiamen University, Xiamen, in 2009.

3. Goldfajn I., Rodrigo V.: *Capital Flows and the Twin Crises: The Role of Liquidity*. IMF Working Paper, 1997 (No. 97/87).

4. Goldstein I., Ady p.: *Demand–Deposit Contracts and the Probability of Bank Runs*, *The Journal of Finance*, March 2005.

5. Twenty Million Chinese Immigrant Workers Lost Jobs Back Home, a report in Chinese by www.china.org.cn on February 2, 2009. http://news.
qq.com/a/20090202/000592.htm.

Chapter 6. Notes

1. Li Ying, Han Mei: *CASS Unemployment Rate Much Higher than PRC Ministry of Human Resources and Social Securities*, a report in Chinese on *China Youth Daily* on January 2, 2009. http://www.cs.com.cn/xwzx/03/200901/t20090102_1704767.htm.

2. Wang Xu: *Report Shows Real Price of growth*, a report on *China Daily* on September 12, 2008, http://www.chinadaily.com.cn/china/2008-09/12/content_7020515.htm.

3. Wu Yajun, Xuan Xiaowei: *Environment Tax Theory and Its Application in China*, published by Economics Press, Beijing 2002.

4. Sun Linlin, Ren Ruoyu: *Capital Investment in China and Total Factor Productivity Estimation*, an article in Chinese published by World Economy, China, 2005(1): 3-13

5. Wang Xiaolu, Fan Gang, Liu Peng: *Transmission of China's Economic Growth Mode and Growth Sustainability*, an essay on *Economic Studies*, China, 2009(1): 4-16

6. Cai Fang: Green Paper on Population and Work, published by Social Science Document Press, Beijing, 2009.

7. PRC Ministry of Human Resources and Social Securities: *Employment-Oriented Policy Coordination - Report Two on China's Job Plan to Deal with International*

Financial Crisis, a report in Chinese published by *Economic Information Daily*, Beijing, November 4, 2011. http://scbz.lss.gov.cn/disp.asp?ID=1870.

8. Zhang Benpo: *4 T Investment To Bring 5.6 M Long-Term Jobs and 50 M Contemporary Jobs*, a report in Chinese on *China Economic Herald*, July 28, 2009. http://www.ceh.com.cn/ceh/xwpd/2009/7/28/50717.shtml.

9. PRC National Bureau of Statistics: *2009 National Economic and Social Development Bulletin*, February 25, 2010, http://www.stats.gov.cn/tjgb/ndtjgb/qgndtjgb/t20100225_402622945.htm.

10. Chen Jianxin: National Development and Reform Commission to Announce China's Over-Productivity of Steel and Other Industries, a report published in Chinese on www. cnradio.com on December 3, 2009, http://news.iyaxin.com/content/2009-12/03/content_1386299.htm.

11. Ma Hongyu: *The State Council Strongly Restrains Over-productivity to Break Vicious Circle of Steel Industry*, a report in Chinese on *China Securities News* on June 19, 2010. http://www.cnstock.com/index/gdbb/201006/606681.htm.

12. Cheng Siwei: *Recovery Ahead but Hard Work Needed*, a report in Chinese on People's Daily (overseas edition) on July 29, 2009.

13. IUD Leader Decision Data Analysis Center: *Local Funding Platform Debt Repayment Risk and Warning*, a article published on *Leader Decision Information*, China, 2010, (15): 28-29

14. Ba Shusong: *Local Debt Crisis Won't Happen in China*, a report on *People's Daily* (overseas edition) September 3, 2010.

15. Duhigg C.: *Pressured to take more risk, Fannie reached tipping point*. The New York Times, October 4, 2008. http://www.nytimes.com/2008/10/05/business/05fannie. html?pagewanted=1.

Chapter 7. Notes

1. Cheng Siwei: Fictitious *Economy and Financial Crisis*, a article in Chinese published on *Journal on Management Science in China*, 1999.

2. Cheng Siwei: *A Research on Fictitious Economy*, a article in Chinese in *Fictitious Economy Studies*, published by Democracy and Construction Press, Beijing, 2003.

3. Duhigg C.: *Pressured to take more risk, Fannie reached tipping point*, The New York Times, October 4, 2008. http://www.nytimes.com/2008/10/05/business/05fannie. html?pagewanted=1.

4. Leonnig C. : *How HUD mortgage policy fed the crisis*, The Washington Post⊠June 10, 2008. http://www.msnbc.msn.com/id/25053787/.

5. Roberts R.: *How government stoked the Mania*, The Wall Street Journal, October 3, 2008. http://online.wsj.com/article/SB122298982558700341.html.

6. Trehan V. : *The mortgage market: what happened?* National Public Radio(NPR)

Article, August 26, 2007. http://www.npr.org/templates/story/story.php?storyId=9855669.

7. Angell C., Williams N.: *U.S. home prices: does bust always follow boom?* Federal Deposit Insurance Corporation, February 10, 2005. http://www.fdic.gov/bank/analytical/fyi/2005/021005fyi.html.

8. *New home sales fell by record amount in 2007.* MSNBC⊠January 28, 2008. http://www.msnbc.msn.com/id/22880294/#.Twuu3K6lONY.

9. Cheng Siwei: *Systematic Analysis to China Housing Reform in Cities,* a article in Chinese from book *Goal, Mode and Implementation Difficulties in China's Housing Reform in Cities,* Cheng Siwei as chief complier and published by Democracy and Construction Press, Beijing, 1999.

10. Cheng Siwei: *Suggestion and Analysis to China Housing Reform in Cities,* a article in Chinese from Cheng's book *China Economic Reform and Development Studies* (Vol. 3), published by China Renmin University Press, Beijing, 2009.

11. Cheng Siwei: *Systematic Analysis to East Asia Financial Crisis,* a article in Chinese from a book Cheng edited East Asia Financial Crisis: Analysis and Suggestions, published by Democracy and Construction Press, Beijing, 1999.

12. Lasch C.: *The culture of consumerism.* Smithsonian Center for Education and Museum Studies. September 16, 2008. http://smithsonianeducation.org/idealabs/ap/essays/consume.htm.,

13. Zakaria F.: *There is a silver lining,* Newsweek, October 20, 2008, http://www.newsweek.com/id/163449.

14. Zwaig J.: *What history tells us about the market, The Wall Street Journal,* October 11, 2008, http://online.wsj.com/article/SB122368241652024977.html.

15. Steverman B., Bogoslaw D.: *The financial crisis blame game. Business Week,* October 18, 2008. http://www.businessweek.com/investor/content/oct2008/pi20081017_950382.htm?campaign_id=rss_daily.

16. Nocera J.: *First, let's fix the bonuses, The New York Times,* February 21, 2009 (B1)

17. Hu Jintao: Speech at the Conference for 30th Anniversary of Reform and Opening, in Chinese published on www.people.com December 18, 2008, http://cpc.people.com.cn/GB/64093/64094/8544901.html.

18. Wen Jiabao: Every Country Should Deal with Relation between Real and Fictitious Economies, a speech in Chinese Wen gave at a press conference at 7th Asia-Europe Leader Summit, published on www.chinanews.com, October 25, 2008. http://news.sina.com.cn/c/2008-10-25/173016524436.shtml.

19. Cheng Siwei: *Three Directions of Financial Reform,* an article in Chinese published on Beijing Daily, October 6, 2008.

Chapter 8. Notes

1. Obstfeld M, Rogoff K. *Perspectives on OECD capital market integration: implications for U.S. current account adjustment*. In: *Global Economic Integration: Opportunities and Challenges*. Kansas City: Federal Reserve Bank of Kansas City. 2001

2. Zhao Jiangshan, Cao Ying: G20 Holds Close-Door Argument for Judging Unbalanced World Economy, a report in Chinese on Economic Information Daily on October 17, 2005. http://www.mof.gov.cn/zhuantihuigu/czhzhy7/mtbd/200805/t20080519_22046.html.

3. Pettinger T.: *Global Imbalance*, Perma Link, March 9, 2009. http://www.economicshelp.org/2009/03/global-imbalances.html.

4. Cooper R.: *Living with Global Imbalances. Brookings Papers on Economic Activity*, 2007, (2): 91-110.

5. Ricardo C, Emmanuel F, and Pierre-Olivier G.: *An Equilibrium Model of Global Imbalances and Low Interest Rates. American Economic Review* 2008, 98 (3): 358-393.

6. Lorenzo S.: *The Financial Crisis and Global Imbalances: Two Sides of the Same Coin.* Beijing: Speech at the Asia Europe Economic Forum, December 9, 2008.

7. Cheng S.: *Improving world economic order by keeping six balances* on May 13, 2009. http://www.pecc.org/resources/doc_download/809, The Asia Pacific Role in the New Global Economic Order.

8. Bernanke B.: *The global saving glut and the United States current account deficit.* Remarks at the Sandridge Lecture, Virginia Association of Economics, March 10, 2005. http://ideas.repec.org/a/fip/fedgsq/y2005x19.html.

9. Bernanke B.: *The global saving glut and the United States current account deficit.* Remarks at the Homer Jones Lecture, St. Louis, Missouri, April 14, 2005. http://www.federalreserve.gov/boarddocs/speeches/2005/200503102/.

10. Li Yang, He Haifeng: *Imbalance of American Current Account: Performance, Theory and Countermeasures*, an essay on *International Financial Studies*, 2009, (12) 4-13.

11. Zhou Xiaochuan: *Observation and Analysis on Deposit Rate*, the speech at Central Bank Senior Seminar at Malaysia, 2009.

12. Eichengreen B.: *The blind men and the elephant. Issues in Economic Policy.* The Brookings Institution, 2006, (1): 1-24

13. Rostow W W.: *The stages of economic growth, Econ History Review*, 1959, 12(1): 1-16

14. Samuelson P.: *Samuelson Dictionary*, Chinese version, translated by Chen Xun, Bai Yuanliang, and published by Jinghua Press, 2001: 471

15. Roubini N., Brad S.: *The U.S. as a Net Debtor: The Sustainability of the U.S. External Imbalances.* New York: New York University. 2004

16. Truman E.: *Budget and External Deficits: Not Twins but the Same Family.* The Federal Reserve Bank of Boston Annual Research Conference. Boston: 2004-06.

17. Modigliam F., Ando A.: *Tests of the life cycle hypothesis of savings: comments and*

suggestions. Bulletin of the Oxford University Institute of Economics & Statistics, 1957, 19(2): 99-124

18. Friedman M.: *A Theory of the Consumption Function.* Princeton University Press, 1957

19. Du Q, Wei S.: *A sexually unbalanced model of current account imbalances*, NBER Working Paper No. 16000, 2010

20. Cheng Siwei: *Deepen Monetary Reform and Improve Monetary Supervision to Promote*

    Balanced Development of Monetary and Economy, a article in Chinese from *Cheng Siwei on Monetary Reform,* China Renmin University Press, Beijing, 2006 3-11

21. Cheng Siwei: *Outlook of Scientific Development and Fast, Good Development,* a article published on *Journal of China Pudong Administration Institute* 2007, (1) 6-14

22. Cheng Siwei: *New Energy and Low-Carbon Economy,* a article published on Management Review 2010 22 (6) 4-8.

23. Cheng S.: *China and Pacific countries——in the context of regional integration and economic globalization,* the speech at 2005 Pacific Economic Cooperation Conference, 2005, Seoul

24. PRC Ministry of Foreign Affairs: State Leader Conference of ASEAN + China, Japan and Korea, Oct.7, 2011: http://www.fmprc.gov.cn/chn/pds/gjhdq/gjhdqzz/lhg_13/

25. Wu Chengliang, Ji Peijuan: *Breakthrough of 10+3 Cooperation,* a report in Chinese on www. people.com.cn, May 6, 2011. http://world.people.com.cn/GB/57507/14564898.html.

26. Li Xiaoyu, Qi Xing: ASEAN Deputy Secretary-General: *ASEAN Expects More Investment from China,* a report in Chinese on *China Hi-Tech Industrial Herald,* September 5, 2011, http://www.chinahightech.com/views_news.asp?Newsid=634373832323.

27. Information Office of PRC State Council: *White Paper on China Peaceful Development,* September 6, 2011, http://www.gov.cn/jrzg/2011-09/06/content_1941204.htm.

INDEX

352